Property Taxation—USA

Proceedings of a Symposium
Sponsored by the Committee
on Taxation, Resources
and Economic Development (TRED)
at the University
of Wisconsin—Milwaukee,
1965

Property
Taxation

USA

Edited by Richard W. Lindholm

The University of Wisconsin Press
Madison, Milwaukee, and London
1967

Published by
The University of Wisconsin Press
Madison, Milwaukee, and London
U.S.A.: Box 1379, Madison, Wisconsin 53701
U.K.: 26–28 Hallam Street, London, W.1
Copyright © 1967
by the Regents of the University of Wisconsin
All rights reserved
Printed in the United States of America
by Kingsport Press, Inc.
Kingsport, Tennessee
Library of Congress Catalog Card Number 67–20762

Contributors

Paul E. Alyea
Emeritus Professor of Public Finance, University of Alabama

Raleigh Barlowe
Professor of Agricultural Economics and Chairman, Department of Resource Development, Michigan State University

Benjamin Bridges, Jr.
Economist, Social Security Administration

Earl E. Burkhard
Personal Property Taxation Consultant, New York

Yung-Ping Chen
Assistant Professor of Economics, University of California (Los Angeles)

Harold M. Groves
Professor of Economics, University of Wisconsin

Reed R. Hansen
Professor of Economics, Washington State University

Irving Howards
Director of the Bureau of Government Research, University of Massachusetts

Richard W. Lindholm
Professor of Finance and Dean, School of Business Administration, University of Oregon

Arthur D. Lynn, Jr.
Professor of Economics and Associate Dean of Faculties, The Ohio State University

Clarence W. Nelson
Head of Research Department, Federal Reserve Bank, Minneapolis

Joan E. O'Bannon
Assistant Professor of Economics, Agnes Scott College

John Shannon
>Senior Analyst, Advisory Commission on Intergovernmental Relations

Bernard F. Sliger
>Professor of Economics and Dean, Office of Academic Affairs, Louisiana State University

Lynn A. Stiles
>Senior Economist, Federal Reserve Bank, Chicago

Conference Hour

Eli Schwartz, Editor
>Professor of Finance, Lehigh University

Israel M. Labovitz, Coordinator
>Senior Specialist in Social Welfare, Legislative Reference Service, Library of Commerce

Morris Beck
>Associate Professor of Economics, Rutgers, The State University (Newark)

Arthur P. Becker
>Professor of Economics, University of Wisconsin (Milwaukee)

John Henry Denton
>Statewide Coordinator of Real Estate Program, University of California (Berkeley)

Werner W. Doering
>Property Tax Division of the State of Wisconsin

Karl Falk
>Professor of Economics, Fresno State College of California

Mason Gaffney
>Professor of Economics, University of Wisconsin (Milwaukee)

Jewell J. Rasmussen
>Head, Department of Economics, University of Utah

William S. Vickery
>Professor of Economics and Chairman, Department of Political Science, Columbia University

Preface

This is a period of revival of interest in the way the property tax has been applied in the United States and in the way in which the tax may develop in the United States and in other nations of the world. This publication is intended as a contribution to the growing effort to understand how the property tax does work; what can be done to make it work better in the United States; and what should be avoided by new nations interested in developing a strong property tax. In an attempt to realize this goal, a group of some of the world's most knowledgeable persons on the subject of property taxation in the United States were brought together to present papers and to make comments on broad and narrow aspects of this subject.

This book presents the proceedings of the conference, Property Taxation—U.S.A., which took place on the campus of the University of Wisconsin—Milwaukee during the period June 14–16, 1965. Fourteen of the participants presented detailed examinations of a selected aspect of property taxation in the United States. In this volume, these very informative analyses are divided into three groups, and each group is preceded by an introductory section by the editor. Part I is titled "Some Fundamental Considerations"; Part II is titled "Business and Industry"; and Part III is titled "Special Problems." The contributions of all the conference participants through informal discussions have been summarized in the final section. The goal of this presentation of the conference proceedings has been to permit the reader to approach as closely as possible to becoming an actual participant while keeping the quantity of reading to a reasonable level.

The backgrounds of the conference participants cover a wide range of property-tax experience. All aspects of the taxation of property in the United States have not been covered, and no concerted effort has been made to delve into any selected area in a completely comprehensive manner. The goal is to give the general reader and the taxation specialist—including the economist and the government official—a summary of current experience with a number of facets of the property tax in the United States. In working toward

vii

this goal, some important trends are identified, and old and new theories of property taxation are examined to determine their usefulness in reform and improvement of the tax. In most cases, the papers are based on experience with the subject under consideration but cover some theoretical aspects of the subject as well. They also identify policy implications of the facts and analyses presented. Persons interested in the introduction and administration of improved tax systems in the low-per-capita-income developing nations of the world will find the papers and the summary of the informal discussions to be mines of useful advice and information.

The well-publicized weaknesses of the property tax are described, and, when the sources of these weaknesses are explored in paper after paper, a general program for basic property-tax reform emerges. The fundamental reform which appears to be required is the re-emergence of the property tax as a major source of state revenues. These receipts would be used by the states as centrally collected revenues of local governments or as receipts to support state expenditures.

Two other basic policy positions evolve less sharply from the papers, but they are clearly discernible. The first is that a general property tax is much less acceptable than one based largely on land value. The second is that the impacts of income-tax developments in the United States have not been recognized, or have, at best, been considered only intermittently in property-tax legislation.

As the reader goes through these collected papers he will, I am certain, find himself saying (even as I did) that the taxation heritage of the United States—based on sound democratic principles—has been permitted to become heavily encrusted with an overlay of special-interest legislation. It is time these accretions were scraped off so that the clean lines of the original may be seen. When the original purposes and the methods of reaching them are revealed, the property tax becomes much more attractive to businessmen, to economists, to tax specialists, and—most important of all—to taxpayers in general.

The property tax was developed as a general, state-wide tax, and its evolution into a special district and municipal tax was most unfortunate and requires remedy. In the United States, the property tax just does not possess great, unique advantages as a revenue source administered within a small geographical area. Actually, many of the small, independent property-taxing jurisdictions are not required for effective local control of government but are an example of property-tax encrustation through special-interest legislation.

Before the days of the income tax, the property tax was aimed at ability to pay, and many of its current shortcomings arose from efforts to reach income directly. This effort is no longer required. The development of the income tax as the major revenue source of the federal government and the emergence of the federal government as the nation's major tax-gatherer—plus the wide use of the income tax by state and local governments—have largely eliminated the original need to justify the property tax by attempting to base it on individual ability to pay. Individual justice could now be attained if the property tax were based on cost of benefits enjoyed by the property. Social justice could be achieved if the tax took into account society's right to benefit from the exploitation of its natural resources and from land-value increases arising from society's general expansion in numbers and productivity. Recognition of the property tax's strength in helping society to benefit generally from the land and resource values it is creating seems currently to be growing.

The conference and this book owe much to the stimulus and support of the Committee on Taxation, Resources and Economic Development and the Robert Schalkenbach Foundation. In addition, the participants were assisted in making their contributions by the organizations with which they are associated. The School of Business Administration of the University of Oregon was particularly helpful.

Richard W. Lindholm

Eugene, Oregon
March, 1967

Contents

List of Tables

List of Figures

Part I Some Fundamental Considerations

Introduction

This portion of the proceedings of the Property Taxation—USA Conference consists of four general analyses.

The historical development of property taxation in the United States, with some tracing of colonial beginnings to European experience, is summarized by Arthur D. Lynn. He develops the concept of a property-tax cycle from taxation of land to tax coverage of most property and back to taxation exclusively of land. The existence of such a cycle in the past would suggest that the property tax may again become essentially a tax on realty in the future. This possibility is raised again and again by conference participants and is looked upon by some as being involved in what might be called the "urbanization of the property tax." The United States is becoming an urban nation. The property tax, which was introduced as largely a method of taxing the agricultural industry, has become a method for the community to claim a portion of rising land prices and to collect for services provided to those who use and occupy houses and buildings.

In the next paper, Benjamin Bridges establishes through statistical analysis that the property tax does possess an ability to provide additional tax receipts as Gross National Product rises. The property tax has proved to be revenue elastic, i.e., the percentage increase of property-tax collections has been somewhat greater than the percentage increase of GNP. This revenue-elasticity characteristic has meant that property taxes have generally been able to meet local-government expenditure requirements in the United States. Dr. Bridges' highest estimate for the average effective rate to be required in 1975 is 1.65 percent of full and true value of taxable property, an increase of 25 percent from the current rate of 1.32 percent. The 1.65 percent rate was found to be unbearable when previously reached during the depression of 1932, and this might again be the case if this rate were reached in 1975. In Dr. Bridges' opinion, however, 1.39 percent is a better estimate for the property-tax rate to be required in 1975. This rate is only 5 percent above the present

3

level. His estimate of required increase is well within the potential of a United States property-tax base that is rising some 10 percent more rapidly than GNP.

The apparent political necessity of valuing property for taxation purposes at a fraction of its market value has reduced the efficiency of the property tax, however. John Shannon carefully considers the reasons for fractional-assessment patterns, examines the effects of this practice, and develops imaginative solutions to the problem. The results of fractional valuation are a lack of uniformity in assessed valuation and property-tax rates that appear high. Actually, full-value assessment means that the states must make full-value findings which can become the standard to which all autonomous assessment districts can apply their fractional valuations. The difficulty of placing a value on land is sharply reduced when the land is valued in large parcels with no consideration of the structures on the land. The problems arise when an effort is made to place a value on an individual lot. Under these circumstances, the structure on the land or in the immediate vicinity influences judgments on land-site value. The levy of an *ad valorem* property tax * is different from other types of taxes. The base of the tax is visible to all and does not move from one fixed place. The tax liability can exist, however, without a market transaction or a payment for goods or services. Basic collection problems are created by the fact that income for tax payment is not available as a result of the existence of a taxable base, but the pressures developed in the collection process encourage the development of the market economy and the full use of property resources. The property owner is forced to use his property in a manner that will increase income from the property so that he can pay his property taxes. The property owner unable to do this places his property on the market and sells to someone able to utilize the property more completely. The new owner, by utilizing the property to its highest and best use, earns sufficient income from the property to pay the property taxes based on market value of the property.

It is not easy to place a value on a piece of real estate as a whole, and it is even more difficult to separate the value of land from that of the improvements and structures attached to the land. The advocates of site-value taxation, and of property taxation generally, tend to underestimate these problems. Experience has demonstrated, how-

* The term *ad valorem* taxation means the tax rate is applied to a value that is placed on the property. An *in rem* property tax would be a certain tax on each item included in the taxable property list. Today property taxation in the United States is, practically without exception, of the *ad valorem* type.

ever, that, although the administration of the tax may sometimes be rather poor, the tax itself is workable whether the base of the levy includes all wealth or only the value of bare land.

The individual who has had the greatest impact on the attitudes of both professionals and laymen toward taxation of real estate, and particularly toward land-site values, has been Henry George. Reed R. Hansen's careful examination of that social reformer and his views finds him to have been a challenging and articulate writer who said "much which is pertinent and useful to our current society . . . . " But this is not the end of the story. Dr. Hansen is faced with the same problem in his discussion that has confronted the writers of similar studies. As he becomes involved in an analysis of George's theories, he finds that insufficient data exist to allow him to determine, for example, how important the control of land is in the power of monopolies or what the impact on the efficiency and beauty of our urban areas would be if the real estate tax were based entirely on the value of land. The United States today is very different from the United States of George's experience. The less-developed areas today bear a marked resemblance to the United States in George's time, however, and his analysis is still very pertinent to these areas. United States economists in the 1960's have found the George approach most provocative in considering urban sprawl or the taxation of oil and mineral resources.

Richard W. Lindholm

1. Arthur D. Lynn, Jr.

Property-Tax Development: Selected Historical Perspectives

The defects of the property tax are, it would appear, beyond remedy . . .

C. F. Bastable [1]

The history of the property tax in the United States provides a not inconsiderable area for review. Over an extended period of time, both the theoretical and the practical defects of the property tax have attracted the sustained attention of a large number of fiscal specialists. The resultant literature appears to be second in quantity only to that generated by the confrontation of the American scholar with the antitrust laws. If bibliographic bulk alone, with or without invective, could rid a tax of defects, the property tax would be pure indeed. Yet in reality there would seem to be ample reason for continued consideration and analysis of this ancient revenue source; this paper will note several historical perspectives which appear relevant. It obviously could not, and clearly does not, make any pretense of completeness.

In discussions of property taxation, it is conventional to note this pithy evaluation of the tax by E. R. A. Seligman.

Practically, the general property tax as actually administered is beyond all doubt one of the worst taxes known in the civilized world. Because of its attempt to tax intangible as well as tangible things, it sins against the cardinal rules of uniformity, of equality and of universality of taxation. It puts a premium on dishonesty and debauches the public conscience; it reduces deception to a system, and makes a science of knavery; it presses hardest on those least able to pay; it imposes double taxation on one man and grants entire immunity to the next. In short, the general property tax is so flagrantly inequitable, that its retention can be explained only through

ignorance or inertia. It is the cause of such crying injustice that its altera-
tion or its abolition must become the battle cry of every statesman and
reformer.[2]

Our predecessors in the discipline did not suffer overmuch from
inhibitions restricting the scope of their normative conclusions. Despite the frequent repetition of Seligman's colorful statement and the
expression of similar opinions by many others, the property tax has
changed at only a glacial rate. Reduced interest in its problems is the
result of increased attention to new developments in other areas
rather than of the elimination of persistent tax defects. It may even
be that some fiscal scholars have relied too much on theory and have
failed to note some of the lessons possible from experience.[3] In any
case, a brief review of past tax usages relevant to our study is made
here.

Property Taxation in Ancient Times

Despite Jens P. Jensen's contention that the American general
property tax is primarily an indigenous fiscal development,[4] some
consideration of its European antecedents is relevant to any study of
American property taxation.[5]

Land and tangible personal property have provided a tax base
since ancient times. Haskell P. Wald states that:

> In its origins, the land tax was doubtless conceived as a method of per-
> sonal taxation. In primitive economies, which were agricultural for the
> most part, land value or produce was the best available measure of the
> taxpaying capacity of the citizens. The ancient institution of the tithe, the
> progenitor of an important group of land taxes, was certainly grounded
> in ability-to-pay thinking. As the forms of tangible wealth multiplied and
> intangible property made its appearance on a large scale, the land tax was
> converted to an essentially impersonal levy. The latest trend toward
> personalization of the tax is thus completing a cycle.[6]

Property areas, values, or incomes, despite variation in their satisfaction of concepts of tax equity, provided—at least to some degree—
a tax base within the administrative capability of primitive governments. This, coupled with the fact that land and tangible personalty
were the principal indices of wealth during ancient and medieval
times, explains the frequent use of land and tangible personal
property as a subject of taxation.

Seligman notes that a land tax, formally a classified property tax,
was levied in Athens in 596 B.C. He also indicates that the early
Roman property tax applied only to realty. Later Roman property
taxes sought to reach personal property, but after a time it slipped

out of assessment. The imperial tax system which developed later included a variety of direct and indirect taxes rather than a general property tax.[7] Thus the ancient world provides an example of an often-observed fiscal phenomenon—the property-tax cycle from land to general property and back to land again. This pattern will be considered later after discussion of the medieval tax practices— especially those in England—which appear to have particular relevance to the development of property-tax institutions in the United States.

Property Taxation—Medieval Period

It is hazardous to generalize about taxation in the confused and diverse medieval period. Royal fiscal policies often amounted to the King's getting what he could—that being limited, in part, by the constraints of the right-duty relationships which characterized the feudal system. The strictly feudal revenue of the Crown—the incidents of tenure such as scutage, relief, tallage, and wardship [8]—were often inadequate revenue producers [9] and appear to be related only indirectly to subsequent tax developments.

It is probable that the Englishman of the twelfth century had no very precise notion of appropriate sources of taxation. Yet from the accession of Henry II to the death of Henry III (1154–1272), significant developments took place in the English tax pattern.[10] The Saladin Tithe of 1188, designed to support the third crusade, applied a 10 percent rate to rents and movable property. Similar taxes, known as the subsidy and the tenth (on personalty) and fifteenth (on realty), were later levied by the Crown when appropriate consent was registered by the *curia regis* and, subsequently, by the Parliament.

These medieval property taxes were considered the equivalent of a general property tax by Seligman.[11] They became stereotyped apportioned taxes after 1334. Revenue yields declined, exemptions multiplied, and once again, *as in ancient times,* personal property slipped out of assessment and dropped from the tax rolls. The general-property levy gradually became, in effect, a land tax and, given the typical lag of the law, was first so called in 1697. Thus medieval English general-property taxation became fossilized. Periodic valuation of the tax base apparently proved to be too hard for existing administrative machinery, and effective public support of this tax was insufficient to maintain it as originally conceived.[12] As a result, the medieval property tax passed through a cycle not unlike that of earlier and later times.

While the taxation of personal property had not been completely abandoned in England at the time America was colonized, the American colonists may have arrived with an interesting dichotomy in their conception of the property tax: ideally the tax should cover all property, but practically it could be expected to apply only to land. Presupposing such a disparity between theory and practice, along with a well-developed individualism and a distinct aversion to taxes in general, it is probable that colonial fiscal decisions were indeed difficult.

Of more immediate relevance to local property-tax developments in the English colonies of North America was the poor-law rate pattern such as that established by 43 Elizabeth c. 2 in 1601 and described by Edwin Cannan. The parish poor rate was not necessarily assessed consistently as an equal pound rate but took estimated ability into account in determining tax liability. Cannan points out that, despite tendencies toward standardization, as late as 1698 a King's Bench decision noted that "the rent is no standing rule, for circumstances may differ, and there ought to be regard *ad statum et facultates*." [13] He observes that, in fact, the old practice of forming a general estimate of ability lingered on as late as 1823 in some parishes. In 1739, during the reign of George II, all local rates were consolidated with the poor-law rate and based on ability. This pattern, naturally enough, had a significant effect upon the development of local taxation in British America.

Property Taxation in America

The Colonial Experience

Expenditures by the colonial governments were modest, allowing gradual development of provincial and local tax patterns. While the fiscal ideas and institutions of England were influential forces, the colonists developed their own particular variations upon received themes. Three related taxes—on polls, property, and faculty (potential income-earning capacity)—were used, especially in New England.

Because there were no material inequalities in wealth, each man's value "was fairly measured by his head and hands," [14] and a poll tax had a degree of logical justification. The first internal tax in the colonies was a poll tax, payable in tobacco, levied by Virginia in 1619.[15] As differences in wealth and income developed, however, alternative taxes were desired by at least some citizens. Responses varied somewhat by colony, by region, and in terms of the economic interest of the dominant decisional groups. Selected examples will necessarily suffice here.

Massachusetts.—The case of Massachusetts provides an example of colonial tax development which is not atypical of New England. A poll tax was levied from the beginning of the colony. During the 1630's incidental property taxes were levied as needs arose. Finally, in 1646, the property tax was put on an annual basis.[16] It should be noted that while contemporary property taxes are *in rem* levies— objective taxes on the property itself—colonial property taxes were frequently essentially personal in character and also were often specific rather than *ad valorem*. In effect, the combination of poll, property, and faculty taxes sought to use ability, as it was then conceived, as a tax base. This overlapping tax triad constituted a colonial equivalent of the nineteenth-century general property tax and is the fiscal institution out of which that levy evolved. The General Court of Massachusetts stated the relevant tax principle in 1634 as follows: "In all rates and public charges the towns shall have respect to levy every man according to his estate, and with consideration all other his abilities whatsoever and not according to the number of his persons." [17]

Massachusetts applied the property tax to the "visible estate," real and personal; this was supplemented by poll and faculty taxes. As Bullock put it, "The Act of 1646 . . . definitely established a system of direct taxation upon property, income and polls, which continued in operation without fundamental changes until 1862, and for the most part lasted until the twentieth century." [18]

Over time, personal income, or faculty, supplied only a negligible amount of revenue; the concept, so intriguing to scholars and so clearly derived from Tudor England, came to be of minor fiscal significance. In the 1700's, it was customary to levy one-third of direct taxes on polls and two-thirds on property. The tax history of other New England colonies recapitulates, in general, that of Massachusetts.[19] This pattern also applies to Maine at a later time.[20] Similarly, after property taxation was established in New York in 1683, that jurisdiction appears to recapitulate the usual property-tax developmental pattern.[21]

Unlike New England, the Southern Colonies did not initially accept property taxation. In general, they preferred to rely upon polls, import duties, and indirect taxes. This is explained, no doubt, by the fact that provincial governments were generally controlled by plantation owners. Tax developments in Virginia, Maryland, and North

Carolina provide adequate examples of taxation in the South.

Virginia.—As indicated earlier, the first levy in Virginia was the poll tax of 1619. A property tax was levied during 1645–48; this type of levy was not used again until 1755 at the time of the French and Indian War. The land-tax rate was 1s. 3d. per hundred acres. In 1763, a year for which data are available, total revenue was £43,000, of which polls produced £24,000 compared with £10,000 from land.[22]

Maryland.—In 1641 a "subsedye" for the "better support" of the Lord Proprietor was passed. This was a poll tax of 15 pounds of tobacco on every person over 12 years of age. Similar revenue devices were used until 1756 when the first property tax on realty was imposed. The scope of this levy was extended to all property in 1777, after the declaration of rights by the state convention of 1776 condemned poll taxes. After the Revolution, the property tax was less used, except during the period of the War of 1812, and income from licenses, fines, and transfer taxes supplied the state fisc. From 1826 until 1841 no significant property tax was levied in Maryland.[23] Thereafter, circumstances, including debts derived from state internal improvements policy, dictated use of the general property tax.

North Carolina.—Before 1715, North Carolina relied upon customs and tonnage duties for revenue. In that year, however, the first direct taxes were levied; both poll and land taxes were adopted, the latter at a rate of 2s. 6d. per hundred acres.[24] The poll tax was the largest source of revenue during the colonial period. Reluctance to rely heavily upon land taxes was intensified by the levying of quit-rents due the Lords Proprietors. Local revenues were obtained by poll taxes on the tithables. A property tax was levied in 1777. After the Revolution, transfer from the states to the federal government of the right to levy import duties necessitated greater use of property taxation in the southern states in general and in North Carolina in particular. In 1784, rural land was taxed by the acre and town lots *ad valorem*. By 1819, all realty was taxed according to value.[25] North Carolina, therefore, while somewhat differently circumstanced initially, began the nineteenth century with a property-tax system not unlike that of her neighbors.

Thus, prior to the Revolution, the American colonies tended to follow the pattern previously established by the English land taxes and poor rates except that the use of property as a tax base was, in some instances, deferred. By the beginning of the nineteenth century, derivative state and local tax systems were more complex, more diverse, and generally well on the way to the development of the full-blown general property tax.

Nineteenth-Century Property Taxation

By the end of the American Revolution, most of the states had levied poll and property taxes. Collections were poor and public attitudes nonsupportive. Administrative organization was inadequate, and the will to develop an effective tax system was not yet apparent. Fortunately, however, the 1790's were a financial "golden age" [26] during which states were able, for the most part, to rely almost entirely upon non-tax revenue. This happy situation continued until 1812 for the older states; new territories and states necessarily depended upon taxation for what were relatively modest expenditure requirements.

While state and local governments, no doubt reflecting popular attitudes, were often fiscally exuberant during the first half of the nineteenth century, this period saw the general property tax become the norm for state and local tax patterns. As Richard T. Ely put it, in a much-quoted statement, the period

. . . witnessed the complete establishment of the American system of state and local taxation. The distinguishing feature of the system may be described in a single sentence. It is the taxation of all property, movable and immovable, visible and invisible, or real and personal, as we say in America, at one uniform rate. This is the only direct tax known in most of our commonwealths, and it is only recently that certain special forms of taxation have assumed greater importance in some of our state budgets than this.[27]

This period, then, saw the property tax assume its mature character. Developments included (*a*) a shift from area-measurement bases or from assessment based upon probable income to the market-value assessment standard; (*b*) general adoption of an all-inclusive statement of taxable property and specification of broad exemption categories; (*c*) the development of improved, though still often rudimentary, administrative and equalization organization; and (*d*) the initial development of special supplemental and/or in-lieu taxes for newly developed institutions and for types of property which did not easily came under the general-property-tax rubric.

Limitations of space, time, and relevance preclude a state-by-state consideration of nineteenth-century property-tax developments; two states, Ohio and Illinois, are selected arbitrarily as examples.

The Ohio Story.—From 1803 to 1825, Ohio derived the main part of its revenues from a land tax. Realty was not taxed *ad valorem* but was listed for tax purposes in one of three classes by local assessors, and a specific rate per acre was applied for each class.[28] It is not particularly surprising to be informed by the fiscal historian of the period, E. L. Bogart, that gradually more and more property found its way into the lowest-rate class.[29] This system of land classification and specific rates caused much dissatisfaction, and numerous suggestions for adoption of an *ad valorem* system were made prior to 1825. In that year, the General Assembly adopted "An Act establishing an equitable mode of levying the taxes of this state" which abolished the old system of land classification and provided for the valuation of real property at its true value in money.[30] The market-value standard has been a component of Ohio property-tax law since that time. Of possible interest to those concerned with land-value taxation is Section 15 of the 1825 Act, which provided that land should be valued "without taking into consideration the value of actual improvements made thereon." [31] Apparently no formal economic analysis was devoted to the possible results of this pragmatic policy decision; it did not, in any event, long survive the trend to the general property tax.

The period 1825–1846 in Ohio property-tax history may be described as one in which the legal property-tax base was extended to include more and more categories of property. This process culminated in the adoption of the Kelley Act in 1846, which applied the uniform rule of taxation according to value to all property not specifically exempted.[32] An evident desire to remove it from the area of potential legislative caprice led to the inclusion of the uniform rule as Section 2, Article XII of the Ohio Constitution of 1851. The uniform rule remained applicable to realty and personalty alike until the adoption in 1929 of the classification amendment of Article XII, which became effective in 1931. Thereafter, both tangible and intangible personalty were classified for *ad valorem* tax purposes, leaving the uniform rule applicable only to land and the improvements thereon.[33] This abbreviated version of the Ohio story is reasonably representative of developments in many other places.[34]

Illinois Development.—As a territory, Illinois used a classified land tax with specific rates per 100 acres just as Kentucky and Ohio did.[35] The first state constitution (1818) authorized a general property tax; only land and certain enumerated property categories were made taxable prior to 1839, however.

A number of expensive circumstances, including an aggressive internal improvements policy, an unsuccessful state banking venture, the panic of 1837, and subsequent depressed business conditions, impaired the state financial situation. This by no means atypical situation stimulated development of a full-blown general-property-tax system in Illinois. The tax did not prevent temporary defaults on the state debt but was a significant factor in allowing the state to avoid repudiation of its debt. The Constitutions of 1848 and 1870 provided for a general-property-tax system with a uniform market-value assessment standard and for what amounted to local administration coupled with some state equalization authority. Thus, the early history of property taxation followed much the same pattern in Illinois as it did in other jurisdictions.[36]

These examples are representative of the evolution of the general property tax up to, and in some instances beyond, approximately the time of the Civil War.[37] While prolixity is by no means novel in the voluminous literature of property taxation, it would seem sufficient here to describe, in very general terms, developments since the Civil War. Many of the topics related to this period are subjects of other papers in this symposium and merit treatment in more depth than possible here.

Survey: Post-Civil-War Property-Tax Developments

Although the general property tax had achieved ascendancy in state and local tax systems, there was growing recognition, after the Civil War, of its limitations and inadequacies. Early responses to this attitude were (a) increased centralization of property-tax administration; (b) central assessment of railroad property or special taxation of such property; (c) the creation or revival of state equalization agencies; and (d) the developing realization that uniform-rule, ad valorem taxation of special property categories was inadequate and that alternate fiscal arrangements were needed because of the increasing heterogeneity of property.

In 1902, state and local revenues were still derived principally from the general property tax. The period around the turn of the century, however, saw the development of state tax commissions and the recognition of the increased importance of effective administration.[38] Rising tax rates at this time stimulated renewed interest in effective assessment and in equalization. Most significant, however, was the development of new revenue sources which, in due course, would permit reduced reliance upon property taxation at the state level.

Twentieth-Century Developments

Since 1900, and more particularly since 1930, property-tax development has included (a) the repeal or modification of uniform-rule provisions and the classification of property for tax purposes; (b) the exemption of particular types and categories of property from ad valorem taxation and, in some instances, the substitution of in-lieu taxes so that the property tax has steadily lost its *general* character; (*c*) the supplementation and/or replacement of property-tax revenues by other forms of taxation at either the state or local level; (*d*) new administrative patterns involving either increased state administrative responsibility or additional state supervision of local property-tax administration; and (*e*) increased federal and state aid to local governments. Despite these developments, the prevalence of gross inequalities in assessment, the frequent inadequacies of property-tax administrative organization, and the characteristic tendency of officials and taxpayers to ignore property-tax law as it is written were noted, in 1963, by the Advisory Commission on Intergovernmental Relations.[39] Centuries of property-tax experience have failed to produce either perfection in, or scholarly satisfaction with, existing property taxation. Rather clear prescriptions for property-tax reform have been made repeatedly, time out of mind. Yet significant changes have come primarily in periods of crisis or under the impact of quite glaring inequities.

Multiple interpretations obviously can be made and have been made about the historical sweep of property-tax development here described. The volume of criticism has been loud, the rate of change slow, and reform often dictated by unrelated external events. These facts do not detract from the validity of property-tax-improvement proposals. They do emphasize the inertia of mankind; the high premium often placed upon the certain, the known, and the predictable; and, lastly, the vitality of accepted fiscal institutions as long as the stress they induce is not extreme.

This paper has surveyed some aspects of property taxation over a long span of history. Necessarily, detail has been minimized and relevant background omitted. Certain tentative conclusions emerge.

a) Property has been much used as a tax base since ancient times.
b) The property-tax cycle (observed by Bastable, Seligman, and others) appears repeatedly in history—i.e., as a particular society and economy develops, property taxation moves from a specific to an *ad valorem* rate; from taxation of land to tax coverage of all or most property. Thereafter, as property becomes more heterogeneous in character and ownership distributed less equally, other taxes are substituted in relation to some categories of property, and the property tax reverts to a levy essentially on realty. A study of the past illustrates the continual recurrence of such a pattern.
c) Prediction of future tax patterns is obviously hazardous. Effective

property taxation is dependent in part, however, upon the generation, recording, retrieval, and effective use of a quite considerable bank of ownership and value-descriptive data. In the past, data-processing capabilities have been inadequate for the information-handling tasks implicit in property taxation. Modern data-processing capabilities and potentials remove this bar to effective *ad valorem* property taxation. Accordingly, its use will be more a function of human decision-making, tastes, and rational (or irrational) choices among tax alternatives than in the past. Repetition of past cyclical behavior in the property-tax base does not, therefore, appear automatically necessary merely because of developing socio-economic complexity.

d) Property taxation has developed out of an essentially agrarian background and, despite the efforts of many over a rather extended period,[40] is not yet well adjusted to an essentially urban society. This challenge remains, not only for the scholar and the lawmaker, but for all society.

Notes

1 C. F. Bastable, *Public Finance* (London: Macmillan, 1892), p. 424.

2 Edwin R. A. Seligman, "The General Property Tax," in *Essays in Taxation* (9th ed.; New York: Macmillan, 1921), p. 62.

3 See O. W. Holmes, Jr., *The Common Law* (Boston: Little, Brown, 1881), pp. 1–5; and Thomas S. Adams, "Ideals and Idealism in Taxation," *American Economic Review*, 18 (March, 1928), 1.

4 Jens P. Jensen, *Property Taxation in the United States* (Chicago: University of Chicago Press, 1931), pp. 19 ff.

5 See, e.g., Jens P. Jensen, *Government Finance* (New York: Thomas Y. Crowell, 1937), pp. 233–38.

6 Haskell P. Wald, *Taxation of Agricultural Land in Underdeveloped Economies* (Cambridge, Mass.: Harvard University Press, 1959), p. 45.

7 Seligman, "The General Property Tax," p. 34.

8 See, e.g., Theodore F. T. Pluckett, *A Concise History of the Common Law* (5th ed.; Boston: Little, Brown, 1956), pp. 531–45; see also William Blackstone, *Commentaries on the Law of England*, ed. J. W. Ehrlich (San Carlos: Nourse Publishing, 1959), pp. 136–57.

9 Sir John Clapham, *A Concise Economic History of Britain* (Cambridge: Cambridge University Press, 1949), p. 174.

10 This story is well told in Sydney Knox Mitchell, *Taxation in Medieval England* (New Haven, Conn.: Yale University Press, 1951); see also Joseph R. Strayer and Charles H. Taylor, *Studies in Early French Taxation* (Cambridge, Mass.: Harvard University Press, 1939).

11 Seligman, "The General Property Tax," p. 45; but see William Kennedy, *English Taxation, 1640–1799* (London: G. Bell and Sons, 1913), for a possibly more reasonable interpretation.

12 See also W. R. Ward, *The English Land Tax in the Eighteenth Century* (London: Oxford University Press, 1953); detailed coverage is provided in Stephen Dowell, *A History of Taxation and Taxes in England* (London: Longmans, Green, 1888), esp. Vol. 2, bks. 1 and 2; local rates are covered most effectively in Edwin Cannan, *The History of Local Rates in England* (2nd ed.; London: P. S. King and Son, 1912).

13 Comerbach, *Reports,* p. 478, as cited in Cannan, *History of Local Rates,* p. 79.

14 William J. Shultz and M. R. Caine, *Financial Development of the United States* (New York: Prentice-Hall, 1937). p. 15.

15 Paul Studenski and Herman E. Kroos, *Financial History of the United States* (2nd ed.; New York: McGraw-Hill, 1963), p. 20.

16 E. E. Day, "History of the General Property Tax in Massachusetts, 1630–88" (thesis, Harvard University Library), reported in Charles J. Bullock, *Selected Readings in Public Finance* (3rd ed.; Boston: Ginn, 1924), pp. 305 ff.

17 *State and Local Taxation of Property* (New York: National Industrial Conference Board, 1930), p. 3.

18 Bullock, *Selected Readings in Public Finance,* p. 304.

19 M. Slade Kendrick, *Public Finance* (Boston: Houghton Mifflin, 1951), p. 95.

20 Fred E. Jewett, *A Financial History of Maine* (New York: Columbia University Press, 1937).

21 Kendrick, *Public Finance,* pp. 96–98, also citing J. C. Schwab, *History of the New York Property Tax* (Publications of the American Economic Association, Vol. 5, No. 5; Baltimore, 1890), and Frederick D. Bidwell, *Taxation in New York State* (Albany: J. B. Lyon, 1918).

22 William Z. Ripley, *Financial History of Virginia, 1609–1776* (Columbia College Studies in History, Economics, and Public Law, Vol. 4, No. 1; New York: Columbia College, 1893), pp. 38, 41.

23 Thomas S. Adams, *Taxation in Maryland* (Studies in State Taxation with Particular Reference to the Southern States, Johns Hopkins University Studies in Historical and Political Science, Series 18, No. 1; Baltimore, Md.: The Johns Hopkins Press, 1900), pp. 26, 29.

24 Coralie Parker, *The History of Taxation in North Carolina During the Colonial Period, 1663–1776* (New York: Columbia University Press, 1928), p. 98.

25 George E. Barnett, *Taxation in North Carolina* (Studies in State Taxation with Particular Reference to the Southern States, Johns Hopkins

University Studies in Historical and Political Science, Series 18, No. 2; Baltimore, Md.: The Johns Hopkins Press, 1900), p. 84.

26 See Shultz and Caine, *Financial Development,* pp. 159 ff.

27 Richard T. Ely and John H. Finley, *Taxation in American States and Cities* (New York: Thomas Y. Crowell, 1888), p. 131.

28 This practice followed the precedent established with the first tax on land levied for the purpose of financing the government of the Northwest Territory. See Act of May 1, 1798, I CHASE, STATUTES, 208; I LAWS OF THE NORTHWEST TERRITORY, 1788–1800, 307 (Illinois State Bar Assoc. Reprint, 1925).

29 E. L. Bogart, *Financial History of Ohio* (Urbana: University of Illinois Press, 1912), p. 183.

30 Act of February 3, 1825, 23 Ohio Laws 58, II CHASE, STATUTES, 1476.

31 This interesting statutory provision was noted by Ely in Ely and Finley, *Taxation,* p. 135.

32 Act of March 2, 1846, 44 Ohio Laws 85, 2 CURWEN 1260.

33 114 Ohio Laws 714 (1931).

34 This section is based upon Bogart, *Financial History of Ohio,* and Arthur D. Lynn, Jr., and Clinton V. Oster, "Real Property Taxation of Farm Lands and Structures," *Ohio State Law Journal,* 17 (1956), 75–88.

35 Robert Murray Haig, *A History of the General Property Tax in Illinois* (Urbana: University of Illinois Press, 1914), p. 37.

36 This section derives from: Haig, *Property Tax in Illinois;* Constance C. Einhorn and H. K. Allen, "Development of the Illinois Revenue System," in *Report of the Revenue Laws Commission* (Springfield: State of Illinois, 1949), pp. 1–51.

37 See, for example, comments in Arthur P. Becker, "The Wisconsin State Tax Dilemma," in National Tax Association, *1963 Proceedings of the Fifty-Sixth Annual Conference on Taxation,* ed. Walter Kress (Harrisburg, 1964), pp. 307–8; and Lawrence A. Leonard, "Property Taxation in Kansas, An Historical Analysis," *National Tax Journal,* 11 (September, 1958), 230. The literature is legion and completeness is beyond the scope of this summary paper.

38 See Harley L. Lutz, *The State Tax Commission* (Cambridge, Mass.: Harvard University Press, 1918).

39 Advisory Commission on Intergovernmental Relations, *The Role of the States in Strengthening the Property Tax,* Vol. 1 (Washington, D.C.: U.S. Government Printing Office, 1963). The staff work for the report was conducted by Frederick L. Bird and Edna T. Bird.

40 For general coverage of other views of property-tax development, see Jensen, *Property Taxation;* Simeon E. Leland, *The Classified Property Tax in the United States* (Boston: Houghton Mifflin, 1928); Harold M. Groves, *Financing Government* (6th ed.; New York: Holt, Rinehart and Winston, 1964); William J. Shultz and C. Lowell Harriss, *American Public Finance* (8th ed.; Englewood Cliffs, N.J.: Prentice-Hall, 1965).

2. Benjamin Bridges, Jr.

Past and Future Growth of
the Property Tax

The property tax is the backbone of the local revenue system in the United States. In 1963 property-tax revenue accounted for approximately 88 percent of the tax revenue of local governments, 68 percent of their general revenue from own sources, and 47 percent of their general revenue from all sources. Furthermore, the property tax is an important part of the federal-state-local revenue system. Property-tax revenue accounted for approximately 15 percent of all 1963 tax revenue and 13 percent of all 1963 general revenue. (See Table 2.3, p. 30.)

Forecasts of the future growth of this very important tax are needed to aid in the formulation of tax and expenditure policies. This paper attempts, by examining the past growth of this tax, to shed some light on its future growth. The first section of the paper deals with the growth of the property-tax base; the second section deals with the growth of property-tax revenue.

Growth of the Property-Tax Base

One method of making forecasts of the growth of the property-tax base is the income-elasticity method. This method is as follows: First, the future income elasticity of the property-tax base is forecast on the basis of estimates of income elasticities for the past. The elasticity coefficient shows the relationship between percentage changes in the tax base and percentage changes in income. Second, the percentage change in income is forecast. (There are numerous methods of forecasting income change.) Third, the growth of the tax base is derived from the two forecasts above. In this paper, the term "income elasticity of the property-tax base" always refers to the elasticity of the market value of the property-tax base with respect to Gross National Product (GNP).

In this section, elasticities of the property-tax base and its components for various periods between 1899 and 1961 are examined.[1] Estimates of elasticities for various periods between 1899 and 1957 are based on Raymond Goldsmith's annual wealth estimates; estimates for the period 1956–61 are based on Census of Governments data on market values of taxable property for 1956 and 1961.[2]

Elasticities for 1899–1957

The estimates of the market value of the property-tax base used in Table 2.1 are based on Raymond Goldsmith's wealth estimates. My estimated market value of the real-property-tax base is equal to Goldsmith's estimate of the market value of all privately owned land and structures minus his estimate of the market value of institutional structures; my estimated market value of the personal-property-tax base is equal to the sum of Goldsmith's market values of privately owned producer durables and of privately owned inventories. Goldsmith's wealth estimates are rather crude. Since the tax treatment of real property does not vary greatly from state to state, my estimates of the real-property-tax base are about as reliable as the wealth estimates upon which they are based. The tax treatment of personal property varies greatly from state to state. Producer durables and inventories are taxed in most, but not in all, states; motor vehicles and other consumer durables are taxed in some states. My estimates of the personal-property-tax base are thus considerably less reliable than the wealth estimates upon which they are based.

In this section, elasticities are presented for the periods 1899–1957, 1899–1929, 1929–48, 1948–57, 1948–53, and 1953–57. The first and last year of each of these periods is the peak year of a National Bureau of Economic Research reference cycle. Peak-to-peak periods were chosen in an effort to remove business-cycle effects from my elasticity estimates. The first peak year for which the Goldsmith wealth estimates are available is 1899; 1929 is the last peak year before the Great Depression; 1948 is the first postwar (World War II) peak year; 1953 and 1957 are the only other postwar peak years for which Goldsmith wealth estimates are available.[3]

Table 2.1 shows that the 1953–57 and 1948–57 elasticities of the real-property-tax base, 1.4 and 1.0 respectively, both exceeded the 1899–1957 elasticity of 0.9. The elasticities were 0.9 and 0.7 for the periods 1899–1929 and 1929–48 respectively.

The elasticities of different types of real property differed markedly. For 1953–57 the elasticities of non-farm residential property, non-farm non-residential property, and farm property were 1.2, 1.8, and 1.0 respectively. For 1948–57 the corresponding elasticities were 1.0, 1.2, and 0.8 respectively, and for 1899–1957 they were 0.9, 0.9, and 0.6 respectively.

The 1953–57 and 1948–57 elasticities of the personal-property-tax base, 1.3 and 1.1 respectively, both exceeded the 1899–1957 elasticity of 0.9. The elasticity coefficient was 0.9 for both 1899–1929 and 1929–48.

Table 2.1—GNP Elasticities of the Market Value
of the Property-Tax Base and its Components [a]

	Real Property					
Period	Non-farm non-residential property [b]	Non-farm residential property [b]	Farm property [b]	Weighted all real property [c]	Personal property [b]	Weighted all property [d]
1899–1957	0.9	0.9	0.6	0.9	0.9	0.9
1899–1929	1.0	0.9	0.6	0.9	0.9	0.9
1929–1948	0.8	0.5	0.6	0.7	0.9	0.7
1948–1957	1.0	1.2	0.8	1.0	1.1	1.1
1948–1953	0.9	0.9	0.7	0.8	1.0	0.9
1953–1957	1.2	1.8	1.0	1.4	1.3	1.4

[a] The property-value estimates are for ends of calendar years; the GNP estimates are for calendar years.

[b] Elasticities were calculated using the following formula.

$$E = \frac{\log (B_1/B_0)}{\log (Y_1/Y_0)}$$

Where E is the coefficient of elasticity, B_1 is the tax base for the ith year, and Y_i is GNP for the ith year. The above formula for E was derived by forcing the equation $\log B = \log A + E \log Y$ through our two observations (B_0, Y_0) and (B_1, Y_1). A is a constant term.

[c] Weighted by estimated proportion which each component is of 1961 assessed value of real property.

[d] Weighted by estimated proportion which each component is of 1961 assessed value of all property.

Sources: Raymond W. Goldsmith, *A Study of Saving in the United States*, 3 (Princeton: Princeton University Press, 1956), 12–15, 426–27; Goldsmith, *The National Wealth of the United States in the Postwar Period* (Studies in Capital Formation and Financing No. 10; Princeton: National Bureau of Economic Research, Princeton University Press, 1962), pp. 177–82, 184–89; U.S. Department of Commerce, Office of Business Economics, *U.S. Income and Output* (Washington, D.C.: U.S. Government Printing Office, 1958), pp. 118–19; U.S. Department of Commerce, Office of Business Economics, *Survey of Current Business*, 44 (July, 1964), 8; and U.S. Bureau of the Census, *Taxable Property Values*, Vol. 2 in *Census of Governments: 1962* (Washington, D.C.: U.S. Government Printing Office, 1964), pp. 28–29 and 32–33.

The 1953–57 and 1948–57 (weighted) elasticities of the property-tax base, 1.4 and 1.1 respectively, both exceeded the 1899–1957 elasticity of 0.9. The elasticities were 0.9 and 0.7 for the periods 1899–1929 and 1929–48 respectively.

Elasticities for 1956–61

Census of Governments publications present data on market values of the property-tax base for the years 1956 and 1961. Market values were derived from assessed values by the use of assessment-sales ratios.[4]

For the period 1956–61 the elasticity of the property-tax base was 1.5. The elasticities for all real property, non-farm residential real property, non-farm non-residential real property, and farm real property were 1.6, 1.6, 1.9, and 1.0 respectively.

Elasticities in the Future

In the years since World War II, the elasticity of the property-tax base has been greater than unity. Using the Goldsmith data, I found elasticities for 1948–57 and 1953–57 of 1.1 and 1.4 respectively; using the Census of Governments data, I found an elasticity for 1956–61 of 1.5. On the other hand, according to the Goldsmith data, the long-term elasticity (for the period 1899–1957) was 0.9, or less than unity.

On the basis of similar findings for the postwar period Dick Netzer, Robert Lampman, Otto Eckstein, and Selma Mushkin forecast elasticities of 1.0 to 1.5 for the decade or so following their studies. In his projections, Netzer used an elasticity of 1.0 for the period 1957–70 but stated that his forecast was probably too low.[5] Lampman forecast an elasticity in the range 1.0 to 1.5 (1.2 most probable) for the period 1960–70.[6] Eckstein forecast an elasticity of 1.4 for 1958–68.[7] Mushkin forecast an elasticity of 1.2 or 1.3 for the 1961–69 period.[8] She argued that independent projections of construction for 1961–69 indicate a similar elasticity.

On the other hand, Eugene McLoone forecast an elasticity of less than unity for the decade following his study (1960–70).[9] McLoone argued that independent projections of non-farm residential construction and non-farm non-residential construction indicated an elasticity for the decade of less than unity and one very similar to the long-term elasticity of the past fifty or sixty years.

Forecasters seem to agree that the future elasticity of the property-tax base will be above the 1929–48 elasticity of 0.7. This low elasticity was caused by the Great Depression and World War II. Forecasters differ, however, concerning the relative weights to be

given to the long-term elasticity and to the various postwar elasticities
in forecasting the future elasticity.

The elasticities for 1948–57, 1953–57, and 1956–61 all exceeded the
long-term elasticity. This fact suggests that the future elasticity will
also exceed the long-term elasticity of 0.9. On the other hand (as can
be seen in my *National Tax Journal* article), the 1953–61
elasticity of 1.4 to 1.5 (estimated by splicing together Goldsmith and
Census of Governments data) exceeded the elasticities of all earlier
periods of similar length. This fact suggests that the future elasticity
will be below that of 1953–61. Thus, giving weight to both the recent
past and the less-recent past, my best guess is that for the next decade
or so the elasticity of the property-tax base will be in the range 1.0
to 1.2.

Forecasting Methods

In my view, the income-elasticity method (described above) does
not produce very reliable forecasts of the growth of the property-tax
base. The income-elasticity method is essentially a simple regression
method. Tax base is the dependent variable, and income is the only
independent variable. The elasticity coefficient shows the relationship
between percentage changes in the tax base and percentage changes
in income. As shown in Table 2.1, this coefficient has not been a very
stable one. In addition, there is the problem of forecasting percentage
changes in income.

Other methods of forecasting the growth of the property-tax
base have not been very reliable either, however. For example, some
researchers have derived forecasts of residential construction (and
hence of the growth of the residential component of the property-
tax base) from forecasts of household formation and of cost per new
housing unit. Such forecasts have not been very accurate.[10] Other
researchers have used multiple regression methods to explain the
growth of the housing stock. Housing stock is the independent variable and the dependent variables include consumer income, the
relative price of housing, an interest rate, and mortgage credit
terms. The estimated regression coefficients differ markedly from
study to study, however.[11] Unfortunately, the poorness of available data
seriously hampers this approach. In addition, there is the problem
of forecasting the independent variables.

Since no one method of forecasting the growth of the property-
tax base has shown great reliability, forecasters would do well to
employ several different methods. Forecasters would also do well to
make separate forecasts for each of the major components of the

base, because the growth patterns of the various components of the property-tax base have differed markedly.

Growth of Property-Tax Revenue

The growth of the property-tax base is only one of a number of factors influencing the growth of property-tax revenue. Local expenditure pressures and the availability of other local-revenue sources (particularly aid from federal and state governments) are also important factors in influencing the revenue growth of this predominantly local tax. In round numbers, local governments in 1963 received 97 percent of all property-tax revenue. The local property tax financed approximately 46 percent of local direct general expenditure; revenue from federal and state governments, non-tax general revenue from own sources, revenue from other local taxes, and increases in debt financed approximately 30 percent, 15 percent, 7 percent, and 3 percent respectively of these local expenditures.

Over the next decade or so, an increasing emphasis on property-tax reform and on tax relief, along with the expansion of industrial property-tax exemptions, may significantly affect the choice among more expenditure, more property-tax revenue, and more revenue from other sources. Greater equalization of assessment will tend to bring down assessments of classes of property now assessed at a relatively higher proportion of their market value than other classes of property. Reforming the taxation of personal property by legally exempting from taxation classes of personal property that are now fractionally taxed will also reduce property-tax revenue. Because of the regressivity of the property tax, some additional tax relief for low-income taxpayers will be granted. The adverse effect of the property tax on urban redevelopment will cause some additional tax relief for slum redevelopment projects. Increased interarea competition for industry will limit the revenue productivity of the property tax.[12] On the other hand, greater equity in property-tax administration should help somewhat to lower taxpayer resistance.

The importance of political factors in determining the growth of property-tax revenue makes forecasting the growth of this revenue considerably more difficult than forecasting the growth of the property-tax base. In an effort to shed some light on the future growth of property-tax revenue, I have derived the property-tax implications of various assumptions with regard to some of the factors which will affect the tax's revenue growth over the next decade. This approach is of some help in making policy decisions with regard to the future growth of the tax's revenue.

Before discussing the future growth of property-tax revenue, however, the past growth of the tax's revenue will be dealt with briefly. Tables 2.2 and 2.3 show that from 1902 to 1927 there was little change in the relative importance of the property tax but that from 1927 to 1948 the relative importance of the property tax declined drastically. The rapid decline of the property tax did not continue during the 1948–63 period, however. During this period its roles in the local and the combined state-local revenue systems declined only slightly, while its role in the combined federal-state-local revenue system increased appreciably. From 1948 to 1963 property-tax revenue decreased from 51 percent to 47 percent of local general revenue and from 36 percent to 32 percent of state-local general revenue, but increased from 10 percent to 13 percent of federal-state-local general revenue. In addition, property-tax revenue increased from 1.03 to 1.32 percent of property value and from 2.61 to 3.61 percent of GNP.

The property-tax implications of various sets of assumptions with regard to the GNP elasticity of the property-tax base, the growth rate of GNP, and growth rate of local expenditures will now be examined. As stated in the previous section of the paper, a property-tax base elasticity coefficient of 1.0 to 1.2 seems reasonable for the period 1963–75. The most careful and recent projections of state-local expenditures were made for the Council of State Governments (CSG). The Council's expenditure projections are based upon a GNP growth rate for 1962–70 of 5.7 percent per annum.[13] In these projections, the assumed annual growth rates of real GNP and the GNP price deflator are 4.1 and 1.5 respectively. The annual GNP growth rate for 1963–75 should be similar to that for 1962–70. Thus, a GNP growth rate of 5 to 6 percent per annum seems reasonable for 1963–75. The CSG projects a growth rate of combined state-local expenditure for 1962–70 of 7.2 percent per annum.[14] This is a projection of what the economic and political processes are likely to produce, not necessarily of what is considered desirable. The CSG did not give separate projections for local expenditure. After a study of the composition of the state-local expenditure increases projected by the CSG, however, I conclude that, if there are no important changes in allocation of functions between the state and local levels of government, the growth rate for local expenditures would be about 0.7 percent per annum lower than that for combined state-local expenditures. The annual local expenditure growth rate for 1963–75 should not be too different from (although perhaps slightly lower than) that for 1962–70. An annual growth rate for local expenditure of 6 to 7 percent seems reasonable, therefore, for 1963–75.

Three sets of assumptions with regard to base elasticity, growth rate of GNP, and growth rate of local expenditure are discussed in the

Table 2.2—Relationship of Property-Tax Revenue to GNP [a]
and to Market Value of Property [b]: 1902–63

Fiscal [c] year	Property-tax revenue as a percentage of GNP	Property-tax revenue as a percentage of market value of real and personal property [d]	Real-property-tax revenue as a percentage of market value of real property [e]
1902	3.47	0.91	0.92
1913	3.71	0.99	1.02
1922	4.58	1.32	1.38
1927	4.88	1.54	1.60
1932	5.88	1.67	1.69
1934	7.28	1.66	1.67
1936	5.65	1.63	1.65
1938	4.89	1.59	1.63
1940	4.86	1.56	1.59
1942	3.61	1.36	1.43
1944	2.39	1.24	1.31
1946	2.33	1.21	1.26
1948	2.61	1.03	1.10
1950	2.85	1.13	1.23
1952	2.63	1.05	1.17
1953	2.70	1.10	1.21
1954	2.73	1.13	1.24
1955	2.96	1.17	1.28
1956	2.96	1.20	1.30.
1957	3.07	1.21	1.32
1958	3.17	1.23	1.34
1959	3.37	1.25	1.36
1960	3.40	n.a.	n.a.
1961	3.58	n.a.	n.a.
1962	3.67	n.a.	n.a.
1963	3.61	1.32 [f]	1.43 [f]

n.a.—Not available.

[a] GNP of the previous calendar year.

[b] Market value of property at the end of the previous calendar year.

[c] In this table data are shown for all years of this century for which property-tax revenue data are available.

[d] Real property consists of privately owned land and all structures except institutional structures. Personal property consists of privately owned producer durables and inventories.

[e] Real property consists of privately owned land and all structures except institutional structures. Real-property-tax revenue estimated as 80 percent of all property-tax revenue.

[f] Estimated as 107 percent of the 1958 rate. According to Census of Governments data, the rate for locally assessed real property increased by 7 percent from 1957 to 1962 [U.S. Bureau of the Census, *Property Taxation in 1962*, State and Local Government Special Studies No. 47 (Washington: U.S. Government Printing Office,

(Notes to table continued on following page)

1964) , p. 19.] The rates for 1957 and 1962 were 1.35 percent and 1.44 percent respectively.

Sources: U.S. Bureau of the Census, *Historical Statistics on Governmental Finances and Employment,* Vol. 6, No. 4, in *Census of Governments: 1962* (Washington, D.C.: U.S. Government Printing Office, 1964) , pp. 32–34; Raymond W. Goldsmith, *A Study of Saving in the United States,* 3 (Princeton: Princeton University Press, 1956), 12–15, 426–27; Goldsmith, *The National Wealth of the United States in the Postwar Period* (Studies in Capital Formation and Financing No. 10; Princeton: National Bureau of Economic Research, Princeton University Press, 1962) , pp. 177–82, 184–89; U.S. Department of Commerce, Office of Business Economics, *U.S. Income and Output* (Washington, D.C.: U.S. Government Printing Office, 1958) , pp. 118–19; U.S. Department of Commerce, Office of Business Economics, *Survey of Current Business,* 44 (July, 1964), 8; and U.S. Bureau of the Census, *Governmental Finances in 1963,* Series G-GF 63—No. 2 (Washington, D.C.: U.S. Government Printing Office, 1964) , p. 22.

paper. These three hypothetical cases are denoted as the high-rate, medium-rate, and low-rate cases. For the high-rate case the base elasticity is 1.0, the annual GNP growth rate is 5.0 percent, and the annual local expenditure growth rate is 7.0 percent; for the medium-rate case the corresponding figures are 1.1, 5.5 percent, and 6.5 percent; for the low-rate case the corresponding figures are 1.2, 6.0 percent, and 6.0 percent. For any given share of local expenditure financed by the local property tax, the high-rate case requires the highest effective property-tax rate; the medium-rate case a lower effective rate; and the low-rate case the lowest effective rate. In my judgment, the medium-rate case is the most reasonable set of assumptions. The other two cases provide reasonable outer bounds. The property-tax implications of these three sets of assumptions are illustrated in Table 2.4, and the implications of these and other sets of assumptions (some reasonable and some not so reasonable) can be seen in Table 2.6.

Medium-Rate Case

For the period 1963–75 assume a base elasticity of 1.1, a GNP growth rate of 5.5 percent per annum, and a local-expenditure growth rate of 6.5 percent per annum. If the 1975 share of local direct general expenditure financed by the local property tax is to equal the 1963 share, approximately 46 percent (Table 2.3) , the effective property-tax rate of 1.32 percent (Table 2.2) must increase 5 percent, to 1.39 percent (Table 2.4) .[15] The 1975 effective rate would be the highest rate since 1940, but it would be well below the highest rate ever achieved during prosperity—the 1927 rate of 1.54 percent (Table 2.2) . The 1963–75 annual increase of 0.4 percent in the effective rate (Table 2.4) would be far below the 1954–63 annual increase of 1.7

Table 2.3—Relationship of Property-Tax Revenue to Other Revenue Sources

Fiscal Year	Local government property-tax revenue as a percentage of			
	Direct general expenditure	General revenue from all sources	General revenue from own sources	Tax revenue
1902	71.0	73.1	78.2	88.6
1913	67.5	72.8	77.4	91.1
1922	71.0	76.9	83.9	96.9
1927	74.8	73.9	82.3	97.3
1932	71.7	73.1	85.2	97.3
1934	73.5	65.3	86.1	96.7
1936	71.3	62.6	85.3	94.7
1938	67.9	63.1	84.5	93.8
1940	64.2	60.1	83.3	92.7
1942	66.5	60.0	80.8	92.4
1944	70.4	59.4	79.7	92.7
1946	60.2	57.6	77.9	91.9
1948	50.9	51.4	74.3	88.6
1950	47.7	50.2	73.5	88.2
1952	47.5	48.9	71.0	87.5
1953	48.4	49.0	71.0	87.0
1954	46.5	49.0	70.3	87.2
1955	45.8	48.9	70.0	86.9
1956	46.3	48.8	69.5	86.8
1957	46.3	48.5	69.3	86.7
1958	46.0	48.7	69.9	87.4
1959	45.7	48.7	69.5	87.2
1960	46.3	47.8	69.0	87.4
1961	46.7	48.4	69.5	87.7
1962	46.2	48.0	69.0	87.7
1963	45.8	47.1	68.0	87.5

Source: U.S. Bureau of the Census, *Historical Statistics on Governmental Finances* U.S. Government Printing Office, 1964) , pp. 32–34, 38–40, 44–46; and U.S. Bureau ton, D.C.: U.S. Government Printing Office, 1964) , pp. 22–23.

percent (Table 2.5). The required 1963–75 GNP elasticity of other local revenue (local direct general expenditure minus local property-tax revenue) of 1.2 (Table 2.4) would be well below the 1954–63 other-revenue elasticity of 1.7 (Table 2.5). Although the rate increase required to maintain the property-tax share is not large, it seems likely that the growth of other revenue will permit a significant decline in the property-tax share.

On the other hand, if the 1975 effective rate is to equal the 1963 effective rate of 1.32 percent, the share of local expenditure financed and to Local Direct General Expenditure: 1902-63

State and local government property-tax revenue as a percentage of			Federal, state, and local government property-tax revenue as a percentage of	
General revenue from all sources	General revenue from own sources	Tax revenue	General revenue	Tax revenue
71.6	72.1	82.1	43.3	51.4
69.7	70.1	82.8	46.5	58.7
69.5	71.1	82.7	37.3	45.0
65.1	66.1	77.7	40.9	50.0
61.7	63.8	72.8	46.8	56.2
53.1	61.2	68.9	39.0	46.0
48.8	55.0	61.1	32.7	38.7
48.1	52.7	58.4	29.6	34.3
46.1	51.1	56.7	29.8	34.9
43.5	47.5	53.2	18.6	21.8
42.2	46.3	52.5	7.9	9.4
40.4	43.4	49.4	9.0	10.8
35.5	39.8	45.9	10.3	12.0
35.1	39.9	46.2	12.6	14.4
34.4	38.3	44.8	9.7	10.9
34.3	38.4	44.8	10.1	11.2
34.2	38.3	45.2	10.4	11.8
34.5	38.4	45.7	11.5	13.2
33.9	37.5	44.6	11.2	12.8
33.7	37.5	44.6	11.4	13.0
34.1	38.6	46.2	12.5	14.3
33.1	38.5	46.3	13.1	15.0
32.5	37.7	45.4	12.6	14.5
33.3	38.4	46.3	13.4	15.5
32.7	37.8	45.9	13.4	15.4
31.9	37.1	45.4	13.2	15.3

and Employment, Vol. 6, No. 4, in *Census of Governments: 1962* (Washington, D.C.: of the Census, *Governmental Finances in 1963,* Series G-GF 63—No. 2 (Washing-

by the local property tax must decrease 5 percent, from (in round numbers) 46 percent to 44 percent (Table 2.4) .[16] Thus, the property-tax share would be slightly below the lowest share ever achieved— approximately 46 percent. (Table 2.3). The required 1963–75 elasticity of other revenue, 1.2 (Table 2.4), would be well below the 1954–63 elasticity of 1.7 (Table 2.5). It seems likely that the growth of other revenue will permit a decline in the property-tax rate as well as a decline in the property-tax share.

Table 2.4—Property-Tax Implications of Three Sets of Assumptions

	High-rate case [a]	Medium-rate case [b]	Low-rate case [c]
Property-tax share constant at 1963 level: [d]			
1975 effective rate	1.65	1.39	1.15
1963–75 percentage change in property-tax rate	25	5	— 13
Average annual percentage change in property-tax rate	2.0	0.4	— 1.2
GNP elasticity of other revenue [e]	1.4	1.2	1.0
Property-tax rate constant at 1963 level: [f]			
1975 property-tax share	37	44	53
1963–75 percentage change in property-tax share	— 20	— 5	15
Average annual percentage change in property-tax share	1.8	—0.4	1.2
GNP elasticity of other revenue [e]	1.7	1.2	0.8

[a] Base elasticity of 1.0, GNP annual growth rate of 5.0 percent, and local-expenditure annual growth rate of 7.0 percent.

[b] Base elasticity of 1.1, GNP annual growth rate of 5.5 percent, and local-expenditure annual growth rate of 6.5 percent.

[c] Base elasticity of 1.2, GNP annual growth rate of 6.0 percent, and local-expenditure annual growth rate of 6.0 percent.

[d] Property-tax share is ratio of local property tax to local direct general expenditure.

[e] Other revenue is local direct general expenditure minus local property-tax revenue.

[f] Property-tax rate is the ratio of state-local property-tax revenue to the market value of real and personal property.

High-Rate Case

Assume a base elasticity of 1.0, a GNP annual growth rate of 5.0 percent, and a local-expenditure annual growth rate of 7.0 percent. If the 1975 property-tax share is to equal the 1963 share, the effective rate must increase 25 percent, from 1.32 percent to 1.65 percent (Table 2.4). The 1975 effective rate would then almost match the highest rate ever achieved—the 1.67 percent of 1932 (Table 2.2). The 1963–75 annual percentage increase of the effective rate, 2.0 (Table 2.4), would be somewhat above the 1954–63 annual percentage increase of 1.7 (Table 2.5). The required 1963–75 elasticity of other revenue, 1.4 (Table 2.4), would be somewhat below the 1954–63 elasticity of 1.7 (Table 2.5). Since the rate increase required to maintain the property-tax share is quite large, it seems likely that the property-tax share will decline significantly.

Table 2.5—Changes in Property-Tax Rates, Changes in Property-Tax Shares, and GNP Elasticities of Other Revenue: 1902–63

Period [a] (fiscal years)	Annual percentage change of property-tax rate [b]	Annual percentage change of property-tax share [c]	GNP elasticity of other revenue [d]
1902–1958	0.5	— 0.8	1.3
1902–1927	2.1	0.2	1.1
1927–1948	— 1.9	— 1.8	1.5
1948–1958	1.8	— 1.0	1.6
1948–1954	1.6	— 1.5	1.5
1954–1958	2.1	— 0.3	1.9
1902–1963	0.6	— 0.7	1.4
1948–1963	1.7	— 0.7	1.6
1954–1963	1.7	— 0.2	1.7
1958–1963	1.4	— 0.1	1.6

[a] Periods in this table were chosen to correspond as closely as available data permitted with the periods used in Table 2.1.

[b] Property-tax rate is ratio of state-local property-tax revenue to market value of real and personal property.

[c] Property-tax share is ratio of local property-tax revenue to local direct general expenditure.

[d] Other revenue is local direct general expenditure minus local property-tax revenue. Elasticities were calculated using the formula given in Table 2.1. GNP of the previous calendar year.

Sources: U.S. Bureau of the Census, Historical Statistics on Governmental Finances and Employment, Vol. 6, No. 4, in Census of Governments: 1962 (Washington, D.C.: U.S. Government Printing Office, 1964), Tables 2.2 and 2.3, pp. 44–46; U.S. Bureau of the Census, Governmental Finances in 1963, Series G-GF 63—No. 2 (Washington, D.C.: U.S. Government Printing Office, 1964), pp. 22–23; Raymond W. Goldsmith, A Study of Saving in the United States, 3 (Princeton: Princeton University Press, 1956), 426–27; U.S. Department of Commerce, Office of Business Economics, U.S. Income and Output (Washington, D.C.: U.S. Government Printing Office, 1958), pp. 118–19; and U.S. Department of Commerce, Office of Business Economics, Survey of Current Business, 44 (July, 1964), 8.

If the 1975 effective rate is to equal the 1963 effective rate, however, the property-tax share must decrease 20 percent, from (in round numbers) 46 percent to 37 percent (Table 2.4). The property-tax share would thus be far below the lowest share ever achieved—approximately 46 percent (Table 2.3). The required 1963–75 elasticity of other revenue, 1.7 (Table 2.4), would equal the 1954–63 elasticity of 1.7 (Table 2.5). It seems likely that the property-tax rate will show little change.

Table 2.6—Ratios of 1975 Property-Tax Rate to 1963
Property-Tax Rate for Various Sets of Assumptions [a]

Annual percentage increase	GNP elasticity of the market value of the property-tax base				
	0.8	1.0	1.1	1.2	1.4
Property-tax revenue: 7.5%					
GNP: 4.5%	1.56	1.41	1.33	1.27	1.14
GNP: 5.0%	1.49	1.33	1.25	1.18	1.05
GNP: 5.5%	1.43	1.25	1.18	1.10	0.97
GNP: 6.0%	1.35	1.18	1.10	1.03	0.89
GNP: 6.5%	1.30	1.12	1.04	0.96	0.83
Property-tax revenue: 7.0%					
GNP: 4.5%	1.47	1.33	1.27	1.19	1.08
GNP: 5.0%	1.41	1.25	1.18	1.11	0.99
GNP: 5.5%	1.35	1.19	1.11	1.04	0.92
GNP: 6.0%	1.28	1.12	1.04	0.97	0.85
GNP: 6.5%	1.23	1.05	0.91	0.78	0.67
Property-tax revenue: 6.5%					
GNP: 4.5%	1.39	1.25	1.19	1.12	1.02
GNP: 5.0%	1.33	1.19	1.12	1.05	0.93
GNP: 5.5%	1.27	1.12	1.05	0.98	0.86
GNP: 6.0%	1.22	1.05	0.99	0.92	0.80
GNP: 6.5%	1.16	1.00	0.93	0.86	0.74
Property-tax revenue: 6.0%					
GNP: 4.5%	1.32	1.19	1.12	1.06	0.96
GNP: 5.0%	1.27	1.12	1.05	1.00	0.88
GNP: 5.5%	1.20	1.06	0.99	0.93	0.82
GNP: 6.0%	1.15	1.00	0.93	0.87	0.76
GNP: 6.5%	1.10	0.94	0.88	0.81	0.70
Property-tax revenue: 5.5%					
GNP: 4.5%	1.25	1.12	1.06	1.01	0.91
GNP: 5.0%	1.19	1.06	1.00	0.94	0.84
GNP: 5.5%	1.14	1.00	0.93	0.88	0.78
GNP: 6.0%	1.09	0.94	0.88	0.82	0.71
GNP: 6.5%	1.04	0.89	0.83	0.77	0.66

[a] The ratio of the 1963 property-tax share to the 1963 share for a constant property-tax rate is the reciprocal of the ratio of the 1975 property-tax rate to the 1963 rate for a constant property-tax share.

Low-Rate Case

Assume a base elasticity of 1.2, a GNP annual growth rate of 6.0 percent, and a local-expenditure annual growth rate of 6.0 percent. If the 1975 effective rate is to equal the 1963 effective rate, the property-tax share must increase 15 percent, from (in round numbers) 46 percent to 53 percent (Table 2.4). Thus, the property-tax share would be the highest since 1946 (Table 2.3). The required 1963–75 elasticity of other revenue, 0.8 (Table 2.4), would be far below the 1954–63 elasticity of 1.7 (Table 2.5). It seems likely that the growth of other revenue will permit a sizeable decrease in the property-tax rate.

If the 1975 property-tax share is to equal the 1963 share, the effective rate must decrease 13 percent, from 1.32 percent to 1.15 percent (Table 2.4). The 1975 effective rate would, therefore, be the lowest rate since 1954 (Table 2.2). For 1963–75 the effective rate would decrease by 1.2 percent per year (Table 2.4); the effective rate for 1954–63 increased by 1.7 percent per year (Table 2.5). The required 1963–75 elasticity of other revenue, 1.0 (Table 2.4), would be far below the 1954–63 elasticity of 1.7 (Table 2.5). The growth of other revenue may well permit a decline in the property-tax share as well as in the property-tax rate.

Summary

For each of the three hypothetical cases, the property-tax share seems more likely to decrease than to increase. For the medium-rate and low-rate cases, the property-tax rate also seems more likely to decrease than to increase. For the high-rate case the property-tax rate seems unlikely to change appreciably. In my judgment, the medium-rate case is the most reasonable of the three cases.

Thus, the data presented in this section suggest that over the period 1963–75 property-tax revenue will decline significantly in relative importance. Bear in mind, however, that forecasting the growth of property-tax revenue is extremely difficult. The revenue-growth trends suggested by the data in this section should be interpreted accordingly.

Notes

1 For a more detailed examination, see Benjamin Bridges, Jr., "Income Elasticity of the Property Tax Base," *National Tax Journal*, 17 (September, 1964), 253–64. See also Bridges, "The Elasticity of the Property Tax Base: Some Cross-Section Estimates," *Land Economics*, 40 (November, 1964), 449–51.

2 Raymond W. Goldsmith, *A Study of Savings in the United States*, 3 (Princeton: Princeton University Press, 1956), 12–15; Goldsmith, *The National Wealth of the United States in the Postwar Period* (Studies

in Capital Formation and Financing No. 10; Princeton: National Bureau of Economic Research, Princeton University Press, 1962), pp. 177–82, 184–89; U.S. Bureau of the Census, *Taxable Property Values*, Vol. 2 in *Census of Governments: 1962* (Washington, D.C.: U.S. Government Printing Office, 1963), pp. 40–43; and U.S. Bureau of the Census, *Taxable Property Values in the United States*, Vol. 5 in *Census of Governments: 1957* (Washington, D.C.: U.S. Government Printing Office, 1959), pp. 28–31.

3 Elasticity estimates for other subperiods of the 1899–1957 period are presented in Bridges, "Income Elasticity of the Property Tax Base," pp. 259–60.

4 For a discussion of the reliability of these ratios, see *ibid.*, p. 256.

5 Dick Netzer, "Needs and Resources over the Next Decade: State and Local Governments," *Public Finances: Needs, Sources, and Utilization* (Special Conference Series No. 12; Princeton: National Bureau of Economic Research, Princeton University Press, 1961), pp. 33–36.

6 Robert J. Lampman, "How Much Government Spending in the 1960's?" *Quarterly Review of Economics and Business,* 1 (February, 1961), 15–16.

7 Otto Eckstein, *Trends in Public Expenditures in the Next Decade* (Supplementary Paper; New York: Committee for Economic Development, 1959), p. 44.

8 Preliminary estimate. Revised estimate to appear in the Project '70 publications of the Council of State Governments.

9 Eugene Peter McLoone, "Effects of Tax Elasticities on the Financial Support of Education" (Ph.D. dissertation, University of Illinois, 1961), Chap. 3.

10 Two such forecasts are George W. Pinnell, "Residential Real Estate Finance in the 1960's," *Journal of Finance,* 15 (May, 1960), 250–62; and Burnham O. Campbell, "Long Swings in Residential Construction: The Postwar Experience," *American Economic Review,* 53 (May, 1963), 508–18. Campbell's forecast for the 1960's is much more pessimistic than Pinnell's. Thus, at least one of these forecasts will prove to be very inaccurate.

11 For two such studies see Tong Hung Lee, "The Stock Demand Elasticities of Non-Farm Housing," *Review of Economics and Statistics,* 46 (February, 1964), 82–89; and Richard F. Muth, "The Demand for Non-Farm Housing," Chap. 2 in *The Demand for Durable Goods,* ed. Arnold C. Harberger (Chicago: University of Chicago Press, 1960), pp. 29–96.

12 For a discussion of industrial property-tax concessions, see Benjamin Bridges, Jr., "State and Local Inducements for Industry: Part 1," *National Tax Journal,* 18 (March, 1965), 1–14; and Bridges, "State and Local Inducements for Industry: Part 2," *National Tax Journal,* 18 (June, 1965), 175–92.

13 See Selma J. Mushkin and Robert Harris, *Transportation Outlays of States and Cities: Projections to 1970* (Chicago: Council of State Governments, 1965), pp. 41–42.

14 Preliminary estimates. Revised estimates to appear in the Project '70 publications of the Council of State Governments. In an earlier and less detailed study, the National Planning Association projected a constant dollar growth rate for 1959–76 slightly in excess of 6 percent per annum. See U.S. Outdoor Recreation Resources Review Commission, *Projections to the Years 1976 and 2000: Economic Growth, Population, Labor Force and Leisure, and Transportation* (Study Report 23; Washington, D.C.: U.S. Government Printing Office, 1962), pp. 160–217. The economic growth section was prepared by the National Planning Association.

15 Throughout this section, the term effective property-tax rate means state-local effective rate. For 1963–75 it is assumed that the percentage growth rates for local and for state-local property-tax revenue are equal. Row 13 of column 3 of Table 2.6 indicates that the 1975 effective rate would be 1.05 times the 1963 effective rate.

16 The ratio of the 1975 property-tax share to the 1963 share for a constant property-tax rate is the reciprocal of the ratio of the 1975 property-tax rate to the 1963 rate for a constant property-tax share. Thus, .95 is the reciprocal of the 1.05 which appears in row 13 of column 3 of Table 2.6.

3. John Shannon

Conflict between State Assessment
Law and Local Assessment Practice

Although most states still have full-value assessment laws on the statute books, they have demonstrated a chronic inability to secure local compliance with these laws. The 1961 assessment-ratio study made by the Bureau of the Census reveals that the national average for locally assessed real estate was 29 percent of 1961 market value.[1] Perhaps of even greater significance is the finding that most state tax administrators have been unable to equalize local assessment levels at any uniform fraction of current market value.

In any evaluation of this conflict, it is important to note that, because of the essentially static nature of real property assessments, the extent of deviation from the market value standard during assessment hinges primarily on the dynamic fluctuations of the price level. It was the interaction of rapidly falling real estate values and fairly rigid tax assessments between 1929 and 1933 that raised assessment levels to the closest approximation of market value since 1900. It was the interaction of steadily rising property values and relatively static assessments since World War II that has now plunged real estate assessment ratios to their lowest recorded level. There are certain cynical observers of the property-tax scene who contend that only a catastrophic decline in property values can bring relatively rigid assessments into line with the market-value concept.

The usual state requirement calling for the annual assessment of all taxable property can be realized in administrative practice only in a highly static economic situation. Because of the dynamic character of real estate values, particularly in the metropolitan market, even those assessors with large appraisal staffs and extensive administrative support can only hope to keep within hailing distance of current

39

market values. In the rapidly developing urban areas, assessors have difficulty adding new construction to the tax rolls, let alone keeping up-to-date on the annual assessments of older properties. Municipal assessors ordinarily take the position, therefore, that they are doing a creditable mass-appraisal job if they actually reappraise 25 to 33 percent of the taxable properties each year.

Thus, administrative factors can account for a part of the gap between state law calling for full-value assessments and the administrative practice of fractional valuation—but for only a small part of that gap. In the average situation, property is being assessed at approximately 30 percent of current market value, and there is a 70-percentage-point gap separating administrative behavior from the full-value law. When analyzing this gap, perhaps 10 to 15 percentage points can be attributed to the strictly administrative factors noted above. Or, to view the matter more positively, under the most ideal enforcement conditions, assessors in metropolitan areas can hardly be expected to maintain a general assessment level above 90 percent of current market value.

Table 3.1 illustrates just how wide the gap is between state assessment law and local practice, and Table 3.2 summarizes state assessment standards.

Table 3.1—Conflict between Assessment Law and Practice: 1961
(percent)

State	Legal assessment standard [a]	Statewide ratios of assessed value to sales price [b]	Median area ratio [c]	Coefficient of interarea dispersion [c][d]	Coefficient of intra-area dispersion
United States	*n.a.*	*29.0*	*n.a.*	*n.a.*	*25.8*
Alabama	60	18.6	19.4	19	28.9
Alaska	100	n.a.	n.a.	n.a.	n.a.
Arizona	100	12.0	14.9	18	35.4
Arkansas	20	12.4	14.7	23	35.6
California	100	17.5	21.2	12	22.5
Colorado	100	23.1	26.9	13	23.3
Connecticut	[e]	52.1	52.8	15	14.9
Delaware	100	53.2	57.0	6	15.3
District of Columbia	100	50.5	—	—	—
Florida	100	41.2	44.5	25	22.3
Georgia	100	20.0	22.0	33	30.5
Hawaii	[f]	48.1	52.9	6	27.5
Idaho	100	11.5	9.4	13	30.1

(Table continued on following page)

Table 3.1 (continued)
(percent)

State	Legal assessment standard [a]	Statewide ratios of assessed value to sales price [b]	Median area ratio [c]	Coefficient of interarea dispersion [c][d]	Coefficient of intra-area dispersion
Illinois	100	44.7	49.0	11	29.9
Indiana	100	20.8	23.3	11	34.0
Iowa	60	23.9	22.8	10	24.4
Kansas	100	18.5	22.4	16	34.6
Kentucky	100	25.4	26.0	17	27.3
Louisiana	100	17.9	18.6	28	36.8
Maine	100	43.0	33.8	68	19.9
Maryland	100	44.9	49.1	11	21.3
Massachusetts	100	36.7	35.2	22	19.2
Michigan	100	32.6	31.2	21	25.5
Minnesota	100	9.6	7.8	18	34.4
Mississippi	100	12.8	12.7	34	33.8
Missouri	100	25.0	25.3	13	30.1
Montana	30	6.7	7.8	17	25.2
Nebraska	35	24.5	28.7	12	27.5
Nevada	100	21.4	21.4	21	18.5
New Hampshire	100	41.4	37.1	29	20.8
New Jersey	100	28.6	21.8	39	[g]
New Mexico	100	14.8	21.6	17	26.5
New York	100	47.0	28.9	34	[g]
North Carolina	100	32.3	36.2	29	24.9
North Dakota	50	14.3	13.2	47	33.9
Ohio	100	29.5	37.3	12	23.5
Oklahoma	35	18.6	19.7	12	36.0
Oregon	25	22.1	23.1	11	24.7
Pennsylvania	100	32.2	27.9	27	28.7
Rhode Island	100	67.6	60.7	19	16.6
South Carolina	100	5.4	5.7	28	31.4
South Dakota	60	41.7	48.6	15	23.2
Tennessee	100	26.4	17.6	40	28.0
Texas	100	16.1	16.5	28	28.7
Utah	30	14.4	14.8	15	21.7
Vermont	[e]	25.1	25.1	25	25.4
Virginia	100	29.0	30.5	34	22.5
Washington	50	14.3	16.3	13	25.0
West Virginia	100	30.9	32.3	21	27.1
Wisconsin	100	46.6	47.2	31	15.9
Wyoming	100	18.9	19.6	15	29.2

n.a.—Not available.

[a] For more detailed information on state assessment law see Table 3.2.

(Notes to table continued on following page)

Notes to Table 3.1 (continued)

[b] Based on locally assessed taxable real property. Average weighted by type and size of property.

[c] Computed from a distribution of selected local areas according to a median assessment ratio for non-farm houses.

[d] Average deviation per area divided by median area ratio and expressed as a percentage.

[e] All taxable property to be assessed at a uniform percentage of market value within each local assessment district—each local assessor makes his own assessment level determination.

[f] State director of taxation has the authority to specify the uniform percentage of market value appraisal to be used for assessment purposes.

[g] Data not comparable.

Source: Commerce Clearing House, *State Tax Reporter* (Chicago, 1964); and U.S. Bureau of the Census, *Taxable Property Values,* Vol. 2 in *Census of Governments: 1962* (Washington, D.C.: U.S. Government Printing Office, 1963).

Table 3.2—State Assessment Standards

Jurisdiction	Full value	Other than full value		Legal valuation concept (for all taxable property except as noted)
		Percent	Year effective	
Alabama		60	n.a.	Fair and reasonable market value
Alaska	X			Full and true value in money
Arizona	X			Full cash value
Arkansas	X [a]	20 [a]	1960	See note a
California	X			Full cash value
Colorado		30 [b]	1964 [b]	See note b
Connecticut		1–100	1957	Uniform percentage of market value within local district
Delaware	X			True value in money
District of Columbia	X			Full and true value in lawful money
Florida	X			Full cash value
Georgia	X			Fair market value
Hawaii				Fair market value or a percentage thereof
Idaho		20 [c]	1966	Full cash value
Illinois	X [d]			See note d
Indiana		33⅓ [e]	1962	See note e
Iowa		60	1941	Actual value
Kansas		30 [f]	1964	See note f
Kentucky	X			Fair cash value
Louisiana	X			Actual cash value; land at not less than $1 per acre

(Table continued on following page)

Table 3.2 (continued)

| Jurisdiction | Full value | Other than full value | | Legal valuation concept (for all taxable property except as noted) |
		Percent	Year effective	
Maine	X			At just value in compliance with the laws of the state
Maryland	X			Full cash value less an allowance for inflation
Massachusetts	X			Fair cash valuation—in practice a 100 percent valuation is used
Michigan	X			Full cash value
Minnesota		X [g]	n.a.	True and full value in money
Mississippi	X			Assessed in proportion to its value
Missouri	X			True value in money
Montana		30 [h]	1919	Various percents ranging from 7 percent to 100 percent for 7 other classes of property
Nebraska		35	1957	Required to be valued at its actual value and assessed at 35 percent
Nevada		35	1963	Full cash value
New Hampshire	X			Full and true value in money
New Jersey		20–100	1964	Of true value; in a multiple of 10 as established by each county board of taxation
New Mexico	X			Assessed in proportion to its value
New York	X			Full value; in practice at a portion of actual value
North Carolina	X			True value in money
North Dakota		50 [i]	n.a.	Full and true value in money
Ohio	X			True value
Oklahoma		35	1958	Fair cash value
Oregon		25	1961	True cash value
Pennsylvania	X [j]			Actual value
Rhode Island	X			Full and fair cash value
South Carolina	X			True value in money
South Dakota		60 [k]	1957	True and full value in money
Tennessee	X			Actual cash value
Texas	X			Full and true value in money
Utah		30	1961	Reasonable fair cash value
Vermont		1	n.a.	See note 1
Virginia	X			Fair market value
Washington		50	1944	True and fair value
West Virginia	X			True and actual value
Wisconsin	X			Full value at private sale

(Table continued on following page)

Table 3.2 (continued)

| Jurisdiction | Full value | Other than full value | | Legal valuation concept (for all taxable property except as noted) |
		Percent	Year effective	
Wyoming	X			Fair value in conformity with values and procedures prescribed by the State Board of Equalization

n.a.—Not available.

ᵃ All property, including taxable intangibles, is required to be assessed at its true market value in money or, in the case of personal property, at its usual selling price. The assessed value of property is placed on the tax record at 18 percent of market or actual value for the assessment year 1959 and at 20 percent for subsequent years.

ᵇ All taxable property must be assessed at 30 percent of its actual value. If on August 1, 1964, the assessed valuation of any property was more or less than 30 percent of actual value, annual adjustments were to be made in 1965, 1966, and 1967 so that the assessed valuation of the property in 1967 would be 30 percent of actual value. Oil and gas leaseholds, lands, and royalty interests are assessed at an amount equal to 87.5 percent of the gross value or selling price of the oil or gas produced, saved, and sold during the preceding calendar year.

ᶜ After 1965, real property is required to be assessed at 20 percent of full cash value, personal property at 20 percent of full cash value, and operating property (inventories) at 40 percent of full cash value.

ᵈ The statutes provide that real property shall be assessed at its fair cash value which is declared to be the price it would bring at a fair, voluntary sale. In actual practice, however, these statutes are not strictly adhered to. The ratio of assessed value to fair cash value has been found by the State Department of Revenue to average as low as 20 percent in some counties.

ᵉ The statutes provide for the assessment of all property at a rate which is uniform, equal, and based on a just valuation at true cash value. After January 1, 1962, all property shall be assessed at 33⅓ percent of true cash value.

ᶠ All property is to be valued at its true value in money. After January 1, 1964, all real and tangible personal property is required to be assessed at 30 percent of its value.

ᵍ The legislature assigns various percentages of the true and full value appraisal to be used for the assessment of the various classes of property.

ʰ On realty.

ⁱ After the equalization of assessments, the county auditor reduces the assessed values to 50 percent before taxes—except those imposed to pay bonded or improved warrant indebtedness—are computed.

ʲ Except in fourth- to eighth-class counties where real property is assessed at a predetermined ratio, not to exceed 75 percent of actual value.

ᵏ All property shall be assessed at its true and full value in money, and the assessor shall retain in his files a record of such full and true value, but taxable value to be entered on the assessment rolls shall be 60 percent of the full value.

(Notes to table continued on following page)

Notes to Table 3.2 (continued)
[1] One percent of the listed value of real estate taxable to a person plus one percent of the listed value of his personal estate, plus the amount of his taxable poll, if any, constitute his assessment statement. Listed value is a proportionate part of appraisal value as determined by each town. Appraisal value is the estimated fair market value.
Source: Commerce Clearing House, *State Tax Reporter* (Chicago, 1964).

Rationalizations for Static Fractional Assessments

As a prelude to the formulation of a hypothesis to explain the conflict between assessment law and practice, the various technical arguments or theories that have been advanced either to oppose an increase in assessments or to condone the administrative practice of fractional valuation will be briefly analyzed.[2]

Uniformity Argument

By stressing the uniformity argument, many property-tax students and administrators have attempted to dismiss or minimize the conflict between the full-value-assessment law and the practice of fractional valuation.[3] Those who advocate uniformity claim that, as long as the local assessment official makes a reasonably successful effort to assess all property at the same percentage, it really does not make any difference whether property is assessed at 1 percent, at 50 percent, or at any other uniform percentage of market value.

The weakness of this argument is revealed simply by pushing it to its logical conclusion. If the percentage is of so little consequence, why, for example, have state and local assessment officials systematically ignored their sworn duty to enforce the full-value law? The validity of the uniformity argument may be questioned on the basis of administrative convenience as well as of legal compliance. There would appear to be much to recommend a full-value-assessment policy. Before it is possible to assess property at a uniform percentage of the market value, it is first necessary to estimate the market value. Why complicate the procedure needlessly with fractions?

The uniformity rationalization in support of underassessment has two very practical limitations also. First, there is evidence that assessment uniformity deteriorates as the general assessment level declines (Table 3.3). To put the issue more bluntly, this means that the lower the assessment level, the larger becomes the administrative graveyard in which the assessor can bury his mistakes. Second, it must be noted that the percentage of market-value appraisal used for tax-assessment purposes can have a profound fiscal effect on local governments. Because tax exemptions and local tax and debt limits are often tied to assessed valuations, it is readily apparent that deep under-assessment can both radically constrict the fiscal powers of local governments and expand the value of partial tax exemptions.

Table 3.3—Relationship of Assessment Ratio to Assessment Uniformity

Median assessment ratio	No. of areas	Percent of areas having a coefficient of intra-area dispersion of		
		Less than 20 percent	20 percent to 39.9 percent	40 percent or more
Less than 20	25	20.0	72.0	8.0
20–29.9	48	35.4	60.4	4.2
30–39.9	18	38.9	61.1	—
40–49.9	16	56.3	43.7	—
50 or over	9	55.6	44.4	—
All areas	*116*	*37.1*	*59.5*	*3.4*

Source: Jacob M. Jaffe, "The 1962 Census of Governments Report on Taxable Property Values," *National Tax Journal,* 16, No. 3 (September, 1963), 274.

Although the uniformity argument appears plausible and makes excellent grist for the public relations mill, there is no validity to the contention that, as long as they assess all property at a uniform rate, it does not make much difference if assessment officers ignore the full-value-assessment mandate. If this were the only rationalization used to support fractional-static assessment policy or to oppose any state action to raise depressed local assessment levels, the case for condoning local failure to comply with state full-value-assessment law would be weak indeed.

The Normal-Value Argument

No analysis of the failure of local assessors to gear tax assessment to the great post-depression advance in property values can overlook the persistence of the widely held contention that "property is selling for more than it is worth." It followed from this line of reasoning that property-tax assessments should not be geared to post-World War II inflated prices because these prices did not represent the normal or intrinsic value of the property. This theory undoubtedly made a deep impression on assessment officials; it also provided them with a convenient, and apparently plausible, rationalization for failing to adjust tax assessments to the dramatic advance in valuation.

Although the advocates of the normal-value approach to tax assessment could find no essential theoretical justification for pegging assessments to pre-war price levels, they certainly realized that this rationalization shielded them from political retribution. This fact was indicated by an editorial writer for the *Louisville Courier Journal:* "To assess property at its market value at a time when inflation has skyrocketed the cost of small homes might easily increase the cost of real estate to the point where many lower-income and middle-income people could not afford homeownership. *The tax assessor undertaking such a project would be inviting political if not personal disaster."* [4]

Although the normal-value theory may have had some theoretical justification immediately after World War II, it has since become thoroughly discredited. When examined solely from the technical standpoint, this theory possesses no more validity than does the uniformity argument for fractional assessments. The normal-value theory appears to be a convenient rationalization advanced by many assessment officials (particularly during periods of rapidly rising or high-level price conditions) to obscure their unwillingness to accept the political consequences inherent in any decision to comply with the constitutional market-value mandate.

The Aggravation Argument

Since World War II, many state tax administrators have justified their failure to raise depressed local assessment levels to the legal standard by contending that a blanket increase in local assessment levels would serve to aggravate inequities in the original assessment. This argument is a property-tax myth. It rests on the belief that horizontal adjustment of the assessment base would place the taxpayer with a relatively high assessment at a disadvantage in comparison with the property owner with a low assessment. Because the property tax is a proportional levy, however, horizontal adjustments of the base cannot further distort or aggravate inequalities caused in the tax load by the lack of uniformity in the original assessment process. The invalidity of this aggravation argument was clearly exposed in a publication issued by the California State Board of Equalization.

We hear it said that no intercounty equalization orders should be issued until intracounty equalization has been achieved—that when properties are unequally assessed within a county, an intercounty order increases the inequality. This is a delusion. A percentage increase or decrease of assessed valuation "across the board" adds or detracts from previously existing inequalities no more than the size of the hills and valleys is increased or decreased by viewing them from either end of a telescope.[5]

To be consistent, the exponents of the aggravation theory should oppose all tax-rate increases on the same grounds, because any horizontal adjustment of either a tax rate or a tax base would exert the same proportional effect on the determination of both the size and the distribution of the tax load.

Defective Administrative Machinery

As a corollary to the aggravation argument, there emerged the belief that local administrative reforms were an absolute prerequisite to more equitable local assessment, and that the elimination of gross inequities between property valuations within a local assessment jurisdiction would thereby create a situation more conducive to raising local assessment levels to the state valuation standard.

This point of view was fostered by the common spectacle of untrained, ill-equipped, poorly paid, locally elected assessors preparing the assessment rolls by accepting without much question the valuations submitted to them by their taxpaying constituents, or by transferring with little or no revision the assessment figures entered on the previous year's tax roll. In many localities, the local board of review was either unable or unwilling to bring even a semblance of assessment uniformity out of this type of "voluntary" taxation. Moreover, effective state valuation assistance and supervision were conspicuously absent.

Immediately following World War II, California, Kentucky, Oregon, and Maryland developed rather sophisticated programs for providing technical assistance to local assessors and for generally strengthening their supervisory position on the local-assessment front. In addition, many cities, particularly the larger jurisdictions, placed increasing reliance on well-trained appraisers selected and promoted on the basis of merit.

These post-World War II attempts to strengthen the assessment process have undoubtedly worked in the direction of greater uniformity within local assessment jurisdictions. They have not, however, brought local assessment levels substantially closer to alignment with state valuation law except in Oregon, and, in that state, it was first necessary for the legislature to abandon the full-value standard and adopt in its place a 25-percent-assessment provision.

In summary, it is probably safe to assume that the appointment of local assessors and stepped-up programs of state technical assistance cannot come to grips with the fundamental problem—that of bringing local valuation practice substantially into alignment with state law when the ratio of legal requirement to actual practice reflects a great disparity between the two. These administrative reform efforts, however, do provide an opportunity to replace "roll copying" with a more sophisticated and uniform method of fractional assessment.

Political Barriers to Full-Value Assessment

Although the various rationalizations employed to justify administrative deviation from the state full-value-assessment laws lack substantive validity, they do point up the presence of political obstacles to the attainment of full-value assessment. These political barriers, in turn, raise serious doubts concerning the basic theoretical premise underpinning full-value-assessment laws—that the assessment process in all of its aspects is simply a ministerial or technical task of market-value estimation which can be divorced completely from the policy function of tax-load determination.

Misdirection of Political Responsibility

The misdirection of political responsibility is a primary obstacle to administrative realization of the full-value mandate. The locally elected assessors have been extremely reluctant to gear assessed valuations to steadily rising price levels, because they fear that they will be held politically responsible if the local rate makers—city councils, county boards, and the school boards—fail to cut back their tax rates commensurate with the increase in the tax base. They usually adopt the safer strategy of freezing assessments in times of rapidly rising market values, thus forcing the local legislative bodies to raise their rates if additional revenue is needed to meet increased expenditure requirements.

Even the locally appointed municipal assessor is not untouched by political pressures. The officials who appoint the assessor often take the position that raising tax rates has political ramifications far less adverse than sending out individual notices of assessment increases to thousands of property owners. Moreover, municipal officials often fear that the city school board will take advantage of a full-value-assessment policy by failing to cut back school rates in proportion to the increase in the assessed valuation. Thus, by adopting a static fractional-assessment policy, the city fathers force the school board members to raise tax rates if additional revenue is necessary to meet their budgetary needs. Moreover, once a static assessment policy forces school tax rates to the legal limit, this strategy can then give those who control local assessment policy far-reaching control over local school budgets.

By the same token, state officials charged with the responsibility for raising depressed local assessment levels to the full-value standard fear that the state administration in general, and the governor in particular, will be blamed for the increase in the local property-tax load that would inevitably accompany the state order dramatically increasing the local property-tax base. They have no more assurance than do the local assessment officials that the local legislative bodies would cut back their rates to offset the higher base level. Because state tax authorities are usually directly responsible to the governor, they will not disturb the local status quo without first securing the governor's approval. Most governors have been extremely reluctant to pull local fiscal chestnuts out of the fire by ordering blanket increases in local assessment levels.

In view of this basic misdirection of political responsibility, it is not difficult to understand why assessment officials or those who control local assessment policy tend to freeze assessed valuations during periods of rising property values rather than run the risk of becoming political scapegoats by constantly increasing assessed valuations. "If it is suggested that the officials are lacking in courage, there is the obvious rejoinder that it takes extraordinary courage to do something that is predestined to have an undesirable development for which you are not responsible, but for which you know you will be blamed." [6]

The Tradition of Local Assessment Autonomy

The tradition of local autonomy of assessment is the second major barrier to administrative compliance with state assessment law. This tradition of home rule in assessment matters is reflected in:

a) The selection of local assessors by the electorate or—especially in cities—the appointment of assessors by local officials.
b) The perennial conflict between state law calling for full-value assessment and the pervasive use of fractional assessment by local administrators.
c) The lack of public support for proposals, such as state assessment of taxable property, which would give state tax authorities effective control over the local assessment process.

Since the latter part of the nineteenth century, state legislative bodies have struggled unsuccessfully to bring a measure of order to the local assessment process. Their approach to this problem was coercive.

State legislatures created various state tax agencies and vested in these bodies the power to equalize local property-tax assessments, to initiate discharge proceedings against incompetent local assessors, to order horizontal adjustments of local assessment levels, and to reassess local property in jurisdictions where the original assessments proved highly unsatisfactory.

State property-tax experience indicates that, in the absence of effective political support, it is futile to give state tax authorities coercive authority over local assessment officials. Most state tax authorities are keenly aware of the distinction between legal authority and political power. Because they do not receive the requisite political support from the governor and state legislatures, state property-tax officials must handle local assessors with kid gloves. The law that directs state officials to equalize local assessment levels at full value is ordinarily not worth the paper it is printed on. Under such circumstances, decisive authority vanishes and those on the state property-tax firing line find themselves in the frustrating position of having to convince local officials that "good assessment is good politics."

Extra-Legal Classification of Property

It is not unusual to discover that various classes of property are being assessed at different rates. A local assessor may be attempting, for example, to assess residential property at 30 percent of current market value, automobiles at 100 percent, and merchants' inventories at 60 percent. In addition, a state tax department may be assessing utility property subject to local taxation at approximately 50 percent of current market value. This extra-legal system for distributing the property-tax burden among various classes of property owners takes on special political significance because any decision to raise all assessments to full value would cause a radical redistribution of the tax load. Homeowners in particular might be forced to pay higher taxes. Much of the reluctance of state officials to enforce a full-value-assessment policy stems from fear that the resultant collapse of this extra-legal system of variable assessment classification would bring political repercussions.

Extra-Legal Limitations on State and Local Tax and Debt Powers

A state decision to force local officials to raise their depressed assessment levels to the full-value standard would also destroy another curious fiscal institution in many states—the power of the conservative forces within the community to restrain the local spenders, particularly the school boards. For example, state law may provide that no school board can levy a rate in excess of $1.50 for each $100 of assessed valuation unless such a rate is approved by the electorate in a special referendum. Thus, if the assessor decides to assess property at 25 percent of its current market value, he automatically constricts the tax power of the local school board to one-fourth of its legal entitlement, and the school board is soon forced to "go to the people" in the form of a special referendum in order to obtain authorization for a rate in excess of the statutory limit. In short, deep underassessment permits those persons controlling local assessment policy both to intensify the tax and debt restrictions imposed by the state and to force local legislative bodies thereby to seek the approval of the electorate for tax-rate increases.

It should be pointed out that this extra-legal system for restricting local governments in general, and school boards in particular, seems to represent a method of compensating for the fact that local property-tax policymakers do not appear to be impeded by as many political barriers as state tax policymakers do. There are several factors responsible for this situation.

First, because of the widespread diffusion of responsibility for the setting of local property-tax rates, it is usually difficult for property owners to single out the person or persons directly responsible for the decision to increase the property tax. A property-tax increase may stem from the decisions of one or more of the following local legislative bodies—the school board, the county board, the city council, or, possibly, a special district agency. In striking contrast, the governor is usually held politically accountable for a decision to raise a state sales or income tax.

Second, the conventional system of political sanctions appears to operate less rigorously at the local level. When a governor decides to advocate a sales- or an income-tax increase, he must calculate the effect such a decision may have on his future political ambitions and the repercussions for his party at the next election. The system of political sanctions operates with such efficiency at the state level that the governor's position has become the most hazardous within our political system, and one student of state politics, Robert Pitchell, has noted that "incumbency which in virtually every other electoral office in the land is in odds of advantage for re-election is a liability in the office of Governor." [7] In contrast, locally elected representatives—*particularly school board members*—need, apparently, to be less concerned about the effect which a tax rate decision will have on their political futures.

Third, largely because no alternate method exists for raising local revenue, a decision to raise a local property tax does not precipitate a bitter partisan debate between the spokesmen for labor and management. A proposal to increase the state sales tax can be expected to cause a hostile reaction from labor, while a proposal to increase the graduated income tax ordinarily elicits strong opposition from the business community.[8]

Fourth, while local policymakers can adjust property-tax rates to meet relatively small increases in their budgets, state lawmakers do not possess such a finely calibrated revenue instrument. Thus, in sharp contrast to the relatively slow and steady rise in property-tax rates, increases in state taxes on sales and income are usually abrupt and dramatic. An increase in the state sales tax from 2 to 3 percent, for example, represents a 50 percent hike in the tax rate and compounds the problem of generating sufficient consensus to authorize such a major departure from the status quo. As a result, both the state sales-tax and the state income-tax movements have alternated between periods of coma and convulsion. It is usually necessary for a fiscal crisis to develop at the state level before the requisite political support can be mustered for expanded use of one or both of these two revenue instruments.

Fifth, property-tax increases are more directly related to visible needs for local public expenditure. Property owners can, at least, take satisfaction in the fact that their dollars are staying at home to meet their educational needs and other community requirements.

Because the decision to raise the property rate operates under a different set of political rules than a decision to increase a state sales tax or a state income tax does, a decision to raise all local assessment levels to the full-value standard would both destroy this extra-legal system for restraining local expenditures through the practice of fractional assessment and force the state legislature to construct a new control system—a prospect that operates in many states to preserve the fractional-assessment status quo.

In summary, the presence of four political factors—misdirection of political responsibility for tax-load determination, the tradition of local assessment autonomy, the extra-legal system for classifying property for taxation, and the use of fractional assessment to constrict local tax and debt powers—have blocked local and state administrative compliance with the full-value laws. More importantly, they negate the basic premise underpinning a fixed-valuation assessment standard: the assumption that the assessment process can be effectively divorced from tax policy considerations.

The Need for a Solution

The conflict between law and administrative practice is at the heart of the property-tax-equalization issue, and a resolution of this conflict should receive the highest priority on any agenda dedicated to property-tax reform. The uncertainties and deficiencies caused by the extra-legal character of the assessment process can be illustrated in several ways.

Because state and local property-tax officials are often reluctant to publicize the extent to which they actually deviate from the law, property owners are usually denied access to objective data needed to evaluate the equity of their assessments. In the absence of a clear legal standard, there is a strong incentive for each property owner to attempt to beat down his assessment in order to obtain preferential tax treatment; and the assessment process, especially in the case of a major industrial or commercial property, often takes on the character of a negotiated settlement.

The failure of local and state tax officials to place property on the tax rolls at the legal level has also undermined the financial integrity of many local governments and school districts. The amount of tax revenue which can be raised and spent by local governments is dependent upon the percentage of market value used in assessment by the tax official. Continued underassessment has reduced the effective tax power of many counties, school districts, and cities to only a fraction of that allotted them by the state constitution or statutes; low assessments and rising costs may combine to force their tax rate to its legal limit. It is important to note that, in such a situation, it is the assessor, rather than the state legislative body, who sets the metes and bounds of local fiscal policy: the assessment official has become, in effect, a budget officer.

It should also be noted that administrative deviation from the law tends to create an environment conducive to the assessment of different types of property at varying percentages of market value. This differential assessment policy, of course, distributes the local tax load among the various classes of property owners in a manner not intended by law. By departing from the legal valuation standard in this way, the assessor again usurps the authority of the state legislative body, which alone should have the power to classify property and to determine the distribution of a tax load.

Resolving the Conflict—The Coercive Approach

From a strictly legal standpoint, the coercive approach provides the obvious and forthright method for resolving this perennial conflict between law and assessment practice. State tax administrators would merely exercise their present authority and direct local assessment officials to raise their depressed valuations to the level prescribed by state law.

In the view of state political leaders, however, such a drastic solution to the conflict is totally unrealistic. Because local assessment levels have dropped so far below the legal valuation standard, it would require blanket assessment increases of truly staggering dimensions. In a typical state with local assessment levels ranging anywhere from 20 to 50 percent of current market value, a strict enforcement policy would require state tax officials to order an increase in the assessment of every property in the state of from 100 percent to 5 percent—and, depending on the local assessment ratio, the percentage of increase might, in some cases, be still greater.

Because there is no effective public demand for such radical action, a crash program to raise depressed local assessment levels to the legal level would probably generate such strong public alarm and property-owner opposition as to place the political fortunes of the state administration in real jeopardy. Commenting on the possible consequences of a blanket assessment increase, the Advisory Commission on Intergovernmental Relations stated that this would be a good way to start a political revolution. "Leadership that could induce the legislature to make all the essential supporting legal adjustments and convince a rebellious public that the policy was desirable would be almost a miracle." [9]

Extraordinary Judicial Action

While there is little likelihood that state and local assessors will *voluntarily* raise assessments to the full-value standard, the coercive approach can work, at least temporarily, if the state court orders the state tax department to raise local assessment levels to the legal valuation standard. Courts in Florida and Kentucky have recently directed assessment officials to comply with a state mandate calling for full-value assessment.[10] Because it is quite possible that the state legislative bodies may enact substantial changes in the property-tax law in order to prevent the implementation of these court orders, it is not possible to predict the final outcome of these extraordinary judicial actions.[11]

There are several reasons for believing that this type of extraordinary judicial action will not provide a general solution to the problem posed by the inability of the state tax officials to secure local compliance with state valuation law. First, in most states the courts have sanctioned assessment uniformity at less than full value, following the ruling of the United States Supreme Court in *Sioux City Bridge Co.* v. *Dakota County*, 260 U.S. 441 (1923). Why should a property owner be anxious to have the courts order all property-tax assessments raised to full value if he has only to prove disproportionate assessment of his own property in order to have his tax valuation reduced to the prevailing assessment level? Thus, it is not necessary for the aggrieved taxpayer to issue a writ of mandamus, ordering the state and local officials to raise all assessments to the prescribed legal valuation level in any normal assessment controversy involving a claim of disproportionate assessment.

Second, the courts in some states might follow the logic of the fractional valuation judgment recently articulated by the California District Court of Appeals and sustained by the California Supreme Court. The California District Court of Appeals ruled, in effect, that the continual violation of the full-value law has developed into a right of the assessor to assess property at a uniform fraction of full value.[12]

Third, the political and public relations implications of obtaining a court order to raise depressed local assessment levels to the full-value standard would tend to dampen the ardor even of those who would stand to benefit most directly from taking such action. Because of possible adverse public reaction, local officials might ponder a long time before they were willing to exercise their constitutional tax and debt prerogatives by setting the legal machinery in motion to have assessments raised to full value throughout the county and state.[13]

The fourth, and most basic, reason for doubting the efficacy of judicial intervention is that such an action could have no lasting results unless it were accompanied by other, more basic, reforms. It is extremely difficult, for example, to imagine full-value assessment becoming a permanent part of property-taxation unless the state is willing to overthrow the tradition of local assessment autonomy. It would soon become apparent that the state tax department could not hold local assessment levels at the prescribed state standard unless that agency had effective control over the persons making the original assessment. In short, the judges can resolve the conflict between law and practice only if state political leadership is willing to create an administrative environment compatible with enforcement of state assessment law. For all practical purposes, the state tax department would have to become the assessor, or, at least, the senior partner in the assessment process.

It must be conceded, however, that there are certain conditions under which the courts might be confronted with a demand for a writ of mandamus to force administrative compliance with the full-value law. A petition for a writ could be based on the contention that assessments must be raised to the legal level in order (a) to prevent illegal constriction of the fiscal powers of local governments and local school districts through the process of fractional valuation—the Kentucky situation; (b) to prevent the assessor from expanding a tax-exemption privilege by fractional-assessment practices, thereby discriminating against property which does not have the benefit of such exemption—the Florida situation; and (c) to insure the equitable distribution of the state property-tax load among the local jurisdictions.

A Fractional Standard

Although still within the coercive context, a far less radical method for bringing state law and local assessment practice together would necessitate a change in the assessment law, making it conform more nearly to the prevailing local practice. For example, a state could abandon the full-value standard and substitute for it a 25 percent requirement—the procedure employed by Oregon.

While this approach would dramatically lessen the great gap between law and practice, it too bristles with policy problems. As indicated by the data set forth in Table 3.1, most of the states that have taken this fractional approach have not been able to bring local assessment levels into line with state legal requirements. As previously noted, only Oregon has achieved a close approximation of law and administrative practice. Abandonment of the full-value standard in favor of a fractional-assessment law will not solve this problem unless the states are also willing to overthrow the tradition of local assessment autonomy by giving the state tax department both the legal authority *and* the political support necessary to prevent significant deviation from the prescribed state standard. This means that it is equally important that the state tax department be given effective control over the person making the original assessment when the state law specifies a fixed percentage of full value for assessment purposes as when a full-value standard is prescribed.

A Non-Coercive Solution

A non-coercive approach for resolving the conflict between assessment law and practice is based on the assumption that the state tax department will not receive sufficient political support to enable it to raise and to hold local assessment levels at a fixed percentage of current market value under all price conditions. This non-coercive policy seeks, therefore, to reconcile assessment law and administrative practice by creating a dual system—often designated as the variable-ratio equalization system [14]—based on local fractional assessment and state full-value determinations.

This dual system has two distinct features. First, it authorizes the local assessor to assess all property at any uniform percentage of current market value he deems expedient. Second, in order to prevent local fractional assessment policies from undercutting state fiscal objectives, the legislature would direct the state tax department to make an independent determination of full value in each local assessment jurisdiction. These full-value estimates would be derived from assessment-sales ratio studies and/or sample appraisals made by the state tax department.

These full-value findings can then be used to realize a wide range of interdistrict equalization objectives such as apportioning taxes in joint school districts; equalizing the valuations of centrally and locally assessed property; distributing state fiscal aid fairly to local governments; and securing uniform application of state restrictions on the tax and debt powers of local governments and school districts, thereby stripping local assessors of their *de facto* role of budget officers for local government and school districts. The effectiveness of the dual system in the interdistrict equalization of assessment has been clearly demonstrated in Wisconsin. There are now over eighty statutory uses for the full-value determinations made by the Wisconsin state tax department.

The dual system can also attack the more serious problem of inequitable assessment of individual property parcels within each local assessment jurisdiction. When each local assessor is permitted to determine his own assessment ratio, a full-disclosure policy becomes imperative. Only in this way can property owners determine the fairness of the assessment of their own property.

A full-disclosure policy should have three components. First, legislation could provide copper-riveted assurances that the state tax department will make an annual study of local assessment ratios. Second, there should be legislative insistence that the state tax department publicize the results of their assessment-ratio findings. Perhaps the day will come when all property-tax bills will carry a notation like the following:

Based on assessment ratio studies made by the state tax department, property in your district is being assessed generally at [————] percent of current market value. If you believe that the assessed valuation on your property is not in line with the prevailing assessment level, contact the [county clerk's office] for information concerning the time and place for registering an assessment appeal.

Third, the legislature should provide that the assessment ratios established by the state tax department may be introduced by the taxpayer as evidence in appeals to the review agency on the issue of whether his assessment is inequitable.

There are two reasons for believing that a full-disclosure policy might be able to trigger more far-reaching assessment reforms. First, while the majority of taxpayers may not be particularly interested in beating the drums for the selection of assessment officials on the basis of demonstrated ability, they can be expected to be more receptive to a policy which would enable them to judge the fairness of assessments of their own property. Second, a full-disclosure policy would dramatize assessment inequalities. In so doing, it would also generate more support from the general public and the tax officials for proposals calling for basic institutional and administrative reforms—the most important of which is the appointment of assessors on the basis of merit.

In effect, this dual system—local fractional assessment and state full-value determination—reconciles the demand for local assessment autonomy with the state's need for a reliable measure of the local property-tax base. It also meets the property owner's need for accurate information concerning the fractional-valuation policies of the local assessor.

Pointing out the political advantages of this approach, the National Tax Association's Committee on State Equalization of Local Assessments noted:

The major advantage of the system is immediately obvious. Variable-ratio equalization requires no equalization orders from a state agency to a local agency. The assessment roll for local tax purposes need not be changed. The local assessor is in no sense coerced by the state agency. Other state agencies (such as those responsible for distributing state school aid and for assessing public utility enterprises) will carry out more or less automatic adjustments every year as they are informed by the ratio-study agency what the assessment ratios are in each jurisdiction.[15]

This non-coercive approach has worked well in Wisconsin, and the Advisory Commission on Intergovernmental Relations has recommended that all states not willing to take over the assessment function completely consider the adoption of this dual system in order to make the property tax more equitable and more effective as a revenue instrument for local government.[16]

Summary

For states interested in reconciling the conflict between assessment law and practice there are three basic policy alternatives:

a) State enforcement of its own full-value mandate.

b) The creation of a dual system which would permit a local assessor to assess property at any uniform fraction of market value he deems expedient but would require the state tax department to make full-value determinations for each local assessment district in order to effect both interdistrict *and* intradistrict equalization.

c) The repeal of the full-value-assessment law and the enactment of a fractional-assessment standard.

If a state can overcome the massive political obstacles, state enforcement of its own full-value mandate stands out clearly as the most efficient way to secure equalization in both interdistrict and intradistrict assessment. No state has yet been able to muster the political leadership necessary to put this ideal solution into practice, however.

If a state is not willing to overthrow the tradition of local assessment-ratio determination, the dual system of local fractional assessment and state full-value determination represents the "second-best" policy because it can reconcile the demand for local assessment autonomy with the state's need for a reliable means of judging equality of interdistrict and intradistrict assessment. The point must be emphasized that the dual system can do much to promote intradistrict assessment equalization *provided* the state is willing to pursue vigorously a policy of full disclosure of local-assessment-ratio findings. The chief weakness of the dual system is its apparent complexity, and its designation as a variable-ratio equalization procedure only adds to this appearance of complexity.

Paradoxically, the most popular (and the simplest) solution to the problem—abandonment of the full-value law in favor of some fractional standard—can be rated as only the "third-best" approach because it has not worked well in practice. State legislative bodies have often been willing to jettison the full-value law but have been reluctant to grant state tax officials the political support necessary to enforce the fractional-assessment standard any more effectively than its predecessor.

Thus, while formal abandonment of the full-value standard and the adoption of a fractional-assessment law can dramatically reduce the gap between law and practice, this policy has not ordinarily promoted the cause of interdistrict or intradistrict assessment equalization. As previously noted, it may actually aggravate intradistrict assessment inequalities, because state officials may be reluctant to publicize local-assessment-ratio findings and thereby reveal the extent to which local assessors and state tax officials are deviating from the fractional-assessment law. Individual property owners are the real victims when this happens, because they are denied access to the information they need to determine the fairness of their own assessments.

In the final analysis, the conflict between state assessment law and local administrative practice boils down to one basic political question—should state officials or local officials determine the general ratio for assessing taxable property in each local assessment jurisdiction? If state political leadership is unwilling to pay the political price necessary to overthrow the tradition of local assessment autonomy and to enforce the most logical standard—full-value assessment—the dual system stands out as the most practical way of maximizing equalization possibilities while minimizing political turmoil. It can maximize equalization possibilities because all local assessment decisions down to the last individual assessment can be evaluated and controlled by the full-value findings of the state tax department. It can minimize political turmoil because it does not force local officials to comply with assessment-equalization orders issued by state officials. On the surface, at least, local officials retain their traditional right to chart their own assessment course.

Notes

1 U.S. Bureau of the Census, *Taxable Property Values*, Vol. 2 in *Census of Governments: 1962* (Washington, D.C.: U.S. Government Printing Office, 1963), Tables 8–10, pp. 40–42. The corresponding 1957 report is U.S. Bureau of the Census, *Taxable Property Values in the United States,* Vol. 5 in *Census of Governments: 1957* (Washington, D.C.: U.S. Government Printing Office, 1959).

2 For a detailed examination of these arguments, see John Shannon, *Conflict Between Law and Administrative Practice in the Valuation of Property for Taxation in Kentucky* (Lexington: Bureau of Business Research, University of Kentucky, 1957), pp. 32–54.

3 Leslie E. Carbert, "Full-Value Assessment Versus Fractional Value Assessment," in National Tax Association, *1953 Proceedings of the Forty-Sixth Annual Conference on Taxation,* ed. Ronald B. Welch (Sacramento, 1954), p. 174.

4 *Louisville Courier Journal,* February 5, 1953, editorial page.

5 California State Board of Equalization, *What Does Intercounty Equalization Mean to You?* Folder A (Sacramento, September, 1955), p. 2.

6 California State Board of Equalization, *Annual Report, 50–51* (Sacramento, 1951), p. 5.

7 Robert J. Pitchell, "The Role of State Tax Policy Commissions," in National Tax Association, *1963 Proceedings of the Fifty-Sixth Annual Conference on Taxation,* ed. Walter J. Kress (Harrisburg, 1964), p. 213.

8 For a detailed analysis of public reaction to the perennial income-sales tax controversy see Leon D. Epstein, *Votes and Taxes* (Madison: Institute of Governmental Affairs, University of Wisconsin, 1964).

9 Advisory Commission on Intergovernmental Relations, *The Role of the States in Strengthening the Property Tax,* 1 (Washington, D.C.: U.S. Government Printing Office, 1963), 61. The staff work for the report was conducted by Frederick L. Bird and Edna T. Bird.

10 Florida Supreme Court, *Irving G. McNayr, as County Manager of Dade County* v. *The State of Florida, on the relation of Dupont Plaza Center, Inc.,* 166 So.2d 142 (1964). On June 8, 1965, Kentucky Court of Appeals ordered the Kentucky Department of Revenue to raise local assessments to the full-value standard—*Russman* v. *Luckett,* 391 S.W.2d 694 (1965).

11 For example, the New Jersey legislature recently repealed the full-value law and authorized a fractional-assessment policy when confronted with a court order requiring 100 percent assessment. It is probably safe to assume that, if constitutional considerations preclude their adoption of a fractional-assessment standard, the Kentucky and Florida legislatures will attempt to roll back local tax rates roughly commensurate with the assessment increase.

12 California District Court of Appeals, Second District, August 31, 1964—*Michels* v. *Watson* 229 AcA 497 (1964); *Hanks* v. *State Board of Equalization,* 229 AcA 520 (1964).

13 Nevertheless, the friends of public education will undoubtedly follow the Kentucky situation closely. If efforts to strengthen local school financing by means of the writ of mandamus prove successful in that state, attempts might be made to use this same strategy in other states in which extremely low assessment levels have caused a fiscal crisis in local education.

14 For a more detailed exposition of this approach see John Shannon, "A Non-Coercive Plan for Resolving Interdistrict Assessment Problems," in National Tax Association, *1958 Proceedings of the Fifty-First Annual Conference on Taxation,* ed. Walter J. Kress (Harrisburg, 1958), pp. 357–64.

15 Report of the Committee on State Equalization of Local Property Tax Assessments, in *ibid.*, p. 348.

16 Advisory Commission on Intergovernmental Relations, *The Role of the States,* pp. 7–25. It should be noted that the Advisory Commission did not accept unconditionally the non-coercive approach. The Commission urged the states to eliminate all constitutional and statutory requirements for fixed levels of assessment *"except* for specifying the minimum assessment ratio (in relation to market value) below which assessments may not fall." The basis for the Commission's recommendation that a minimum assessment ratio be set as high as practicable was the finding that the quality of the assessment apparently tends to deteriorate as the assessment level becomes lower. It should also be noted that, while Wisconsin has used the dual system to achieve a very high degree of interdistrict assessment equalization, it has not fully exploited the potential use of its full-value findings in intradistrict equalization. Only the more sophisticated property owners are aware of the local-assessment-ratio findings of the Wisconsin state tax department.

4. Reed R. Hansen

Henry George:
Economics or Theology?

Henry George lived from 1839 to 1897. He was a printer, an editor-publisher, a world traveler, and a fluent, persuasive journalist; he was also a politician and lecturer, but he was not an economist. He might be classified as a philosopher who evaluated life as he saw it. His writings and speeches were a moral outcry against the social injustice of his day, and it was perhaps as a moral philosopher and politician, capable at times of Churchillian rhetoric, that he entered the sphere of economic discussion. Although George did not possess a Ph.D., his writings were finally assembled and published in a ten-volume series, the very weight of which would guarantee an honorary degree from some administrators.[1]

George wrote extensively on many social problems, but undoubtedly he is best remembered as the advocate of the single-tax doctrine. To understand adequately this one part of his broader program, however, it is first essential to become familiar with the philosophy and purpose of George's writings.

The Philosophy and Program of Henry George

The central theme in the George literature was a plea for a competitive capitalism which would provide a suitable environment for individual effort. His primary objective was the conservation of a laissez faire capitalism, with its freedom of opportunity. This objective was consistent with his ever-present opposition to monopoly and his continual attack upon monopoly restrictions. Understandably, his support of free trade was an anti-monopoly measure—and his anti-Asian immigration policy was an exception.

As a critic of the society which existed 100 years ago, George opposed federal land subsidies to railroad monopolies, liquidation of public lands through the Morrill Act, and other legislation which served to transfer national wealth into private hands. He lived in California where the landed barons were particularly influential. He witnessed first hand the restrictions on freedom of the press resulting from a telegraphic monopoly, and he vigorously opposed the other developing monopolies in gas, heat, telephone, etc. In cases where monopolies could not, or should not, be dissolved, he advocated public control or public ownership.

This was the period in American history when many utopian crusades promised relief from the serious ills of the day, and the Henry George movement was another ideological attempt to show mankind the way to nobler achievements. Like other crusades, it was presented with the apostolic fervor characteristic of the times. The social problem of major concern to George was the appalling poverty developing in the growing cities and resulting in the rising amount of crime, ignorance, and ugly human misery. The intense poverty of the cities was associated with rapid technological change and great accumulations of wealth; hence, the pessimistic conclusion that greater urbanization and wealth meant greater poverty in the cities. This problem is a familiar one today, only the current jargon refers to technological and hard-core unemployment, urban sprawl, and social disorder. One must concede that the title of Henry George's best-known book, *Progress and Poverty*, is indeed timely, and the substance is an early war on poverty.

His explanation for the advancing poverty among growing riches was based upon the behavior of the monopolists owning land and resources. The men who controlled the land also controlled the people who must live on the land. As population grew, the land grew in value, and the men who worked the land paid for the privilege of doing so. In *Progress and Poverty*, George stated: "Thus wages and interest do not depend upon the produce of labor and capital, but upon what is left after rent is taken out . . . . And hence, no matter what be the increase in productive power, if the increase in rent keeps pace with it, neither wages nor interest can increase." [2] Thus, by raising his rent, the monopolist reduced the proportional shares to labor and capital.

In addition to identifying this unearned income—the expropriation by the landlord of the fruits of economic growth—George used his land-value theory to explain depressions. During a boom period, people held unused land expecting higher prices. When the speculative rent line rose too far above the normal rent line, the ensuing depression brought them together, and idle land was again returned to production.[3]

George rejected the Malthusian pessimism of the wage-fund theory and its use of the concept of diminishing returns, which advocated not giving more to the poor because they would have more children, resulting later in a larger labor force, in lower wages, and ultimately in greater human misery. George's conception of the real cause of want was described by Edgar Johnson as "The rapacity of man, not the niggardliness of nature." [4] He believed that "It is not the increase of food that has caused this increase of men; but the increase of men that has brought about the increase of food. There is more food, simply because there are more men." [5]

The important role land plays in his economic order can also be appreciated from the following excerpt:

There must be land before labor can be exerted, and labor must be exerted before capital can be produced. Capital is a result of labor, and is used by labor to assist it in further production. Labor is the active and initial force, and labor is therefore the employer of capital. Labor can be exerted only upon land, and it is from land that the matter which it transmutes into wealth must be drawn. The natural order is land, labor, capital.[6]

His solution to the problem of poverty was simply to remove the monopoly restrictions on the use of land. These monopoly restrictions took the form of enormous land holdings by railroad companies, cattlemen, timber and mining corporations, Spanish land grants, outright speculators, and others. George lived in the period of the great land grab, when the government was converting its vast resources into private holdings. George argued that the private holders of vast territories, waiting for better prices, kept out the settlers and prevented cities from developing. He felt that this hoarding of land restricted growth, cut production, and created depressions. For these reasons, Henry George wanted title to the land to remain with the government, available to the highest bidder on a rental basis. The improvements would be privately owned. It was George's opinion that "nothing short of making land common property can permanently relieve poverty and check the tendency of wages to the starvation point." [7] Public ownership of land would appropriate rent for public use, cut taxes on capital and labor, and increase the share to wages and interest. In short, business would prosper, income would rise, and poverty would be abolished.

Henry George realized the difficulty of nationalizing land in the United States, and he suggested alternative ways, more acceptable to the social framework, of controlling monopoly. He recommended direct public control when possible but believed that most of the problems caused by land monopolies could be corrected by taxation. His tax policy was a curious package which included three proposals: (a) a license tax to restrict and discourage liquor and gambling houses, etc.; (b) a high death tax which would have the advantage of not impairing the accumulations and productivity of any individual during his lifetime; and (c) a land-value tax to confiscate all rent, thereby allowing the abolishment of all other taxes except the two mentioned above. His land-value tax would not be a tax upon improvements, and it would provide a minimum exemption for the small homeowner.

The George tax program was solicitous of the need to spare capital from taxation in order to provide accumulation for growth and to stimulate production. His first canon of taxation insisted that taxation bear as lightly upon production as possible, and he expressed considerable concern for incentive effects. George commented on the taxation of production as follows: " . . . tax improvements, and the effect is to lessen improvement; tax commerce, and the effect is to prevent exchange; tax capital, and the effect is to drive it away." [8] He did speak out against income taxes as inquisitorial and a discouragement to accumulation.[9] One might assume he would speak today in opposition to sales taxes as taxes upon commerce and exchange.

To avoid adverse effects, he advocated the taxation of real property, concluding that, if government levied taxes only on rent, then production and labor would be spared harmful effects on incentive. "The whole weight of taxation would be lifted from productive industry. The million dollar manufactory, and the needle of the seamstress, the mechanic's cottage, and the grand hotel, the farmer's plough, and the steamship, would all be alike untaxed." [10]

George thought that the ultimate effect of taxing land and exempting improvements would be threefold: (a) increased productivity, (b) downward redistribution of income, and (c) destruction of land monopolization. He argued that the tax burden would be placed upon landlords; the man who owns a house and lot would, therefore, have less taxes to pay. The speculator and landholder would be forced to liquidate his holdings or to put them to use. Growth, equity, and freedom, as well as removal of the poverty blight, would therefore be possible.

George believed that either the confiscation of rent by taxation or the socialization of land would eliminate speculative pressure and would render land more available. The increased use of land would result in investment and growth in the private sector, while the public sector would have either the rental income from public ownership or high tax revenue from the rent tax to finance what is currently called urban development. New and better cities would be forthcoming, and a "new community splendor" is suggested by Barker: "not common dining rooms, but libraries, universities, parks, and other civic improvements." [11] This tranfer of income from the wealthy private sector to the poor and neglected public sector reminds us of suggestions made in a recent popular seller, *The Affluent Society,* by John Kenneth Galbraith. Like this more recent book, *Progress and Poverty* recommended the use of state taxation to achieve urban renewal. In summary, Henry George's plan for the abolishment of poverty and the creation of a great society included the elimination of taxes upon labor and capital and an increase in government expenditures to resolve the complex problems of the cities.

An Evaluation of the George Program

There are several ways to evaluate George's economic writings of 80 to 100 years ago. One method is to demonstrate smugly the shortcomings which time has exposed: that is, to reveal the inacceptability to this older plan in the current society—a new world George could not imagine. Another evaluation might compare George's economic theories with the economic theories of businessmen in the post-Civil War period and select the lesser of the two evils. Still another approach might dismiss the economic rationalizations of the author as a mere marketing device, not to be confused with the central message—which was a plea for social reform. All three methods are tempting, but a little of each approach is preferable to the exclusive use of one.

The Henry George proposals for free trade, decentralized government, and a freely competitive economy remain worthy goals applauded by most economists. His proposal to nationalize land may seem startling, but it would have been more conservative in his day, when much of the United States was already under government ownership. Today, the political traditions and vocal prejudices against public ownership make the prospects of nationalization of land at best an exciting academic exercise where one can speculate infinitely upon the world that might have been.

A city in which the council holds title to the land, and may or may not own the improvements, would be somewhat comparable to the "company town" owned by a corporation, or the university village on the edge of many campuses, or the vast private developments owned by insurance companies, or the Irvine Company in Southern California whose operation is based on special tax privileges originating under old land grants. There would be no need to exercise the "rights of eminent domain" to get a task performed. The city fathers would be free to plan for comfortable expansion, including development of parks, gardens, shopping malls, and cultural centers, and for a liveable environment free from blatant commercialism.

Government ownership of land implies a faith in the wisdom of the public administrators which may not be justified. The city council might be packed with engineers who would sacrifice the city to the automobile and construct a city of concrete and steel, having the personality of a filing cabinet. To add bitters to this cup, consider the possibilities for other distortions of democracy such as plundering the public domain by granting favorable land rent as political patronage.

The revenue potential of socialized land must also be considered carefully. It is doubtful whether the rental income from public land would be sufficient to provide the tax utopia and the services the George doctrine implies. For instance, the assessed value of real property in the United States in 1961 was $282,000,000,000. Assuming a 30–70 ratio between land value and improvements, the land had an assessed value of $85,000,000,000. Again, assuming a 20 percent ratio between assessed value and market value, the land might have been worth $425,000,000,000. If the 1961 rate of return had been a generous 10 percent, it would have yielded only $43,000,000,000 in revenue as compared to state and local expenditures of $87,000,000,000. If we assume, however, that the $18,000,000,000 in property taxes collected in 1961 were considered when computing the capitalized value of the property, then public ownership would claim not only the current rental estimate, but a share of the current land taxes as well. Under this assumption, public ownership might yield (43 + 6) $49,000,000,000. This estimate ignores, of course, the role of the federal government (income tax deductions as well as expenditures) and the psychological aspects of owning one's own land in an acquisitive society. The estimate also allows for no exemptions in the land-tax base for small homeowners (exemptions which were included in the George proposal). Adequate revenue could be forthcoming if allowance is made for a doubling of property values resulting from a substitution effect of abolishing other taxes.

To turn from the special problems of George's proposals for public ownership of land to the reformer's broader program, Harold Groves has pointed out that history has not been kind to some of George's economic predictions. For example, the landlord's share of the national income seems to have declined rather than to have increased over the years, and the masses are not experiencing the increasing misery he prophesied. In addition, land values have become a diminishing factor in the property-tax base, because of improved transportation, etc.[12] Criticism of George might be extended also to his neglect of the advantages of economies-of-scale and of the subtleties of shifting and incidence.

George's proposal for a land-value tax needs some careful study in order to distinguish between its economic costs and benefits. One might question the adequacy of a tax revenue which relies solely upon a confiscation of rent. This problem was covered earlier in this paper under the nationalization of land. One might also question whether the imposition of a land-value tax would be of much value today in breaking up monopolies. The single tax might have worked 100 years ago, when land was a major form of wealth, but today most of the wealth of the major monopolies or near-monopolies is in something other than land. It is doubtful whether land holdings are a measure of a monopoly's market control or political power, except in a few cases.

There is also the possibility that, in the large, complex society of today, which requires enormous sums of money to promote efficient use of high-value land, a land tax would force small land-holders to sell to the big investors who can finance such projects as the Lloyd and Rockefeller centers. At the moment, real estate investment ranks high in the portfolio of the small investor and is the poor man's hedge against inflation. If higher land taxes were to create greater monopoly in land ownership, the choice between public or private land monopoly might again become important.

Criticism of the single tax often refers to the administrative difficulty of separating the value of the land from the value of the improvements. Furthermore, a land tax which exempts improvements is going to be particularly hard on the farmers and beneficial to the holders of other forms of wealth, including intangibles, improvements, and high-yield educational assets.

An examination of the George philosophy reveals his marked compassion for the welfare of the small businessman and the worker. His program suggests a preference for the redistribution of income from the landed barons to the little man. It is possible, however, that applying the land-value tax today would redirect the flow of income distribution upward. A land-value tax, or a modified property tax that gives special concessions to improvements, is likely to be some-what regressive. Furthermore, in order to provide the needed reve-nue, few exemptions can be given to the homeowner and the small farmer. It is quite likely that land value today represents a higher percent of the poor man's savings than of the rich man's, because the rich hold more of the intangibles, the improvements, and the other forms of wealth exempted from taxation. More specifically, land may be a high percent of the portfolio of the low-income farmer, the small-home builder, and the eternal widow who is always present in tax debates.

The regressive nature of the land tax can be seen more clearly if we consider the impact of an $1,800 Local Improvement District assessment based upon street-frontage, which would descend with devastating force upon the retired couple and, at the same time, would be greeted with pleasure by the affluent suburbanite re-siding at the end of the new pavement.

On the other hand, a more careful study is needed of the land tax before any final judgment can be made concerning its redistri-bution pattern. A cursory examination appears to refute the conten-tion that a land-value tax would have a regressive effect and to indi-cate that George might have been correct in saying a land tax aids the homeowner and increases the burden upon holders of central real estate. One short example will explain my dilemma. Assume a city has $100,000,000 in assessed value of land and buildings and the assessment ratio is 100 percent. $20,000,000 represents the assessed value of commercial property and $80,000,000 represents the assessed value of residential property. If both commercial and residential property are paying a 2 percent rate, we find commercial property paying 20 percent of the total tax bill and residential property paying 80 percent.

The adoption of land taxation and the exemption of improve-ments would produce a shift in the proportion each group pays. If we assume that total commercial property value is split 60 percent for buildings and 40 percent for land, while residential property is split 75 percent for improvements and 25 percent for land, the propor-tions of the total tax bill paid by each would change. The share paid by the commercial property would increase from 25 percent to 28.5 percent, while the share paid by residential property would fall from 75 percent to 71.5 percent. If we assume that the commerical property is held by banks, insurance companies, and the rich and that home-owners represent the man of modest means, then advocates of the ability-to-pay doctrine will cheer. Before accepting the proposal, however, we need to know more about the ownership of property and to quantify the degree of regressivity and hardship.

Underlying the land-value tax is the questionable assumption that all land speculation is evil. Speculation may be one of several factors contributing to the urban sprawl, the need for costly transportation, and the decline in the quality of city life, but land speculation may be contributing also to some priceless conservation, or it may be reserving land for better use at a later time. Possibly it may not be "speculative" at all, but simply the farmer or widow hanging on to the "old ways." On this latter point, we find the typical conflict of interest between human rights and efficient land use and between an individual's rights and the rights of society. We might also conclude with the observations that not all land speculation is profitable and that it does contain some risks.

The Contributions and Effects of Henry George's Economic Theories

In spite of the previous criticisms or qualifications of the mechanics of the Henry George program, it contains much which is pertinent and useful to our current society, and it contains even more which has simply weathered the storms of time. The George doctrine is a useful plea for free trade and a freely competitive society: more importantly, his writings serve to identify the forces which were changing his world and creating the very problems we are struggling to resolve today. George dared to suggest solutions which recognized early the necessity for expanding the role of government participation in order to maintain social justice and a more competitive society.[13]

In the field of taxation, his writings serve to emphasize the need to utilize property taxes and to spare the sales and income taxes. In the area of income taxes, however, George's theories might be used in support of the taxation of capital gains and of the extraction of resources from the land.

When commenting on George's influence upon property taxes in general, it is helpful to remember the difficulty one experiences in attempting to introduce tax reform into the legislative process. One might argue that little tax reform has been introduced by anyone, especially when one recalls the sizeable tax inequities associated with property taxes. One is inclined to see only the problems of property taxation, such as tax limitations, extended exemptions, tax shelters, poor assessments, and the underassessment of bare land in relation to land and buildings. The unsavory record of property taxation in the past makes it difficult to assert that any individual or ideology has had a beneficial influence upon it. Yet, it is possible to find unique areas where the George doctrine found its mark, or where the citizenry fell indirectly into the use of his formula.

The State of Pennsylvania, for instance, allows cities to tax improvements at a lower rate than they tax land. It is interesting to note that only two cities, Pittsburgh and Scranton, practice this differential taxation under the "Graded Tax Plan." This plan permits both land and improvements to be assessed at market value, but the rate applied to buildings is half the rate applied to land. The Pittsburgh plan has now been inaugurated in Hawaii,[14] probably as a means of stimulating city development and of controlling absentee, monopoly ownership.

Because a general precedent has been established in this country for favorable treatment of improvements, such preferential treatment often goes relatively unnoticed. Mason Gaffney refers to the countless frontage assessments, flat acreage assessments levied by special service districts—such as the land taxes levied by irrigation districts.[15] There are also the special exemptions and moratoriums available through state corporations having the authority to grant special tax dispensations. Some tax concessions may take the form of frozen rates or frozen assessed values, but the net result is still preferential tax treatment for improvements.[16]

Gaffney asserts that property taxes adversely affect new investment in improvements. From a comparison of property taxes with excise taxes on new construction, he concludes that "each 1% of real estate tax is equivalent to a 19% tax levied as a lump sum payable at time of building. A 3% tax, such as Milwaukee and many other cities now impose, equals a 57% present lump sum tax . . . ."[17] This equivalent of a high sales tax upon new investment in city buildings is said to encourage investors to seek other, less-taxed areas of investment, and the cities suffer as a result.[18]

There is, of course, rising indignation by the American public over the decay and poverty of the large city. Reapportionment may release state legislatures from their traditional concern for the welfare of the rural areas, giving them greater opportunity to breathe new life into the neglected cities. The cities are undergoing internal changes also as racial minorities move in and the owners of property move to the country. The political power shifts, however, as the landlords leave the city council behind. The new city governments will probably resent subsidizing the suburbanite's automobile and providing cheap water and free services; they will prefer taxing the absentee landlord in order to repair the deficiencies in sanitation, transport, water, and protection. City councils have already expressed interest in the doctrine of land taxation and the exemption of the buildings in which they live and work.

The tragedy of the American city can be partially corrected by other means, particularly if tax incentives for improvements meet opposition because of the concept of uniform tax rates on all property. Benefit and penalty taxation must also be considered. For example, additional automobiles add to the cities' congestion and obsolescence; therefore the marginal costs of new automobiles must be estimated, and the auto must be made to pay for its share of the cities' problems. Penalty taxes for pollution, for slums, and for dangerous and unsightly railroad tracks—if sufficiently high—would provide a public awareness that even the most enterprising of our acquisitors would understand.

Even the federal income tax can be enlisted to aid in rebuilding the cities. Not only might federal-income-tax revenue be shared with state and local governments, but the tax might deny deductions for depreciation on buildings beyond a given age or condition, although recently sold, or it might allow the amount claimed as depreciation to be no greater than the amount of new investment in recent improvements. This would penalize those speculating in slums without improvements. Those who wish to penalize large land holders should consider the possibility of allowing no deductions for property taxes on federal-income-tax returns or of requiring *all* capital gains from the sale of land to be declared as regular income. Special tax concessions could be granted for buildings having a green belt (open park land) or meeting other special requirements.

The recent entry of the federal government into welfare legislation and urban renewal is a step toward correcting the poverty problem which George saw developing 100 years ago. Possibly, the advocates of the George doctrine may find they have not been laboring in such a stoney vineyard after all.

Notes

1 *The Writings of Henry George* (Memorial ed., 10 vols.; New York: Doubleday and McClure, 1898–1901).

2 Henry George, *Progress and Poverty* (25th anniversary ed.; Garden City, New York: Doubleday, Page, 1915), p. 171; also quoted in Donald O. Macmillan, 1937), pp. 463–81.

Wagner, *Social Reformers, Adam Smith to John Dewey* (New York:

3 Harold M. Groves, "Philosophers and Philosophies of Taxation" (an early draft of an unpublished manuscript generously loaned to this writer), p. 227.

4 Edgar H. Johnson, "The Economies of Henry George's Progress and Poverty," *Journal of Political Economy,* 18, No. 9 (October, 1910), 715.

5 George, *Progress and Poverty* (25th anniversary ed.), p. 131.

6 *Ibid.,* p. 163.

7 George, *Progress and Poverty* (4th ed.; New York: John W. Lovell, 1883), Preface, p. 3.

8 George, *Progress and Poverty* (25th anniversary ed.), p. 412.

9 Charles A. Barker, *Henry George* (New York: Oxford University Press, 1955), p. 288, discussing George, *Progress and Poverty* (25th anniversary ed.), p. 318.

10 Henry George, *Our Land and Land Policy, Speeches, Lectures, and Miscellaneous Writings* (New York: Doubleday and McClure, 1902), p. 112.

11 Barker, *Henry George,* p. 293.

12 Groves, "Philosophers and Philosophies of Taxation," p. 230.

13 The consequences and influence of the George proposals for land taxation and for the common ownership of land reveal an interesting story. In the book *Land-Value Taxation Around the World* (ed. Harry Gunnison Brown *et al.* [New York: Robert Schalkenbach Foundation, 1955]), there are historical accounts of towns in the United States where land is owned by the city. The cities mentioned are Fairhope, Alabama, the three Ardens in Delaware, and Free Acres, New Jersey.

14 Mason Gaffney, "Property Taxes and the Frequency of Urban Renewal," in National Tax Association, *1964 Proceedings of the Fifty-Seventh Annual Conference on Taxation,* ed. Walter J. Kress (Harrisburg, 1965).

15 *Ibid.,* pp. 277–78.

16 Devices can easily be designated to grant tax privileges. For instance, property taxes can be deductible from other state taxes when certain conditions are met.

17 Gaffney, "Property Taxes," p. 2. Also Mason Gaffney, *Containment Policies for Urban Sprawl* (Government Research Series No. 27; Lawrence: University of Kansas, 1952).

18 Proposals for the use of a "present value of discounted taxes" might conceivably overstate the importance of future property taxes to the potential investor. Consider the intimidating figure one could develop by discounting the federal income taxes paid over the long life of the prospective building—or of any other business expense. Perhaps the discounted present value of taxes would have more utility if accompanied by the discounted present value of profits and revenue. The present discounted value has another weakness. Under conditions of rising assessed values, the 19 percent figure at time of construction could be preferable to the annual 1 percent tax. If the taxpayer had the choice of "prepaying" his taxes and then enjoying a lifetime exemption, the 19 percent would appear smaller indeed.

Part II Business and Industry

Introduction

When land taxation is mentioned, the taxation of farm land comes to mind first. Raleigh Barlowe's paper summarizes American experience and the current situation in this area of taxation. On the basis of this analysis, future developments aimed at confrontation of identified problems within this field are considered. The concluding point of the paper is that "tax policies can be used quite effectively, along with the police, eminent domain, spending, and proprietory powers of government, as a means for controlling and directing future land use." The active use of agricultural-land taxation to aid in reaching planning goals would make the property tax a much more dynamic aspect of rural and near-urban life than it is at present. The rural property tax has always been preeminently a tax for revenue only; however, the tax undoubtedly also possesses attributes useful in creating better land-use conditions.

Earl E. Burkhard has prepared an analysis of the taxation of business personal property for *Property Taxation—USA*. He utilizes the point-of-view of the administrator and the taxpayer. If Professor Lynn's uncertain theory of property-tax cycles is operative, the inclusion of personal property in the property-tax base will continue to decline. The principal value of this paper is in the wealth of administrative information it presents regarding the application of the *ad valorem* property tax to personal property in the United States. This information is helpful in reforming the United States personal-property tax through use of better-qualified administrators and better equipment, as advocated by Burkhard. Its greatest use, however, may be in establishing—or even, perhaps, in deciding whether or not to establish in the less developed nations—an *ad valorem* tax that included personal property as a portion of the base. A side effect, as it were, of Burkhard's analysis is the understanding it provides of why an old revenue raiser continues in use despite serious conceptual and administrative shortcomings.

Harold Groves examines the taxation of intangibles in the United

States and the attempts which were made to include this type of property under the nineteenth-century "tax anything" policy of general, *ad valorem* property taxation. A basic conclusion of his analysis is that: "From the overall view, levies in the ideal tax system would, no doubt, be confined to a personal income tax (including undistributed profits); an inheritance tax; and a property tax *in rem* on economic rent." An ideal tax system does not exist anywhere, however, and, in setting the base for the application of the property tax to businesses, considerable justification exists in the real world for including the value of intangibles—such as monopoly power, know-how, copyrights, and patents—as well as the value of tangibles. Groves concludes that "the only classification of property for special taxation that has solid merit is that which would place a special burden on urban land rent."

Lynn A. Stiles offers a more specialized treatment of the same area considered by Burkhard and Groves. Stiles analyses the taxation of railroad property under the *unit rule* (according to the value of the entire business as an operating unit), a method to which Groves gave favorable consideration in his paper. Stiles finds that, under current conditions, one effect of the unit rule on the taxation of railroad property is that this property is greatly undervalued in comparison with the assessment that would have been made if depreciated value of equipment and buildings and the highest use value of land had been considered. This undervaluation develops under the unit rule because of what might be called the "corporate surplus deficit." Railroad earnings on property owned is frequently less than the 6-percent rate used to capitalize income earned in arriving at the value of property to which the tax rate is applied. In such a case, the unit rule results in a serious undervaluation, which means, in effect, that railroads receive a subsidy not granted to industries operating under " 'brick and mortar,' piecemeal valuation." As a result, railroads can hold large pieces of valuable land more cheaply than other industries can.

The final paper of this group is an effort to evaluate the usefulness of property-tax inducements to attract industry. One of the conclusions Paul E. Alyea reaches is that low property taxes would become much less of an inducement if property taxes were applied only to land, because the price of land would tend to be low where property taxes were high, and the price of land would tend to be high where property taxes were low. High taxes on land would also permit lower taxes on improvements. It is Dr. Alyea's conclusion that the first areas moving toward higher land taxes and lower taxes on buildings and personal property would experience "a temporary advantage" in attracting industry. The advantage might be only temporary because other areas seeing the impact of the shift would try to move toward the same approach; the changeover would be slow, however.

The arguments for including all types of property under the property tax have always been persuasive. In Continental Europe today, where the income tax is not as intensively used as in the United States, a low-rate tax applied to total wealth is gaining favor. In many ways this approach to an overall or all-inclusive property tax is preferable to efforts to continue a general or partially general *ad valorem* property tax.

Areas—such as the United States—in which property taxation is highly developed face quite different problems when considering the use of a general wealth tax than those encountered in Germany, for example, where the property tax as we know it is not used. One approach that might be taken by United States tax leaders who are interested in a general wealth tax is to limit the property tax to land values. In this way the distinctive characteristics of land and natural resources as wealth can be maintained while the taxation of other forms of wealth is not limited to the application of an income tax—which is necessarily restricted to some concept of income realization.

Richard W. Lindholm

5. Raleigh Barlowe

Taxation of Agriculture

Farmers as individuals and agriculture as an industry have had a long and deep-rooted involvement with property taxation. The *ad valorem* property tax, as it has developed in the United States, is essentially the product of an agrarian society. Historically, the general property tax had its American beginnings in the early post-Revolutionary War period.[1] It was devised as a successor to the feudal quit rents used in some colonies and to the specific taxes on land and personalty that had been levied in others. Agriculture was the nation's dominant industry at the time; agricultural land and personalty provided most of the base for the general-property tax for many decades after its acceptance; and property taxes still represent the principal tax paid by most farmers.[2]

Continued acceptance of the property tax over a period of more than a century and a half has made it a traditional fixture in American farming operations. The initial acceptance of the tax by the agricultural community was favored by three important factors: (*a*) tax levies were ordinarily quite low; (*b*) most of the tax revenues were used for local governmental services and improvements; and (*c*) land ownership was closely correlated in most instances with individual wealth and tax-paying ability.

Much could be said here concerning our early experience with farm-property taxation. Tax levies were usually nominal and often involved charges of only a few pennies per acre. Public domain lands along the southern and midwestern frontiers were exempt from taxation for the first five years following their sale.[4] For a long time, tax-supported services were limited primarily to the provision of government and police protection. Public improvements were sometimes financed by taxes but the costs of these improvements were often held to a minimum. Schools were provided for many years on a private-subscription basis, and local roads were constructed and maintained largely by citizen labor crews. Property taxes were sometimes used to encourage the sale and development of speculator-held tracts, but these taxes often went unpaid or were shifted to settler-buyers of the land.[5]

But even though the property taxes of the 1880's may not seem high in comparison with present rates, they often posed problems for land owners. They represented a burden on property ownership in much the same way that they do today. Tax levies were often high in relation to owner incomes. Delinquencies were common, and many properties were forfeited for non-payment of taxes, particularly in the periods following the depressions of 1837, 1857, 1872, and 1893.

Property-tax delinquency was again a major problem for agriculture during the 1920's and 1930's. High taxes and reduced incomes were a problem for all farmers, but the problem was especially acute for farmers on the lower-quality and locationally disadvantaged sites that were marginal or near-marginal for agricultural use. A long period of rising farm incomes and farm-land values, extending from the middle 1890's to 1920, was associated with an upward trend in property tax levies. Farm incomes and farm-land values declined following the agricultural depression of 1920, but farm-property taxes continued their upward climb. This trend led to widespread tax delinquency in marginal agricultural areas, such as the Lake States "cutover" area, during the 1920's.[6] By the 1930's, inability to pay property taxes made tax delinquency a common phenomenon in most agricultural communities, and millions of acres of agricultural land were actually forfeited for non-payment of taxes.

Downward adjustments in property-tax rates were accomplished during the depression years, sometimes through elimination of governmental services or the reduction of operating costs and sometimes by the transfer of governmental functions to other levels of government or by financing these functions with revenue from other taxes. These adjustments, as well as the return of higher prices and expanding markets during the World War II years, made the 1940's something of a golden age in farm-property taxation. Property-tax levies were relatively low in comparison with operator net incomes and with the rising value of farm land. This situation was temporary, and conditions changed rapidly during the 1950's and early 1960's as farm-property taxes climbed to new heights and claimed higher and higher proportions of the net cash incomes realized by farm operators.

The Farm-Property-Tax Situation

Figure 5.1 shows the trend in farm real estate taxes from 1910 through 1963, expressed in terms of average tax levies per acre and average levies per $100 of farm real estate value in the United States. This chart shows a marked increase in average tax levies per acre during the World War I period, slower increases during the 1920's, a decline in average tax levies during the early 1930's followed by 12 years of fairly constant levies, and a steady upward trend in average property-tax levies per acre since 1944. Viewed in terms of farm-land values, tax rates climbed steadily from 1910, and particularly after 1919, until 1933. The ratio of taxes to land values then declined until 1944, since which time it has tended to increase at a rapid rate.

Statistical data concerning the trends in farm-property taxation are reported in Tables 5.1 and 5.2. Analysis of these data and of the

Table 5.1—Trends in Farm Real Estate Taxation in the United States: 1910–63

Year	Average property tax per		Property taxes as a percentage of net farm income before payment of property taxes [a]
	Acre	$100 of property value	
1910	$ .19	$ .47	3.6
1914	.24	.56	4.7
1918	.33	.57	3.1
1921	.54	.94	12.3
1925	.56	1.07	6.7
1929	.58	1.20	7.9
1932	.45	1.52	18.0
1937	.39	1.15	5.9
1940	.39	1.18	7.4
1945	.44	.77	3.3
1949	.66	.95	4.8
1951	.72	.81	4.3
1956	.91	.90	7.1
1958	1.03	.89	6.9
1960	1.22	.97	8.7
1962	1.36	1.02	8.9
1963	1.43	1.03	9.4

[a] Net farm income as used in this table includes the value of all the net income from farming received by farmers in cash, farm products, housing, etc., plus net rent paid to farm landlords, before deduction of real estate taxes.

Source: Lawrence A. Leonard, "Cyclical and Regional Variations in Farm Property Tax Burdens," *Agricultural Finance Review*, 20 (April, 1958), 19; and U.S. Department of Agriculture, Economic Research Service, *Farm Real Estate Taxes* (Washington, D.C.: U.S. Government Printing Office, October, 1962, September, 1963, and October, 1964).

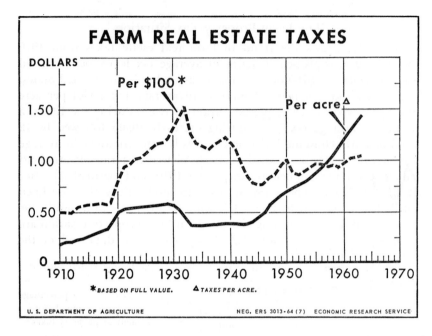

Figure 5.1—Farm real estate taxes.

trends shown in Figure 5.1 shows that farm-property taxes have been moving steadily upward for a period of twenty-one years at an average rate of more than 6 percent a year. Farmers paid an average real estate tax in 1963 of $1.43 per acre, which amounted to a tax of $1.03 on each $100 of real estate value.

The national averages, of course, cover a wide range of different situations. Regional averages per acre ranged from highs of $3.54 in the Northeast, $3.24 in the Pacific States, $2.98 in the Corn Belt, and $2.61 per acre in the Lake States to only $.48, $.57, and $.68 per acre, respectively, in the Mountain, Southern Plains, and Delta regions. (See Table 5.3.) Regional averages per $100 of real estate value in 1963 ranged from $1.72 in the Northeast and $1.59 in the Lake States to only $.45 in the Delta region. State averages per acre ranged from highs of $11.80 in New Jersey and $7.43 in Massachusetts to lows of $.17, $.23, $.30, and $.35 in New Mexico, Wyoming, Nevada, and Alabama respectively, and state averages per $100 of real estate value ranged from averages of $2.37 in Maine and $2.36 in New York to lows of $.34 in Alabama, $.38 in Louisiana and Mississippi, $.46 in Delaware, and $.47 in West Virginia. Similarly wide variations

Table 5.2—Farm Real Estate Tax Situation: 1963

Area	Average tax per acre	Average tax per $100 of property value
United States	$ 1.43	$1.03
Regions:		
Northeast	3.54	1.72
Lake States	2.61	1.59
Corn Belt	2.98	1.22
Northern Plains	1.05	1.23
Appalachian	.92	.56
Southeast	.85	.54
Delta	.65	.45
Southern Plains	.57	.55
Mountain	.48	.86
Pacific	3.24	1.17
Alaska	1.86	1.02
Hawaii	2.01	1.49
Selected States:		
Alabama	.35	.34
Delaware	1.29	.46
Louisiana	.72	.38
Maine	2.28	2.37
Massachusetts	7.43	2.19
Mississippi	.46	.38
Nevada	.30	.65
New Jersey	11.80	2.11
New Mexico	.17	.47
New York	3.67	2.36
West Virginia	.38	.47
Wyoming	.23	.76

Source: U.S. Department of Agriculture, Economic Research Service, *Farm Real Estate Taxes* (Washington, D.C.: U.S. Government Printing Office, October, 1964), Tables 3 and 5.

may be found within individual states where farm lands located in urban fringe areas frequently pay annual taxes in excess of $25 to $30 an acre while forest and range lands in more remote areas have annual levies of as little as $.10 an acre.

A definitive picture of the farm-property-tax situations calls for recognition of the farmer's position in relation to rising property taxes and also of his economic position in the changing American scene. Taxes on farm property almost doubled between 1950 and 1963, while operator's net cash incomes went up by only 17 percent.[7] Farmers find themselves the victims of an unfortunate set of circumstances. As Frederick D. Stocker has observed:

. . . property taxes are a fixed cost of agricultural production. The owner's tax bill does not vary with output or with the price of farm products. Even if he allows his land to lie idle, his taxes are not affected, in the short run at least. Moreover, the farmer is likely to feel particularly helpless in the face of rising property taxes because, unlike other costs that are subject to his personal control, property taxes are governed largely by the will of the community. Finally, opportunities for "shifting" the property tax are limited. Because the farmer typically sells his product in a market in which his individual influence is negligible, he cannot pass the tax on to the consumer in the form of higher prices.[8]

As a generalization, one might assert that the farm operator of today who wishes to remain competitive must apply better managerial practices than ever before to a larger capital investment in land, livestock, and equipment. This combination means higher property taxes. Farm operators must be reconciled to the prospect of fewer people in agriculture, continuation of relatively low returns from agricultural employment, and payment of an increasing proportion of their net cash farm income as property taxes.

The direction of recent trends in this regard is shown by the data reported in Table 5.3. These data show that the number of farms, the total farm population, and the number of workers in American agriculture have all been declining at a rapid rate in recent decades. Department of Agriculture estimates place the total number of farms in the nation at 3,573,000 in 1963 as compared with as high as 6,546,000 in 1930; total farm population at 13,354,000 persons in 1963 as compared with a prewar total of 30,547,000 in 1940; and number of farm workers at 6,518,000 in 1963 as compared with 13,432,000 in 1920 and 10,979,000 in 1940. Farm-land acreage also declined from a peak of 1,159,000,000 acres in farms in 1950 to an estimated 1,124,000,000 acres in 1959, even though the 1959 total included the addition of approximately 4,000,000 acres of farm land in Alaska and Hawaii. Further declines are anticipated in each of these categories.

The decline in the number of farms, in the number of farm residents and workers, and in the land area of farms by no means indicates a decline in the importance of agriculture. The nation's farmers are more productive and operate far more efficiently now than ever before. Food and other agricultural production has more than doubled in the last fifty years. Applications of scientific know-how have made it possible for fewer farmers, operating less acreage, to do a better job of feeding and clothing approximately twice the population we had at the beginning of World War I.

Table 5.3—Trends in Number of Farms, Farm Population, Acreage in Farms, Farm Real Estate Taxes, and Net Cash Incomes from Agriculture in the United States: 1910–63

Year	Number of farms (hundreds)	Farm population (hundreds)	Workers in agriculture (hundreds)	Farm-land acreage (millions)	Average annual income of farm workers	Average annual income of factory workers	Total net cash income from agriculture [a] (millions)	Total farm property taxes [b] (millions)	Property taxes as a percent of net cash income before payment of taxes
1910–14	6,429	32,077	13,561	879	$ 338	$ 547	$2,257	$ 231	9.3
1920	6,518	31,614	13,432	956	660	1,353	3,993	348	8.0
1930	6,546	30,445	12,497	987	456	1,196	2,621	648	10.8
1940	6,350	30,547	10,979	1,061	484	1,298	2,450	451	15.5
1950	5,648	23,048	9,926	1,159	1,598	3,033	8,120	919	10.2
1955	4,654c	19,078	8,364	1,158c	1,698	3,936	7,827	1,149	12.8
1960	3,949c	15,620	7,057	1,124c	2,075	4,665	8,976	1,549	14.7
1963	3,573	13,354	6,518	—	2,375	5,168	9,190	1,789	16.3

[a] Total net cash income includes only the net income received by farmers as cash. Value of farm products consumed and rental value of farm residence are excluded from the total.

[b] Total farm-property taxes includes farm real estate taxes and farm-personal-property taxes.

[c] Data on numbers of farms and total farm-land acreage are for 1954 and 1959 as reported in the U.S. Census of Agriculture for these years.

Source: U.S. Department of Agriculture, *U.S. Census of Agriculture* (1959) (Washington, D.C.: U.S. Government Printing Office, 1961); and U.S. Department of Agriculture, Economic Research Service, *Farm Income Situation* (Washington, D.C.: U.S. Government Printing Office, July, 1964). (Alaska and Hawaii are included in totals for 1960 and 1963.)

Agricultural science and new production efficiencies have freed millions of people for off-farm employment. Meanwhile, the returns to management and labor in agriculture have not kept up with the returns in other types of employment. As Table 5.3 indicates, farm workers had an average income of $2,375 in 1963 as compared with an average income of $5,168 for factory workers, and the income received by farm workers increased only 7-fold during the preceding half-century as compared with a 9.5-fold increase for factory workers.

Net cash income in agriculture rose to $3,993,000,000 in 1920, dropped to approximately two-thirds of that amount in 1930, continued its decline in the 1930's, and then rose in the 1940's, 1950's, and 1960's to $9,190,000,000 in 1963. Property-tax payments, including taxes on both realty and personalty, rose at a faster rate than farm incomes after 1940, with the result that property-tax payments took a gradually increasing proportion of the average farm operator's net cash income. Some 10.2 percent of the average operator's net cash income went for property taxes in 1950, 12.8 percent in 1955, 14.7 percent in 1960, and 16.3 percent in 1963.

A number of variables—including differences in local property-tax rates; differences in assessment policies; the extent of individual property holdings; and ups and downs in farm operator incomes caused by differences in yields, commodity prices, costs, and managerial abilities—affect the proportion of an operator's net cash income required for the payment of property taxes. As one might expect, these proportions vary considerably between farmers living in different localities. They also vary between individual operators living within the same taxing district, and they cause up and down shifts with the year-to-year operations of given operators.

An example of these relationships is provided by the study of property taxes paid as a proportion of net incomes for a sample of 922 Michigan farm account cooperators in 1957, reported in Table 5.4.[9] This analysis shows a regressive relationship between net incomes received and property taxes paid. A study of the same operators in other years would undoubtedly show considerable movement of individual operators from one income bracket to another as they enjoy higher- or lower-income years.[10] Similar studies would show that the net incomes and net worth of farm operators are not always highly correlated for any single year but that there is usually a regressive relationship between current net cash incomes and current property-tax payments. A similar regressive relationship often existed between assessed valuations and actual farm-property values.[11]

Table 5.4—Relationship of Property Taxes Paid to Net Cash Incomes
for 922 Michigan Farm Account Cooperators: 1957

Net income bracket (before payment of taxes)	Number of farmers	Average net income per farmer	Average property taxes per farmer	Property taxes as a percentage of net income before payment of taxes
Negative incomes	32	– $ 1,816	$3.75	—
0 to $1,999	108	1,123	356	31.7
$2,000 to $2,999	93	2,523	356	14.1
$3,000 to $3,999	137	3,495	302	8.6
$4,000 to $4,999	120	4,483	351	7.8
$5,000 to $6,999	186	5,965	420	7.0
$7,000 to $9,999	162	8,278	547	6.6
$10,000 and over	84	12,775	747	5.8
All groups	922	$ 5,248	$430	8.2

Source: Claude Bitner, "The Regressive Impact of Farm Property Taxation on Michigan Farm Families," Quarterly Bulletin of the Michigan Agricultural Experiment Station, 42 (May, 1960), 809-10.

Implications of Property-Tax Trends for Agriculture

With the materials discussed above as background, one might now ask: What are the future implications for agriculture of the present property-tax situation? The property tax will probably continue as one of the two largest taxes paid by agriculture. Barring a major depression, there is little prospect that tax levies will decline. The trend is towards higher and higher taxes. In many taxing districts, tax levies are already at critical levels—levels at which commitments for payment of improvement bonds and of current operating costs could require tax payments above the ability of average property owners to pay in the event of a prolonged business recession. But the demand is for more rather than less public services, and this suggests higher taxes.

Different situations can be expected in different areas. More serious problems will arise in communities in which farm property is already taxed at a high level than in places where property taxes are still low in relation to the value and productivity of the land. The major developments that may be anticipated can best be viewed by classifying agricultural lands into three groups: (a) farm lands that can be expected to remain in farms; (b) farm lands that will shift to grazing, forestry, and other less intensive uses; and (c) farm lands that will shift to more intensive uses.

Current projections suggest a continued decline in the total acreage in farms and in harvested cropland. A Department of Agriculture report in 1962, for example, indicated a need for shifting an additional 51,000,000 acres of harvested cropland out of use by 1980.[12] No one knows how long or how far this downward trend in farm acreage will, or should, continue.[13] For our purposes, it is reasonable to assume that four-fifths or more of our farm land will remain in farming and that most of our forest and range lands will remain in their current uses.

Higher property taxes will represent an added cost for the operators of the lands that stay in agriculture. Insofar as all producers of a given commodity are affected alike by rising taxes, the cost of the higher taxes may be passed on in the form of higher prices. Much of the increase in taxes, however, will be paid out of current incomes. Higher taxes may contribute to greater tax awareness, but, as long as agricultural incomes do not decline, and as long as desired local services are associated with the expenditure of tax revenues, property taxes will probably be accepted as a necessary and routine cost of property ownership.

The trend towards larger but fewer farms suggests that farm land will provide a relatively constant, if not a shrinking, base for property taxation in the future. This situation will complicate the problems many rural communities face in trying to finance public services. The downward trend in rural farm population in some areas may afford opportunities for consolidation of governmental units and for economies in the provision of public services. Major developments along this line, however, cannot be expected without either severe economic pressures that will force changes or political mandates for change from the state or federal levels of government.

Turning to the lands that are shifting out of agriculture, it may be noted that the total land area included in farms in the forty-eight contiguous states dropped by approximately 38,000,000 acres, or by 3.3 percent, between 1954 and 1959. During the same five-year period, the area of cropland in farms used for crop production dropped from 380,000,000 acres to 351,000,000 acres, a decrease of 5.5 percent. Between 5,000,000 and 6,000,000 acres of the decline in total farm land area resulted from a modification of the Census definition of what constitutes a farm.[14] Another 7,000,000 acres is believed to have shifted into highway and urban or suburban uses. The remaining two-thirds of the area lost from farming shifted to lower uses. Some of this area was enrolled as whole farms under the Soil Bank and Conservation Reserve programs. Most of it, however, was farm land which shifted to grass or forest uses, or farms which had been idled because their owners stopped cultivating them.

Serious property-tax problems would undoubtedly arise with the lands that are shifting out of farming at the extensive margin—the lands shifting to lower uses—if the owners of these properties were living under less affluent conditions. Many lands have shifted to lower uses because they are marginal for agriculture under current price and cost conditions and because their owners have seen attractive alternative off-farm opportunities for maximizing their incomes and satisfactions. Property taxes have not been a major factor in forcing these lands to lower uses, and few of these areas involve cases of recent tax delinquency or tax forfeiture.

It is difficult to say how long this situation will continue. During the 1920's and 1930's, property taxes contributed to the abandonment of large areas of marginal and submarginal land. Today, similar areas are shifting out of farm use, and whole farms are disappearing as producing units. But the individual transportation situation and off-farm employment opportunities are such that farm buildings are still being occupied as residences, properties are being held for vacation and recreation purposes, and many properties are held for nostalgic reasons or, sometimes, in the expectation that the land will soon have value for new uses. This situation can continue in an affluent society as long as people are willing to subsidize the ownership of idle or near-idle lands. Complications can be expected if property taxes rise while owner incomes decline. Another type of problem exists when taxes on non-residents or seasonal residents are used to finance local services.

A third important relationship between taxation and land use concerns the farm and agricultural lands that are shifting to more intensive uses. The areas that have shifted from agricultural to urban or suburban, commercial, industrial, and highway uses during the past decade have been variously estimated at between 600,000 and 1,500,-000 acres annually. Some shifting of lands for these purposes is, of course, necessary and desirable. But the shifting process has been both inefficient and wasteful. Large areas have been taken out of agriculture before they have been needed for other uses, and the scattered locations of the lands taken has often blighted surrounding areas for continued agricultural use.

In many respects, the shifting of lands out of agriculture to the so-called more intensive uses represents one of the most critical land-use issues of our time. Several factors are involved, such as need for additional urban space, concern over future food supplies, possibilities for effective land-use planning, and concern over recreational and open-space lands. Local-property-tax and fiscal conditions also affect the situation.

The problem, as it involves the relationship between property taxes and land use, can be visualized as in Figures 5.2, 5.3, and 5.4. Figure 5.2 assumes a central city (A) which, for diagramatic purposes, is shown as occupying a circular shaded area. This area is surrounded by a circumferential band into which the city could easily expand and by a larger circular hinterland. A profile of land rents or of land values for the city can be shown as a cone (BCD). The highest point of this cone (C) represents the rents and values of land at the city's 100-percent point in its central business district, while the sloping sides represent the declining rents and values expected as one approaches the boundaries of the city where land is used for rural rather than urban uses. A triangle (CAB or CAD) can be used to depict a cross section or profile of the land rents (or values) associated with increasing distance from the 100-percent spot, and separate, overlapping triangles (CAD and EAF), indicating the rents associated with different uses (urban and rural in Figure 5.2), can be used to show the approximate points at which higher uses could be expected to supplant lower uses.

In a transportation-constrained society, travel considerations would discourage the rapid outward expansion of the city. Population growth would call for shifting more land around the city's borders to urban use (outward movement of line U from point B to C in Figure 5.3). The areas taken would be expected to lie adjacent to the city, however, and this outward movement would be associated with more intensive use and probably with higher rents from the areas already found within the city.

Increased mobility—caused by such developments as commuter trains, automobiles, and all-weather and limited-access highways—has greatly changed this situation. The modern city is not subject to serious transportation constraints. Cities tend to expand outward, but there is no longer the pressure there once was for relatively restricted and smooth outward growth. People who are willing to move out find that it may actually be less difficult for them to live at point G in Figure 5.3 and to commute to the downtown city than it would have been for them to live at point C under more transportation-constrained conditions. In addition, they may rationalize that certain values in living at site G—such as more open space, lower land costs, and lower taxes—more than compensate them for the cost of their longer journey to work.

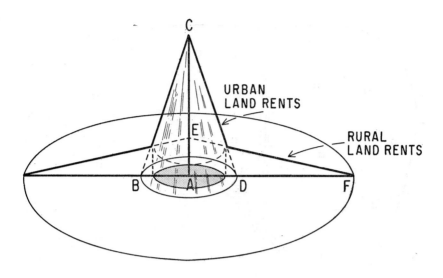

Figure 5.2—Land rent cone.

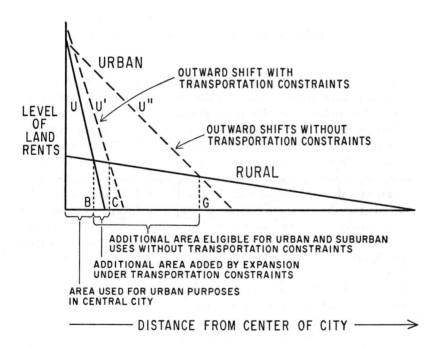

Figure 5.3—Land rent triangles.

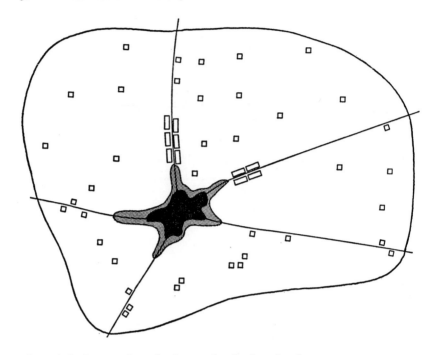

Figure 5.4—Scatteration of urban and suburban developments.

Transportation developments, such as those visualized with Figure 5.3, have greatly expanded the areas around cities which are eligible for urban and suburban development. The area actually needed for urban expansion around a central city may encompass no more than the shaded area shown in Figure 5.4. Opportunities for urban development, however, may appear reasonable for a significantly larger area. As a result, subdividers and others acquire lands at scattered sites for urban uses. In practice, subdivisions and building lots may be laid out first along major highways, but they may occur anywhere. Instead of expanding outward in a compact and orderly fashion, new developments often follow scatteration patterns (see Figure 5.4) which involve a leap frog approach to urban development.

The taxation effects of scatteration are easy to visualize. Prospective suburbanites are charmed by the rural countryside, buy lots, and build houses. Others follow their example. Soon local taxes must rise to provide additional school facilities and other desired public services. Tax assessors note the rising land values associated with the sale of miscellaneous building sites and gradually associate these higher values with all the land within the subdivision zone even though need and a current market exists for the urbanized use of only a fraction of the area. Taxes on farm land rise—sometimes faster on the farm land than on the invading urban and suburban uses. Higher tax costs add to the farmer's operating costs and lead to lower net incomes until the farmer who is interested in farming finds it advisable to sell out to a speculator or subdivider who may be content to let the land lie idle for some years while he waits for a higher market use to ripen.

The taxation problem in the areas where agricultural land is shifting to higher uses is primarily one of keeping tax rates at reasonable agricultural levels until the land is actually needed for urbanized uses. The haphazard policies we have used in the past have too often forced owners to sell out before their lands were actually needed for non-agricultural uses. Such policies have often resulted in idle land and in premature and poorly planned developments.

Needed Developments in Tax Policy

As one looks to the future of agricultural property taxation, it is logical to ask what can be done about the emerging problems. Two important answers call for (a) continuing efforts to secure better administration of the property tax, and (b) measures to limit property-tax levies to levels commensurate with the tax-paying ability of properties and owners.

The plea for better administrative practices is an old one. Progress has been made along this line, but there is still much need for better assessments.[15] Assessment districts often need consolidation, and assessment offices should be staffed by qualified appraisers. Efforts are needed to bring assessments closer to some uniform level of market value and to educate property owners so that they will help police the assessment function. More state supervision is needed in some instances, and thorough reviews are needed in others to update assessment procedures and manuals to make them consistent with modern appraisal practice.

Property taxes are already at dangerously high levels in some areas. Considerable increases are possible in others. Consideration should be given to the placing of upper limits on property-tax levies or, better still, to the reduction of property taxes by finding new sources of revenue for programs which are currently supported by the property tax. The costs of primary and secondary schools provide a prime example. These costs have risen rapidly in recent decades. As the service provided is more beneficial to persons than to property, some tax other than the property tax might logically be designated as a major source of support. Important precedents for this proposal are found in the earlier actions of our states in shifting the costs of highway construction and maintenance from the property tax to automobile, gasoline, and other highway taxes and in shifting the costs of state government to new sources of revenue.

A more questionable area of policy concerns what, if anything, should be done to safeguard agricultural uses of land in areas of urban and suburban expansion. Good assessment practice calls for assessing all lands at values appropriate for their highest and best use. Yet efficient and orderly land-use planning calls for retaining areas in agricultural and open-space uses that may have market-place values for higher uses.

A number of possible policies may be considered. The United Kingdom and some other European countries use tight systems of control to keep land rural until its development for other purposes is approved by public planning agencies. This approach works, and it definitely merits the consideration of American students of land-use problems. Yet it involves more control over individual land-development decisions than most Americans are yet ready to accept.

Land zoning represents a possibility, and the zoning of land for agricultural use can protect it for this purpose. Historically, however, zoning has often provided only a temporary bulwark against demands for the shifting of lands to higher uses.

Sale of conservation easements or of development rights has been suggested as a means of preserving open-space corridors around urban centers. Cities might buy the development rights to agricultural land and leave the operators with full rights to continue the land in its present use. Experience with this approach has, thus far, been disappointing. Development rights for land located near a city often cost almost as much as full ownership, with the result that the city can often buy the land and lease it back to the operator at little, if any, additional cost.

Special taxing arrangements also have been suggested and have been used as a means of handling the problem. A number of states—Connecticut, Florida, Indiana, Maryland, New Jersey, and Oregon—have acted to provide a system of preferential tax treatment for agricultural lands. Maryland's law, which was first enacted in 1956, calls for the assessment of farmland on the basis of agricultural use and without regard for its potential non-farm uses.

Questions can be raised about the effectiveness of these programs.

Limited observations indicate that they are playing a desired role in keeping lands in agricultural use which might otherwise be growing up in weeds. But there also is evidence that preferential taxation arrangements provide a boon to speculators—to owners and investors who hope to develop or sell land at higher values for a higher use in the future and who benefit now from retaining agricultural tax levels.[16]

Perhaps this situation is what it should be. It suggests, however, need for considering the possible use of deferred taxes. If an owner benefits from low taxes now and later sells at an advantage, should he be held for the payment of additional taxes? Considerations of equity and justice dictate an affirmative answer. Tax-deferral arrangements can call for payment of the difference between the taxes actually paid and the amount they would have been without the preferential tax law. If lands which receive preferential treatment in New Jersey are shifted to non-farm uses, payment of this differential is required for the current and the two preceeding years. Oregon requires similar payments for a period of up to five years with accumulated interest charged at a rate of 6 percent.

An alternative, as yet untried, to the tax-deferral, differential-payment approach would require the continued taxation of agricultural land at its agricultural value but would apply a land value increment tax at the time the land shifts to a higher use. This tax could be graduated according to the years of preferential treatment to a maximum of, say, 50 percent of the difference between the assessed value of the land for agriculture and its actual sale or market value for the higher use. This approach would have the value of eliminating need for annual dual assessments and, at the same time, of allowing the governmental unit to share in appreciations in property value.

One other problem associated with preferential assessments should be mentioned. Many lands now in agricultural use around cities should be developed for higher uses. Good planning in these cases may be hindered rather than helped by preferential tax treatment. This situation suggests heed for relating eligibility for preferential tax treatment to master land-use plans or to approval by a land-planning agency. An alternative arrangement, recently approved in California, permits local governments to make inducement payments roughly equal to the higher taxes paid to those owners who agree to keep their lands in agricultural or open-space uses.

As a final comment, it may be observed that preferential tax treatment and tax subsidies represent only a small aspect of the larger problem of public direction of land use. Property taxes are not ordinarily used for non-revenue purposes. It must be recognized, however, that tax policies can be used quite effectively, along with the police, eminent domain, spending, and proprietary powers of government, as a means for controlling and directing future land use.

Notes

1 Cf. Jens P. Jensen, *Property Taxation in the United States* (Chicago: University of Chicago Press, 1931), pp. 26–47.

2 Statistical data are not available concerning income-tax payments by farmers. A general picture of the comparative importance of the property and income taxes paid by farmers can be inferred, however, from the national farm income data for 1963. In that year the 3,573,000 farm operators of the 48 states paid $1,789,000,000 in property taxes, an average of $501 per farm. The average operator's net cash income per farm was $2,572, and the average annual income per farm worker was $2,375. An average operator with a wife and one child would have paid not over $140 in federal income taxes on his farm income.

3 Very little research has been reported on early property-tax levies. An unpublished study by Allan G. Bogue shows that, between 1850 and 1896, millage levies for a typical township in eastern Iowa ranged from 5 to 29.5 mills (between 12 and 18 mills in most years). Total tax levies averaged between 4¢ and 10¢ an acre in the first years and later rose to a high of 32¢ an acre.

4 Cf. Benjamin H. Hibbard, *A History of the Public Land Policies* (New York: Macmillan, 1924), pp. 84–85.

5 Cf. Robert P. Swierenga, "Pioneers and Profits: Land Speculation on the Iowa Frontier" (Ph.D. dissertation, State University of Iowa, 1965). Swierenga makes several references to the non-payment of taxes by land speculators and to their practice of shifting tax delinquency liabilities on to settlers and other land buyers.

6 Cf. R. N. Cunningham and Bernard Frank, "Tax Delinquency and the Cutover Land Problem in Northern Minnesota," in Roy G. Blakey, *et al.*, *Taxation in Minnesota* (Minneapolis: University of Minnesota Press, 1932); Harold Titus, *The Land Nobody Wanted* (Agricultural Experiment Station Special Bulletin 332; East Lansing: Michigan State University, 1945); and Raleigh Barlowe, *Administration of Tax-Reverted Lands in the Lake States* (Agricultural Experiment Station Technical Bulletin 225; East Lansing: Michigan State University, 1951). U.S. Department of Agriculture studies show that 5.1 farms per thousand in the

nation were sold for nonpayment of taxes in 1926. This total rose to 15.3 farms per thousand in 1932 and then dropped to a low of 0.3 farms per thousand in 1950.

7 The term "net cash income" is a more limited concept than "net income." It involves only the cash income received by farmers from marketing of products and from government payments and does not include any allowance for value of housing or farm products consumed.

8 Frederick D. Stocker, "How High Are Farm Property Taxes?" *The Farm Cost Situation* (U.S. Department of Agriculture publication ARS 43–75 [FCS–24]; Washington, D.C.: U.S. Government Printing Office, May, 1958), p. 36.

9 Cf. Claude Bitner, "The Regressive Impact of Farm Property Taxation on Michigan Farm Families," *Quarterly Bulletin* of the Michigan Agricultural Experiment Station, 42 (May, 1960), 808–10.

10 The farm account cooperators included in Bitner's study (*ibid.*) may generally be characterized as better-than-average commercial farmers. Of the 922 operators, 32 had negative cash incomes in 1957 but paid $11,986 in property taxes. Most of the farmers in the lower income brackets were adversely affected by crop failures or by unexpected cost-price squeezes. Over time, these operators would enjoy higher incomes or would drop out of farming.

11 See, e.g., Lawrence A. Leonard, *Assessment of Farm Real Estate in the United States* (U.S. Department of Agriculture publication ARS 43–117; Washington, D.C.: U.S. Government Printing Office, 1960).

12 U.S. Department of Agriculture, *Land and Water Resources: A Policy Guide* (Washington, D.C.: U.S. Government Printing Office, 1962), pp. 4, 38.

13 Wide differences of opinion exist as to whether or not the present trend in agricultural-land use will continue. Some authorities expect the trend towards lower farm-land requirements to continue for several decades; others are much more pessimistic about the future. Hans H. Landsburg, Leonard L. Fischman, and Joseph L. Fisher, in *Resources in America's Future* ([Baltimore, Md.: The Johns Hopkins Press, 1963], p. 24), project a continued decline in cropland acreage until after 1980, followed by an upward trend. Actual future developments will depend upon a number of variables including future agriculture-production trends, developments in synthetic production of food and of other farm products, and the effective demand for farm products both in the United States and abroad.

14 See, e.g., U.S. Department of Agriculture, *A Graphic Summary of Land Utilization*, Vol. 5 in *U.S. Census of Agriculture* (Washington, D.C.: U.S. Government Printing Office, 1959), p. 7.

15 Cf. William H. Heneberry and Raleigh Barlowe, *Assessment of Farm Real Estate for Property Taxes* (North Central Regional Publication

130, Agricultural Experiment Station Special Bulletin 439; East Lansing: Michigan State University, 1962).

16 Cf. Peter House, *Preferential Assessment of Farmland in the Rural-Urban Fringe of Maryland* (U.S. Department of Agriculture publication ERS–8; Washington, D.C.: U.S. Government Printing Office, 1961).

6. Earl E. Burkhard

The Taxation of Business Personal Property

A discussion of personal-property taxation in the United States today is a complex undertaking. The tax differs greatly from state to state, and a detailed examination of the enormous variation is simply beyond the scope of this paper. Any study of this tax is further complicated by the fact that the legal definition of personal property is very broad. If real property is defined by law and custom as "land and everything attached thereto by man and nature," then, conversely, all other property which is created or constructed by man and nature must be classified as personal if it is movable or is not attached to land. This category includes not only all intangibles but agricultural products and nursery stock; bees; boats and vessels; domestic and fur-bearing animals; fisheries; licensed motor vehicles; livestock; mines; oil and gas wells; poultry; public utilities, including merchandising outlets; and standing timber. Items more closely associated with commercial and industrial activity—such as furniture and fixtures, machinery and equipment (including items such as jigs, dies, and patterns), and stock-in-trade or inventory (including supplies and tools, which are part and parcel of the property at and on the premises of manufacturing plants, stores. service establishments and professional offices, and institutions operated for profit, such as hospitals) —are also included in the personal-property category.

This discussion of personal-property taxation is based primarily on attitudes expressed by persons who are directly concerned with personal-property taxation in the United States. This approach seemed to be the only practical way to present a general picture of this tax today. The opinions expressed can be better understood, however, after a brief discussion of tax history and of the background of present-day tax coverage.

Background

Personal-property taxes have been levied since the days of the Pharaoh in ancient Egypt. Such taxes can be traced, in one form or another, through the civilizations of Greece and Rome and of medieval times up to the present day. In the United States, personal property has been taxed since Colonial days. It has only been since the rise of modern commerce and industry during the nineteenth century, however, that machinery and equipment, furniture and fixtures, and inventories have served as the base for a tax on business personal property and have provided most of the revenue derived from such a levy. Before that time, the value of personal property consisted largely of livestock. Assessment of personal property was initially a function of state governments, and the revenue collected was state income. Gradually, however, the assessment function and tax income were allotted first to the counties and eventually to the local municipalities and taxing districts.

Virginia started taxing cattle and slaves (the latter as business personal property) in 1631. New Hampshire's tax schedule of 1680 included some personal property. Maryland enacted the general property tax in 1777. The 1914 revision exempted manufacturing equipment. Oregon enacted in 1843 a personal-property-tax law which allowed contributions to be solicited, but the 1845 legislature passed an enforcement clause, the original act having produced only $81.50 in revenue. Indiana enacted its first codification of tax laws, including a tax on business inventories, in 1852. Most of the other states incorporated the business-personal-property tax into their constitutions upon their entrance into the Union or shortly thereafter. Massachusetts in 1935 took away the right to tax machinery and equipment from the local assessors, in whose province it had been since 1680. New York abandoned the business-personal-property tax in 1933, and Hawaii abandoned the tax in 1948.

Since the beginning of the nineteenth century, the taxation of business personal property has gone through three vaguely discernible cycles: expansion during the early years of that century; stability during the middle and later years; and contraction thereafter. The tax on business personal property has never been popular, however. Ever since Governor Oliver Wolcott, in his May, 1819, message to the Connecticut legislature, characterized that tax and the general property tax as "ill adapted to our needs and detrimental to our growth," the business-personal-property tax has been scorned, ridiculed, and censured as partial, unequal, and unjust; as a sham, humbug, and farce; as lacking uniformity and universality; and as demoralizing and debauching. The opinion that such a tax is detrimental to the growth and prosperity of a state was voiced a century and a half ago, and this argument has been revived in recent years because of the increasing competition for industries among states, principally those in the South. During the past seventy-five years, scarcely a year has passed during which some individual expert or group of experts on economic theory and practice has not gone on record as being opposed to the personal-property tax and recommending the abolishment of all laws which permit its use. During the past several years, the laws dealing with the taxation of business personal property have been subjected to more alterations, amendments, and emasculations than during any period since their inception.

Today there is substantial tax coverage of business personal property in sixteen states—Alabama, Arkansas, Georgia, Illinois, Indiana, Kansas, Missouri, Montana, Nebraska, Nevada, North Carolina, Rhode Island, Tennessee, Texas, Virginia, and West Virginia—although this general coverage is by no means uniform from state to state. There is partial tax coverage in twenty-nine states and the District of Columbia, and personal property is completely exempt from taxation in five states—Delaware, Hawaii, New York, North Dakota, and Pennsylvania. Tangible personal property is taxable in forty-five states, and intangibles are also taxable in twenty-eight of these states. Every state, however, specifically exempts from taxation the property of charitable, public, and non-profit educational and religious organizations; federal, state, and local governments; certain fraternal, labor, and veterans' organizations; and many chartered state institutions as well as most federal institutions.

Unless a state law specifically declares otherwise, personal property is taxed on an *ad valorem* basis, i.e., according to the value of the thing taxed. The term "100-percent valuation" is frequently included in tax legislation. The meaning of this term should not be construed as 100-percent assessment, however, since assessments in all states are a percentage of the valuation. Because assessment depends upon the valuation of the assessor, 100-percent assessment of two objects of equal worth may vary considerably if the value established by an assessor is not in agreement with the cash, fair, market, or use value.

If a law does not spell out in detail which property is taxable, the indication would seem to be that all tangible business personal property is taxed except that which may be specifically exempted by the state constitution or statutes. One exception to this rule is the case of mechanics' tools, which in almost every state are exempted from taxation, in whole or in part, even if their exclusion from the tax base is not mentioned specifically in tax legislation.

There is no uniformity in assessment dates from state to state. Of the thirteen dates used, the most common are January 1, April 1, and October 1. Procedures for the valuation of inventories also vary; in most states, inventories are valued on an average annual basis, but, in some states, the evaluation is computed as of a day certain.

Comments on the Business-Personal-Property Tax

To ascertain the current viewpoints of public and private officials who administer and/or are affected by the business-personal-property tax, a poll was taken which elicited the following comments.[1] (It is understood that these are all personal reflections and do not necessarily represent the policies of the organizations with which the commentator is associated, nor do they necessarily indicate any position taken or to be taken with respect to property taxes.) All comments received are included. The individuals contacted provide a cross section of opinion from persons knowledgeable on the current functioning of the personal-property tax. In order to present attitudes toward the personal-property tax from persons who look at the tax from different points of view, representative persons from three basic professional groupings were contacted. The first group is the assessors. The second group, also tax-collection oriented, is composed of members of state tax commissions. The third group consists of industry tax specialists, a professional group representing taxpayers.

Assesssors

Charles J. Sweeney, Hamden, Connecticut (April 21, 1965): "When, as assessors, we work with real estate values, we have some pretty well defined, useful and reliable benchmarks. In dealing with personal property the assessor is faced with no clear cut definitions or guidelines."

Aldro Jenks, Waterbury, Connecticut (May 4, 1965): "One of the most difficult taxes to administer is that of the assessment of business personal property."

Paul J. Cooley, Muncie, Indiana (April 1, 1965), expresses satisfaction that the State Board, by its assistance, "takes the assessor off the spot with the local taxpayer."

Leslie F. Schwanbeck, Ann Arbor, Michigan, believes that better public relations would eliminate most of the hostility taxpayers have for the personal-property tax (March 31, 1965).

K. G. Greer, St. Johns, Michigan (April 2, 1965): "Personal property taxation is one of our most inequitable, annoying, unfair and administratively impossible frauds of ad valorem taxation ever conceived; but removal or repeal of this source of revenue would create impossible financial problems for our community."

Ida Bradt, Kimball County, Nebraska (April 8, 1965): "I think Nebraska has a good assessment on business with an inventory. Our problem is to come up with something equitable on professional people and service concerns. Even though a business located outside of the city limits pays less tax than one within I have found a number of businesses prefer to locate in the city because of the extra benefits they get, such as fire and police protection, utilities and so on."

Russell T. Wilson, East Orange, New Jersey (April 20, 1965): "Chapter 51 [a recent change in personal-property tax legislation in New Jersey] had a few amendments tacked on making it rather difficult to administer. For example, chemicals and drugs in the hands of a manufacturer are raw materials, exempt until a product ensues. The same materials on the shelves of a druggist are inventory taxed at 25% of the local common level. Many New Jersey assessors have come to the conclusion that personal property would be more effectively assessed at the State level."

Clarence N. Deigado, Ridgewood, New Jersey (March 31, 1965): "The tax situation in New Jersey is still in a muddle. Fortunately I have gotten in all my returns but we did lose $3½ million in assessments on the schedule set up by the State."

A. G. Gus Rockway, Guymon, Oklahoma (April 15, 1965): "Basically the problem in connection with the taxation of business personal property has been equalization. This has been caused by inflation prices on equipment and merchants' inventories. Most of the assessors' offices are not provided with adequate equipment and limited on trained personnel for satisfactory performance. I think that personal property taxation is needed in every state to aid in the burden of taxes with which we are faced today."

Fred C. Vesperman, Austin, Texas (April 21, 1965): "The assessment of personal property is poorly handled by most assessors. A program of good public relations, a continual educational program, and an upgrading of assessment procedures in keeping with modern trends, all lead to a firming up of the personal property assessment roll so that it can bear its proportionate share of the ad valorem tax burden."

State Tax Commissions

C. Jack Cato, Director, Department of Assessment Coordination, Little Rock, Arkansas (April 21, 1965): "As far as I know there has been no movement in our State for exemption or special tax rate for business personal property. Our dealings with the various industries located in the State have been very cordial. We find them more than willing in the majority of cases to pay their share of the local tax burden. We have a constitutional provision whereby any industry producing a product containing cotton is allowed a seven year exemption from ad valorem taxation but I estimate not over 50% of these have asked to be exempted."

Hollis A. Swett, formerly with the Colorado State Tax Commission, now Director of Equalization, State Board of Equalization and Assessment, Albany, New York (March 22, 1965):

If the current trends toward further exemption of personal property continue real property taxpayers are in for a hard time. As one who has worked in property tax administration in three states I have found that the personal property tax is capable of good administration provided the desire to administer it properly exists at the proper levels of government. I think there are moral considerations justifying personal property taxation, for example police and court costs stemming directly from personal property. Real property is rarely subject to theft. In my opinion the argument that competition between states makes it necessary to exempt inventories is highly overrated. When industry relocates there are many compelling reasons for doing so and the property tax does not rank very high.

Harold D. Johnson, Executive Director, State Tax Commission, Boise, Idaho (April 29, 1965): "I feel that the comments from the general public relative to the tax on inventories have been highly over exaggerated. So long as one class of property such as business personal property is not discriminated against or unfairly treated it should stand the same burden as other property."

Eugene Berghoff, Property Tax Division, Department of Revenue, Springfield, Illinois (March 17, 1965): "The assessment of business personal property has become more of a problem since we have transformed from a rural agricultural state to a highly industrialized one. Illinois has been very fortunate in attracting a variety of new industries, brought about by many various programs, one of the mainstays having been the State Board of Economic Development which works very closely with our Department in helping new industry understand our tax program. I believe a property tax program is workable only if properly administered and the taxpayers educated as to the overall program and the results therefrom."

Lewis C. Carter, Chief Attorney, Property Valuation Department, Topeka, Kansas (April 1, 1965): "The assessment and taxation of business inventories has been covered by the State of Kansas for a good many years and we feel it is an important factor in the assessment and taxation of personal property."

Edward Birkenwald, Director, Property Tax Division, Bureau of Taxation, Augusta, Maine (March 16, 1965): "Although there are many exemptions and exceptions to the general rule business personal property has never been considered seriously for exemption. I do not believe the tax itself has a great effect upon the specific location of industry. This, together with all other taxes, might have some effect, but labor and power costs are probably more important."

William H. Riley, Chief Supervisor of Assessments, State Department of Assessments and Taxation, Baltimore, Maryland (March 29, 1965): "The trend, insofar as Maryland is concerned, is toward the abolition of taxation on tangible personal property."

Robert L. Purnell, Chairman, State Tax Commission, Lansing, Michigan (March 30, 1965): "For some time there has been a need of some known approach to the valuation of personal property so that industry might have something concrete to evaluate when anticipating location. The revenue received from personal property in Michigan amounts to 25% of total ad valorem taxes levied; however the taxes on other means of taxation such as corporate tax, business activities tax, etc., certainly would amount to some percentage of the total and would probably have a greater impact on location of an industry."

Stanley D. Jacobs, Supervisor of Equalization, Providence, Rhode Island (April 19, 1965): "Pressure is mounting in many localities for the elimination or reduction of the tax on business and/or industrial personalty, the usual campaign implying the consequent influx of new industry will provide more and better jobs which, it is predicted, will increase individual ability to pay higher real estate taxes, to offset the loss in revenue. An obvious flaw to this theory is the depressing influence on residential values caused by the location of business, particularly industry, in or near residential areas."

Lawrence W. Gauthier, Chief of Property Taxes, Montpelier, Vermont (March 29, 1965): "The taxation of business personal property is somewhat of a problem. In Vermont there has been considerable agitation for the repeal of the business personal property tax during the past three or four years. There is one thing that will hold it up, however, and that is the raising of approximately $7 million of taxes to replace what would be lost. Manufacturers are mainly interested in equality of taxation. Any good firm realizes that towns must have money to support schools, roads, sewers, water, fire and police protection, etc. and most of them are willing to pay their share."

C. H. Morrissett, State Tax Commissioner, Richmond, Virginia (March 24, 1965) : "Tangible personal property has been taxed in Virginia immemorially. There is no movement on foot to relieve business of any personal property taxation. The general opinion is that tangible personal property is income producing and an appropriate subject for taxation."

G. Thomas Battle, State Tax Commissioner, Charleston, West Virginia (May 10, 1965) : "Under the industrial bond arrangement frequently the personal property is purchased by the county and leased to industry, consequently machinery and equipment would not be taxable but inventory would. Because West Virginia is generally considered to have low tax rates I do not feel that this fact has been a major influence in industrial location."

Roland E. Wildes, State Supervisor of Assessments, Rice Lake, Wisconsin (April 9, 1965) : "The only comment I have to make in connection with the assessment of inventories and personal property is the difficulty in their administration."

Industry Tax Specialists

J. G. Van Cleve, Dawson, Desmond and Van Cleve and Associates, Springfield, New Jersey (April 19, 1965) : "Too much attention is being paid to bringing the cost of equipment up to date and too little to the depreciation phase. Probably the most vexing question is the use of the so-called channel of trade assessment against inventories which violates the long proven premise that the highest value of an item is its replacement in kind. Another trend is to exempt inventories from property taxation. To my way of thinking this is an incorrect approach in that it is inventories which make profits; and the fixed assets which do not make a profit and are a drag."

J. P. Smith, Tax Director, The American Tobacco Company, New York, New York (April 4, 1965) : "The various methods of assessment, the lack of uniformity among different classes of personal property and the many views of the states generally on the assessment of inventories all provide a lengthy treatise on this subject."

Edwin G. Fiedler, Assistant Secretary and General Manager, Armstrong Cork Company, Lancaster, Pennsylvania (March 31, 1965) :

"A tax on business personal property is one of the most difficult to administer. Unlike real estate, machinery and equipment and inventories do not lend themselves to a convenient and almost mechanical method of valuation. They exist in infinite variety and appear on the taxpayers' books on the basis of various types of accounting systems."

F. J. Kellman, Tax Department, The Borden Company, New York, New York (May 28, 1965): "Taxation of business personal property is cumbersome, burdensome and not conducive to business enterprise because of the many ramifications encountered in assessment practices."

Paul L. Dillingham, Assistant Head of Tax Department, The Coca Cola Company, Atlanta, Georgia (March 31, 1965): "The taxation of business personal property is a perennial problem. Perhaps the most frustrating problem to companies in many taxing districts is the lack of uniformity and reliable information concerning the basis of taxation."

C. J. Ramage, Assistant Secretary, The Connecticut Light and Power Company, Berlin, Connecticut (April 2, 1965): "It is the feeling of leaders in political and governmental positions that reductions in all forms of taxation are essential if new industry is to be attracted to the State. Of course the big roadblock is the necessity of finding an alternate source of income."

Thomas J. Jubenville, Supervisor Store Services, First National Stores, Inc., East Hartford, Connecticut (March 31, 1965): "Assessors are trying to work out a formula in regard to store areas, with which I do not agree. Each store is individual for its inventories and values are set up for the area the store serves."

J. M. Barker, Director of Taxes, General Mills, Inc., Minneapolis, Minnesota (April 22, 1965): "In my opinion the taxation of personal property, particularly inventory, is not a fair and just tax. The tax is extremely difficult to administer because of the problems of uniformity in valuation. I would not advocate a repeal, however, without a replacement of the lost revenues to the local communities."

H. S. Jones, Land Manager, Kimberly-Clark Corporation, Neenah, Wisconsin (May 11, 1965): "The personal property tax has proven unusually inequitable and burdensome in our State. It is difficult to administer well or equitably. There have been many studies made, the conclusion of most of them being that the tax should be eliminated; but the rub always is 'Where can we replace the $80 million revenue?'"

J. R. Whitmore, Manager, Tax Department, Suburban Propane, Whippany, New Jersey (April 23, 1965) : "The property tax in general should no longer be utilized as a major source of revenue. It is out-moded, regressive, inequitable and excessively costly to administer."

Joseph DiPalma, Manager, Tax Research, Trans World Airlines, Inc., New York, New York (April 14, 1965), makes a thorough and adroit analysis of the assessment and taxation of business personal property and concludes that "It is impossible to administer honestly and equitably."

G. Comas, Insurance Manager, Warner-Lambert Pharmaceutical Company, Morris Plains, New Jersey (April 2, 1965) : "Taxation of Business personal property imposes heavy burdens on industry, to say nothing of the problems of merchandisers at the the retail level."

E. I. Sproull, Jr., Manager, Tax Planning, Commercial Credit Company, Baltimore, Maryland (June 1, 1965) : "The taxation of business personal property is regressive and should be eliminated. It has an adverse effect on the location of industry as well as the expansion of existing industry. Such taxes tend to be incapable of either good administration or equitable results when compared to real property taxation. The tax climate of a particular locality or state is not, in itself, a sufficiently important factor to bring in or keep out industry. Depending upon the nature of the industry there will be other over-riding economic considerations such as markets, availability of skilled labor, etc."

Impact of Personal Property Tax on Industry Location

State and local taxes, particularly the personal-property tax, have been identified as determiners of industry location. It has been believed that industry avoids areas where taxes, especially taxes on personal property, are relatively high. The comments of representatives of state commerce and development commissions are presented below as an indication of what the general situation appears to be and what the attitude seems to be regarding the personal-property tax. These state officials are primarily interested in the economic growth of their respective states. They are not primarily interested in making tax revenues available to government treasuries, as are the tax assessors and the state tax commissioners. Nor are they primarily interested in developing an efficient office that minimizes tax liabilities, as are the industry tax specialists. They are, however, very alert to any factor that affects industry expansion and location. Their opinions are particularly accurate when they comment on the situation within their own state.

Windell R. Adams, Research Consultant, Industrial Development Commission, Arkansas (April 22, 1965): "Personal property taxes, although a cost factor in plant locations, do not seem to demand as much consideration as other factors, such as labor availability, etc."

Willard F. Sprague, Senior Economist, Economic Development Agency, California (May 11, 1965): "The exemption from the property tax is generally only one element in a very attractive package put together for a new investor, and the specific impact of this device is difficult to isolate."

Leonard Leone, Director, Industrial Division, Delaware State Development Department (May 1, 1965): "Many companies have shown interest in Delaware and have progressed to the point of looking for specific sites. Where the company decided to locate somewhere else, our only answer was that a general combination of factors dictated their selecting a site in another state. In no case do I recall that they were the decisive factor. On the other hand taxes have not been indicated as the big plus in Delaware." (Delaware imposes no personal property tax upon business.)

John P. Barron, Industrial Representative, Florida Development Commission (May 19, 1965): "Inventory tax does not present any deterrent with the exception of companies having slow turnover and large inventories."

James E. Bradley, Research Coordinator, Board of Economic Development, Illinois (April 20, 1965): "I have made no specific studies on the importance of tax policy; however, I doubt that any of the studies which have been conducted are too reliable. I can never recall working with any industrial prospect who was not very much interested in the State and local community tax structure."

William P. Tsaffaras, Director, Bureau of Research and Statistics, Department of Commerce and Development, Massachusetts, rates state and local taxes eighth on a scale of eleven factors deciding a new plant location (May 12, 1965).

Paul A. Herbert, Chief, Research, Department of Economic Expansion, Michigan, points out that a company exploring a location is influenced by the total tax burden and not so much by its segments (April 27, 1965).

Marcus Love, Manager, Industrial Department, Mississippi (April 20, 1965): "The tax exemptions here have been a great inducement in our program to attract new industry and it is not hurting our

State financially as our total revenues are rising each year from the steady growth we are experiencing."

Henry Maddox, Division of Commerce and Economic Development, Missouri (April 28, 1965) : "It is very difficult to make a blanket statement that tax laws cause industry to locate in Missouri vis-a-vis other states. Taxation is only one part of the overall picture."

Lloyd K. Allen, Director, Department of Commerce and Industry, Oklahoma (May 1, 1965) : "While the State of Oklahoma has a very favorable tax situation on a total cost basis, particularly as far as industry is concerned, we feel that taxation per se is just one of the many factors influencing the location of industry."

Keith French, Chief of Research, State Development Board, South Carolina (May 5, 1965) : "Generally we feel that the taxation of property does not represent as significant a plant location factor as do corporate income taxes. However, in our experience it can become so."

Ralph W. Emerson, Governor's Staff Director, Staff Division for Industrial Development, Tennessee (May 3, 1965) : "Some cities and counties enforce the business personal property tax while others do not. There appears to be no causal relationship between enforcement of the tax and the location of industry."

Philip Sundal, Research Director, Department of Resource Development, Wisconsin (April 28, 1965) : "Certainly there are cases where the personal property tax has been especially detrimental to industrial expansion, at least a strong psychological deterrent. I believe that for many of the newer space type industries it means little as compared to income taxes."

Conclusion and Recommendations

In my estimation, the business-personal-property tax is equitable, lucrative, and workable if intangibles and personal effects are exempt from taxation and if the tax is administered by qualified assessors, who have experienced and well-compensated staffs as well as modern equipment and business machines. The opinion that the administration of this tax could be improved if assessing were done by the state instead of by the county or the municipal assessor is a debatable one. The use of specialists is necessary, of course. This is often achieved best by employing consultants with nation-wide experience.

The pressure being brought upon legislatures by powerful lobbies and the avid scramble by the states for industries contribute to making it virtually impossible to predict the future of the business-personal-property tax, and the writer, neither a prophet nor the son of a prophet, lacks the courage and temerity to indulge in any forecast.[2]

Notes

1 A letter along the following lines was sent to each individual quoted. The date given in the text is the date of each letter of reply.

   During the June Meeting of the Committee on Taxation, Resources and Economic Development at the University of Wisconsin my assignment will be "The Taxation of Business Personal Property," in which I propose to explore the historical development, current trends, effect on the location of industries, and methods of policy and procedure.

   Your reflections thereon will be appreciated by myself and the Committee, and I hope you will find time to jot down a few, for which accreditation will be given in my paper and the subsequent book *Property Taxation—USA*.

2 See Advisory Commission on Intergovernmental Relations, *The Role of the States in Strengthening the Property Tax*, Vols. 1 and 2 (Washington, D.C.: U.S. Government Printing Office, 1963), staff work conducted by Frederick L. Bird and Edna T. Bird; and Advisory Commission on Intergovernmental Relations, *State Legislative Program* (Washington, D.C.: U.S. Government Printing Office, 1965).

7. Harold M. Groves

Property Taxation of Intangibles

Perhaps taxation is a dull subject; perhaps the property tax is the dullest branch of the tax system; and very likely the intangibles property tax is the dullest member of a dull family. Moreover, the property tax has been declining in relative importance; the retreat from the tangible-personal-property tax is well underway; and the intangibles tax is the least important, least secure, and least respectable of the three. The big question is: How did it or I ever get on this program? Maybe the reason is that I once remarked that, in property taxation as in religion, the things unseen are more important than the visible, and added that, while it is not important to tax everything either seen or unseen, the tax system can sin against neutrality when it taxes one member of a class and not another. No doubt these observations needed more elaboration and defense, and that is why I am here. The major points of my thesis are that much of property is intangibles; that much of this is genuine wealth with taxpaying capacity; and that this wealth cannot be ignored by the tax system without serious breaches of neutrality. The problem is mitigated if an income tax is levied in addition to, or is substituted (in part) for, the property tax.

Concepts of Wealth and Property

Thinking on the property tax must begin with some concept of what there is to tax in a community or perhaps of what we are trying to tax or should try to tax. Here we confront the hypothesis that the proper tax base is all private wealth—all wealth excluding that which is already owned by governments. But this leads us into the difficult assignment of defining wealth.

Stocks and Flows

It is customary to distinguish wealth from income on the score that the former is a stock at a given point of time, and the latter is a flow between two points of time. The distinction is useful, but it is not free from difficulties. Appreciation or depreciation in the value of assets (when exchanged) is often counted, for tax purposes, as income or loss, even though it fits awkwardly into the flow concept and is disregarded in statistical calculations of the national income. A contractual right to receive income of any sort—an annuity, for example—is individual property and wealth in the snapshot exposure and is income in a time exposure. It will often seem incongruous to count it as both, particularly if the time is short. A deceased person's estate is liable for income taxes on pay received after the taxpayer's death and is also liable for death taxes on the portion of this pay which remains to be passed on.

Value of Human Beings Excluded

By convention, those who add up the national wealth—or the property-tax roll—exclude the value of human beings. It is a controversial omission. Even William Petty, the seventeenth-century pioneer estimator of national wealth, recognized that people absorb investment and represent value.[1] Slaves were, of course, recognized everywhere as wealth and property, and, in the era of slavery, a good slave commanded a price in the area of $1,000. Surely the free grandsons of these slaves, even granting the limitations imposed on these people by their environment, are worth, on the average, a much larger figure.

T. W. Schultz, in one of several articles on the human element in economic development, observes that the study of investment in man has long been neglected and that "the mainstream of modern economics has by-passed undertaking any systematic analysis of human wealth."[2] He refers to Alfred Marshall's objection to a concept of capital extended to include human services on the score that economic terminology should minimize departures from the terminology of the market place. Among other reasons for his position, Marshall conceived of wealth as a stock of goods and concluded that human capacities did not qualify because "services . . . pass out of existence in the same instant they come into it."[3] Whether this is an adequate reason for the exclusion and whether the exclusion is an important cause of the neglect Schultz complains about are, no doubt, arguable matters. Certainly, education involves an enormous amount of social and private savings which are ignored by the statistics. And human capacities, with a minor stretch of semantics, could be regarded as an intangible stock in the form of a reasonable expectation of a flow of future income perhaps no more uncertain than many other values. Some work on the theory of a net-worth tax has suggested that this tax should include the discounted value of future income expected from services.[4] This proposal is fraught with many difficulties, to say the least, but one cannot doubt that the quasi-wealth of human faculties in our day is entirely too important to be ignored by the tax system.

It is obvious, of course, that the conventional conception of stocks includes many human services in frozen form. Most tangible wealth involves a great deal of human labor and talent. And subtler forms of intangible property often differ from human services mainly because they can now be bought and sold more or less independently of the persons who created them. This is true of "know-how" created by research and development; of the organizational and nexus values of a going concern; and even, in some cases, of the skill of management.[5] Although an owner-manager could not sell his own skill without committing his future, a corporation might do so. Perhaps this accounts for the fact that efforts have been made not infrequently to capitalize and to tax the success of corporate business while ignoring that of unincorporated business.

Double Counting

A major problem in estimating or taxing the national wealth is double counting. It is obvious that some people's intangible property is but a beneficial interest in other people's tangible or intangible wealth. We are all familiar with the simple case of the farmer and his mortgage, where only the farm constitutes net wealth, but a mortgagee now has a valuable additional piece of paper. In such a situation, another person is, at least, brought into the picture, but even this is not necessary in order to proliferate legal property. Yesterday a farmer owned real estate; today, as a result of sudden inspiration, a trip to the lawyer, and the payment of a small fee to the Secretary of State, a corporations owns the farm, the farmer owns stock, and the property and gross wealth associated with the farm have doubled. If the stock is now used as security for a loan, we get a further proliferation of property—and so on. It is apparent to the naked eye that these legal and institutional changes have not made the country any richer. The new property that has been created is designated as representative intangibles.

Social Wealth and Private Wealth

Professor Ely in his textbook, *The Outlines of Economics* (on which I was weaned), attempted to distinguish social wealth and private wealth,[6] excluding from the former category all claims that could be extinguished without any fundamental loss to the nation. Thus he suggests that we should not count government bonds as social wealth because they are but bondholders' claims upon the taxpayer. A big "bond-fire" would not make the country any poorer. Similarly, he suggests that patents and copyrights are but monopoly privileges at the expense of the consumer. Even land rent is but a claim on the behavior of tenants and, as the followers of Henry George have told us many times, we would still have the land if all land rent were to disappear. Indeed, all property rights are but legally enforceable claims on the beneficial behavior of other people, and the mere act of destroying these rights would not in itself make the country any poorer. If anyone wishes to calculate the social wealth of the nation along these guidelines, he is welcome to the task. As for me, I would be satisfied to get a figure for net wealth, tangible and intangible, which in the degree to which it eliminates double counting, parallels the estate-tax base.

Tangibles and Intangibles in the National Wealth

It has sometimes been said that there are two ways to add up wealth and they should give the same answer: one is to add up the tangibles and the other is to count the paper claims to these tangibles. But, aside from the problem of double counting discussed above, we here confront the fact that, in economics, the whole is not equal to the sum of all of the parts. The difference is the most subtle but genuine form of intangible, called by various names such as goodwill and franchise value. It may be positive or negative.

Professor John R. Commons in his discerning book *Legal Foundations of Capitalism* traces the legal evolution of the concept of intangible property.[7] He cites the notable decision of *Adams Express Co.* v. *Ohio* (164 U.S. 194 [1897]), in which the Court recognized that the company's tangible property in Ohio was only a small fraction of its whole property there. Said the Court:

"Considered as distinct objects of taxation, a horse is indeed a horse; a wagon, a wagon; a safe, a safe; a pouch, a pouch; but how is it that $23,430 worth of horses, wagons, safes and pouches produce $275,446 in a single year?" (165 U.S. 222.) "Whenever separate articles of tangible property are joined together, not simply by unity of ownership, but in a unity of use, there is not infrequently developed a property, intangible though it may be, which in value exceeds the aggregate of the value of the separate pieces of property." (166 U.S. 219.) "If a state comprehends all property in its scheme of taxation, then the goodwill of an organized and established industry must be recognized as a thing of value." (166 U.S. 221.) [8]

Professor Commons concluded that "there are, in fact, not two kinds of value, tangible and intangible; there is but one value and it is intangible." [9] Without going so far, we may reflect that in our day of big business with varying degrees of monopoly power, the type of intangible of which the court speaks must be a very substantial entity.

A Note on Valuation

Presumably, estimators of national wealth, were they to proceed with a fresh appraisal of property, would go at their job much like a local assessor. The standard of appraisal would be market value. Like the assessor, they would have three evidences of value for their items: exchange of similar property (if any) ; capitalized income; and replacement cost. Like the assessor, however, they would soon encounter uncertainties about when and how to use capitalized income. Presumably the building and machinery cannot be worth more than the cost of their replacement. By the rule of substitution, a reproducible object can never be worth more than the cost of reproducing it, but it can be worth less because of economic obsolescence, and the assessor may employ capitalized income in appraising this factor. Were he to treat extraordinary capitalized income as an asset, he would be accused of assessing the business rather than the plant or its constituent items. Thus, the property tax tends to allow for business mistakes but to overlook business successes.

It is a well-known fact that the value of slum property is often made up mostly of intangibles; it represents income-earning power, but it has no counterpart in the reproduction cost of physical structures. In such a case, the assessor is hard put to distinguish between the values of the land, the improvements, and the business. To make matters worse, the taxpayer frequently manages the privilege of writing these intangibles off as depreciation for income tax purposes.

The Property-Tax Base

The pervasive idea underlying late-nineteenth-century property taxation in the United States was that all manifestations of ownership should be taxed at a uniform rate. The rationale for this method of taxation was based on a mixture of a great many ideas and elements: ideas that property pays taxes in its own right (*in rem*) and that property is an index of personal ability to pay; elements of consumption goods and producers' goods; and elements of land, improvements, tangible personal property, and intangibles of many sorts. It made no allowances for the ease of concealing certain kinds of property, for double counting, or for the fact that the incidence of taxing various elements differed. No wonder the period was marked by an ever-increasing discontent with the property tax.

The intangibles which this "tax-anything" policy sought to reach have been classified by Simeon Leland as follows: First, there is strictly representative property, consisting of what is usually described as money and credits: cash, bonds, notes, and book credit. Second, there is the class of intangibles that are wealth in their own right: goodwill, franchises, patents, government bonds. Third, there is an intermediate class, partly representative and partly non-representative, consisting of stocks: their value rests upon tangibles and intangibles, not all of which are usually taxed independently. Finally, he added a class of intangibles, overlapping the others, where claims owned in one jurisdiction were representative of property in another.[10]

Experience of the American States with the Taxation of Intangibles

I shall not attempt an elaborate account of the history of intangibles taxation in the United States. Much of it is a sad story marked by sporadic campaigns for enforcement and repeated recommendations for repeal. Curiously enough, the only kind of intangible that has engaged the attention of most states is the representative variety. A few states, such as Texas and Illinois, still retain the anachronistic general property tax. A recent report from Illinois begins with the observation that, although intangibles constitute more than half the wealth in that state, they contribute only .5 percent to the Illinois tax base.[11] Similar reports are frequently made concerning the tax treatment of intangibles in other areas.

Some states, such as Iowa, Oklahoma, and Nebraska, retreated from the general property tax to the classification of intangibles for a low rate; others, such as Michigan and Ohio, accomplished much the same purpose through a special income tax on the yield of intangibles. Some states, such as New York and Wisconsin, accepted the general income tax as a substitute for the tax on intangibles. Simeon Leland pointed out many years ago that the classified property tax was no substitute for adequate administration but that, with classification, adequate administration is possible.[12] Some states, particularly those with vigorous state administration, have probably vindicated Leland. In others, such as Iowa, the special tax on money and credits is almost as dead a letter as the general property tax which preceded it.[13]

Of more interest to us here is the history of attempts to tax genuine intangibles. The one example of conspicuous success in this area is in the public-utility field where the Commons' idea that there is but one kind of property, and it is intangible, has been quite generally applied.

Public Utilities

States that now apply the *ad valorem* property tax to public utilities generally apply a unit rule of valuation also; that is, they start with valuation of the utility as a whole, without regard for territory and without exclusive regard for the sum of all the tangible and intangible parts. Thus they include in the base the franchise value or the corporate excess (or deficiency) of the firm. In evaluating the franchise, much weight is usually given to capitalized income and the market value of securities. Thus utilities are assessed on *all* their property, tangible and intangible, and this in spite of the fact that, in some jurisdictions—such as Wisconsin—other businesses are assessed on tangibles only, and the state constitution has a uniformity clause precluding classification. The charge of discrimination is seldom heard in our day but it was asserted quite vehemently at one time in Wisconsin, when the state shifted to the present *ad valorem* system and the latter was tested in the courts. Proponents of the system have rejoined that public utilities, like other property, were only being assessed on their market value, and some added the thought—to which moral title is dubious—that the goodwill of monopolistic public service firms must be the goodwill of politicians. The intangibles of utilities are by no means confined to goodwill, however. Especially in the case of railroads, the situation has changed, and franchise value is often negative and a very potent relief from tax burdens. In Wisconsin, moreover, railroads enjoy a special exemption from the state income tax, though other utilities do not.

Corporate-Excess Taxes

The corporate-excess taxes, which several states have tried and a few have retained, attempt to evaluate total business in much the same way that utilities are evaluated and to credit the tangibles independently taxed. This impresses me as admirable in theory. The record of performance in practice, so far as I know it, is hardly better than that of the money and credits tax, however. Thus the feeble and confused corporate-excess tax of Illinois is confined to domestic corporations; a large part of the assessment is still left to local officials;

and the intangibles are all given situs at the place where the corporation has its principal office. A competent recent study recommended
substitution of a corporate-net-income tax.[14] The Massachusetts law,
with state administration, fared better, but it was resented on the
ground that the standards of assessment were ill-defined and left too
much discretion to the Commissioners. For many years it was applied
in addition to the corporate-income tax. Practically all of the corporate-excess feature was repealed in 1962.[15]

Capital-Stock Taxes

Corporate capital-stock taxes probably developed in most cases in
an attempt to tax at the source intangibles held by individuals. They
are thus usually accompanied by the exemption of stock in the hands
of individuals. Often, however, the idea was not applied very consistently, and no exemptions were allowed for stock owned by individuals who did not reside in that state and were, therefore, beyond
its jurisdiction. Moreover, the tax is usually based on book value,
which does not reflect market value with much precision. Capital-
stock taxes involve double counting not only because stock represents,
in part, tangibles already taxed but also because intercorporate ownership proliferates stock. I have elsewhere summarized the situation
with this generalization:[16] "Most states have some sort of capital
stock tax applying a variety of rates to the assets of the company
(tangible and intangible) as indicated by company books. The rationale of these taxes other than that of collecting something extra
from corporations is rarely volunteered."

Many of these capital-stock taxes are legally classed as excises on
the franchise and are not strictly speaking, property taxes. But franchise taxes may take a variety of forms: legislatures may choose, and
have chosen, to measure the corporate privilege by means of capital
stock, authorized, issued, or according to market value; income, gross
or net; corporate excess; and several other criteria. In the case of
domestic corporations, the measure of the privilege need not be confined to the state: witness the Delaware capital-stock tax which reaches
the assets of the Delaware corporations wherever they may be employed. Professor Seligman castigated the system as follows: "Each
commonwealth measures the franchises in its own way: and frequently
the commonwealth measures the franchise of corporations in different ways." [17] He added that the whole concept of franchises is legal
rather than economic; that its meaning defies definition; and that the
frequent discrimination between foreign and domestic companies is
untenable. Seligman concluded that the states might follow European

example and confine corporation taxes largely to net income and to real estate. The ability of firms to survive blows from all sides suggests that a considerable portion of their burdens are passed along to consumers; their other principal defense is the threat to migrate, which they have not hesitated to use freely.

Some Theoretical Considerations

Double Taxation

As we have previously indicated, the record of intangibles taxation in the United States has been filled with double taxation and protests against double taxation. To be sure, the critics have had little enough support from the courts. The issue arose as early as 1865 in *Van Allen* v. *Assessors* (3 Wall 573), where a company was assessed on its intangibles and security owners were also taxed on their interests in the company. Double taxation, thought the court, is not improper: there are two different persons owning two different objects. The shareholder's interest is a distinct and separate interest.

The legal determination that double taxation is permissible does not, of course, settle the matter in terms of moral and economic consequences. In a diverse tax system there is bound to be much duplication of levies; the best test of equity, no doubt, would examine the overall distribution of the tax load. But with the great proliferation of claims that attends modern business, the full taxation of all representative property could hardly meet this test or any other. Henry Simons cautioned against over-concern with the double taxation of income, arguing that, in the case of a gift transfer, both the donor and donee should be taxed. What matter, he said, if this would produce a discrepancy between the tax base and the statistician's total income? [18] But even Simons never argued that the farmer and his mortgagee both be taxed on their gross income with no offsets.

Least serious of the many kinds of double taxation is the application of two different taxes to one person or object. Early proponents of the state income tax favored this measure, in many cases, as a substitute for the personal-property tax, which at that time was the target of much criticism. In the early Wisconsin law, concessions were made to this view, and important classes of personal property—notably money and credits, household goods, and farm machinery—were exempted from the tax. As a further concession, an offset was written into the law under which income taxes might be paid with personal-property-tax receipts. Many people assumed that eventually the personal-property tax itself would be eliminated. As it happened, however, it was the offset, and not the tax, which was repealed. One of the arguments used by proponents of this move was that, if the income from real estate must pay two taxes, the income from personal property might do so also. Perhaps more logical was the experiment made at one time in Utah of allowing an offset of up to one-third of the taxpayer's income-tax bill for all property taxes paid. Most of these experiments have been abandoned; [19] perhaps legislators realized that the present state of knowledge concerning the incidence of these taxes does not allow nice adjustments of this sort to be very meaningful.

Incidence and Equity and Neutrality

The concepts of universality and uniformity have been associated with American general property taxation in the past because they were felt to be the means by which the goals of equity and neutrality might be achieved. This raises the question of how acceptable any exemptions are in this context. It will be said at once that equity is a personal idea and that it is idle to give it much consideration in the case of an *in rem* tax. But can the same be said of neutrality, which has to do with fair competition and with allocation of resources according to the indigenous preferences of consumers? In examining either matter, it would be futile to proceed without an examination of incidence,[20] particularly the incidence of a property tax on business reproducibles—excluding land and including both tangible and intangible capital.

It is generally agreed that the incidence of a tax which strikes one line of business and ignores others tends to be diffused so that, if other factors are equal, the profitability of doing business in the taxed and untaxed lines will, in time, gravitate to the same level. Thus, although the jewelry merchant suffers more from the general property tax than the meat merchant, it does not follow that one of these lines can long remain more profitable than the other. Factors (labor and capital) are constantly entering the two lines, and they will avoid the heavily taxed one until the reduced competition there evens up the returns in the two trades. Thus it appears that, if the short-term effects of changes in the tax system are excluded from consideration, the businessmen in one line of business ought not to complain about a relatively heavy tax. On the other hand, it is also generally agreed that, if most jewelry merchants are assessed at 50 percent of market value but one is assessed at 100 percent, the latter has a genuine grievance, and the differential tax comes out of *his* profits. In such a case, the administration violates the principle of neutrality and, in this instance, that of equity as well.

But it would appear that such situations tend to get mixed and confused. Compare, for instance, the case of the chain store with that of the corner grocer. The chain store tends to be favored by the property tax because, for one reason, much of the chain's property— organizational value, superior management, monopolistic bargaining power, etc.—is intangible. To some extent, the two ways of doing business are distinct fields of competition, and migration of factors may leave relative profits independent of differential tax burdens (as in the case of meat and jewelry merchants). But the independent merchant would certainly be happier if all means of merchandizing were neutrally treated by the property-tax system, and one would be bold indeed to conclude that there is no justification for his preference.

It is a disconcerting fact that intangibles such as research and development and monopoly bargaining power are associated mainly with the larger concerns in business. The point is a major justification for graduation in corporate-income taxation, a system which other-wise rests upon a weak rationale.

I recall a discussion in Wisconsin of whether livestock should be taxed once farm machinery had been exempted from the property tax. The contention was that the tax is unfair to the dairy farmer in comparison with the crop farmer. If livestock is exempted, it will be argued that the tax is unfair to the small farmer whose capital is largely in land and improvements because he cannot afford expensive livestock and machinery.

When economic forces even the returns to the jewelry merchant and the meat merchant, do they do so at the expense of the consumer of jewelry? Opinion differs as to the ultimate incidence of a tax on business capital. Jens Jensen in his monumental work on the prop-erty tax took the view that the incidence lies with the capitalists and that both general and partial taxes tend to reduce the return on capital evenly.[21] In this comfortable view, exemptions and differential burdens have no serious economic consequences as long as they are spread evenly among direct competitors. Jensen's analysis is persua-sive, but it is not sufficient to preclude the possibility of an alternate explanation, namely, that business taxes are shifted forward to con-sumers. According to this alternative view, a differential tax may behave like a selective sales tax, and, while there is ample precedent for the latter, it is open to objection in terms of unneutrality among consumers, being distributed according to their varying tastes. Such taxes are also criticized as interfering with the allocation of resources according to consumers' preferences.

Summary and Policy Conclusions

a) Our first two main sections emphasized the point that wealth and property embrace large and growing elements of intangibles, some illusory (multiple counting), some as genuine as a factory building. Human labor and ingenuity figure largely in all wealth; sometimes they become embodied in a tangible object; sometimes they remain intangible but can be bought and sold without the owner; sometimes they require the owner's direct cooperation and disappear when his activity ceases. Moreover, competition is, in our day, a weak policeman, and monopoly power is a ubiquitous but unevenly distributed factor, providing much highly intangible property often not recognized as such. Our tax system is generally biased to favor tangibles; curiously enough, this bias extends to sales taxes as well as property taxes.

b) Most of American experience with the taxation of intangibles has been an attempt to reach representative intangible property with an impersonal tax—a questionable objective on both theoretical and administrative grounds. The less-ambitious attempts to tax genuine intangibles have been successful in the public-utility field. The attempt to extend the technique of public-utility evaluation to all corporate business—the corporate-excess tax—has been sound in theory but generally unsuccessful in practice. The ubiquitous capital-stock taxes suffer from the absence of a defensible rationale.

c) Business taxes generally are a troublesome area of the tax system. Their incidence is frequently extra-territorial, and the differentials between local levies create unneutral competition and state and municipal tax warfare. From the overall view, levies in the ideal system would, no doubt, be confined to a personal-income tax (including undistributed profits) ; an inheritance tax; and a property tax *in rem* on economic rent. Constrictions of local revenue need, of administrative competence, and of jurisdictional conflict dictate necessary compromises with this ideal system.

d) Once we depart from the ideal system we encounter the issue of universality versus partiality. The main argument of this paper has been that departures from universality do come at a considerable price in terms of the neutrality of the tax system.

e) If it is not practical to tax intangibles under the property tax (as the record seems to indicate) , at least two concessions to universality may be given consideration: one is to forego further erosion of the property-tax base (I see little merit, for example, in taxing a person on his residence and not on his automobile) and the other is to move further in the direction of taxation of income.

f) In my view, the only classification of property for special taxation that has solid merit is that which would place a special burden on urban-land rent.

Certainly, the universality and uniformity goals of the nineteenth-century general property tax were naive. Certainly, they required qualification and supplementation. But it seems that our review has found some merit in them after all. Trends in the opposite direction could go, and perhaps have gone, too far.

Notes

1 See E. A. Johnson, *Predecessors of Adam Smith* (New York: Prentice-Hall, 1937), p. 109.

2 T. W. Schultz, "Investment in Man: An Economist's View," *Social Science Review,* 33 (June, 1959), 110. Schultz also calculated that investment in high school and college education increased from 4 percent of the investment in physical capital in 1900 to 20 percent by 1956 (p. 115). The fact that compensation for services regularly amounts to some 70 percent of the national income supports the hypothesis that wealth in people is a major fraction of wealth in the broadest sense.

3 Alfred Marshall, *Principles of Economics* (7th ed.; London: Macmillan, 1916), p. 56.

4 See Earl R. Rolph and George T. Break, *Public Finance* (New York: Ronald Press, 1961), Chap. 9.

5 See *Measuring the Nation's Wealth* (New York: National Bureau of Economic Research, 1964), pp. 69–70 and Appendix I, Part II, by Vernon L. Smith on "The Measurement of Capital."

6 Richard T. Ely, *The Outlines of Economics* (4th ed.; New York: Macmillan, 1924), pp. 100–101.

7 John R. Commons, *Legal Foundations of Capitalism* (Madison: University of Wisconsin Press, 1959; first published by Macmillan, 1924), Chap. 5.

8 Quoted in *ibid.,* p. 173.

9 *Ibid.,* p. 176.

10 Simeon E. Leland, *The Classified Property Tax in the United States* (Boston: Houghton Mifflin, 1928), pp. 119–21.

11 *Report of the Commission on Personal Property Taxes* (Springfield: State of Illinois, 1959), p. 7.

12 Leland, *The Classified Property Tax*, p. 403.

13 Several sorts of impediments, in addition to inertia and vested interests, have blocked the reform of the general property tax. One is inflexible state constitutions, and another is the federal statute concerning the taxation of national banks, another sad story the pursuit of which would carry us too far afield.

14 Ruth A. Birdzell, "General Corporation Taxes," Chap. 18 in *The Report of the Commission on Revenue of the State of Illinois* (Springfield: State of Illinois, 1963).

15 John Dane, "Remarks," in National Tax Association, *1964 Proceedings of the Fifty-Seventh Annual Conference on Taxation,* ed. W. J. Kress (Harrisburg, 1965).

16 Harold M. Groves, "Institutional Economics and Public Finance," *Land Economics,* 40, No. 3 (August, 1964), 245.

17 Edwin R. A. Seligman, *Essays in Taxation* (10th ed.; New York: Macmillan, 1925), p. 228.

18 Henry Simons, *Personal Income Taxation* (Chicago: University of Chicago Press, 1938), p. 58.

19 The exception is Massachusetts, where the attempt to integrate property and income taxation continues unabated. The Massachusetts income tax is a proportional, classified tax from which real estate income is exempted on the ground that real estate bears the brunt of the property tax. Originally, job income took the rate of 1.5 percent, which approximated the average state rate on property at that time. This model has continued with few fundamental changes, but much informed public opinion dislikes the product. Nevertheless, an attempt in 1959 to amend the constitution to implement a fundamental change was heavily defeated. See Patty Grapel Claunch, "History, Philosophy, and Recent Developments in Massachusetts Personal Income" (M.S. thesis, University of Wisconsin, 1964); Philip Nichols, *Taxation in Massachusetts* (3rd ed.; Boston: Financial Publishing Company, 1938).

20 For our purposes here, the term "incidence" may be defined as "the final burden of a tax."

21 Jens P. Jensen, *Property Taxation in the United States* (Chicago: University of Chicago Press, 1931), pp. 53–61.

8. Lynn A. Stiles

Some Aspects of the *Ad Valorem* Taxation of Railroads

In the past several years, the rail-carrier industry has pressed its complaint of discriminatory treatment at the hands of the states with vigor and a good measure of success. Thanks in part to the real-property assessment ratios made available by the Census Bureau, the railroads have compiled a case for lowering their assessments to the levels officially shown to prevail for the principal classes of non-carrier real estate. The celebrated Doyle Report, published in 1961, presents with tacit endorsement a tabulation compiled by the Association of American Railroads (A.A.R.) that purports to show that if railroad property in some thirty-one states had been assessed in 1957 at the same levels as other property the carriers' *ad valorem* tax bill for that year in those thirty-one states would have totaled $120,000,000 instead of the actual amount of $261,000,000. In presenting the A.A.R. findings, the Report stated that:

The resources available to this committee were not such as to be able to conduct an independent survey to affirm or disprove the specific data presented to us. However, research has been sufficiently extensive to establish that relative discrimination, of considerable magnitude, does in fact exist against the railroads in the assessment procedures of State and local governments for ad valorem taxation purposes. Therefore, the [A.A.R.] data is accepted as confirming the judgment of this study group that State and local assessment procedures do discriminate against the railroads.[1]

The A.A.R. compilation assumes that the legal standard or other formal percentage of value at which railroad property is assessed expresses the *de facto* assessment ratio for carrier property and that this ratio is directly comparable to the sales-based ratios for other property that underlie the Census Bureau's findings in the *U.S. Census of Governments: 1957*.[2] Thus, according to the sales-ratio evidence, railroad property was presumably assessed fully (at 100 percent of value) by Illinois in 1957, while other property was assessed at 45.70 percent of full value. The upshot was that in Illinois the carriers' *ad valorem* tax bill of $35,000,000 exceeded by almost $19,000,000 the $16,000,000 tax bill that would have been imposed if railroad property had been assessed at 45 percent of full value. Illinois stands out in the A.A.R. tabulation simply because, of the thirty-one states covered, it reported the largest of all *ad valorem* tax billings on railroad property and the largest of all absolute tax "excesses"—that is, differences between taxes actually imposed and the tax bills the carriers would have borne if their property had been assessed at generally prevailing levels. The more than two-to-one relationship shown for Illinois between the ratios for railroad assessments and other assessments is matched or considerably exceeded, however, in a number of other states—for example, Arizona (where the ratio was more than five-to-one), California, Idaho (almost nine-to-one), Iowa, Kansas, Michigan, Montana, New Jersey, New Mexico, North Dakota, Oklahoma, Tennessee, Utah, and Wyoming.

The text of the Report at the point where the A.A.R. evidence is presented explains that the reason for confining the enumeration to only thirty-one states is that the other seventeen states (ignoring Hawaii, which has no common-carrier railroad property, and Alaska, which, for all practical purposes, has only a United States Government–owned line) have local assessment rather than central or state assessment, special taxation, or a system of *ad valorem* taxation of a distinctive nature. It is of interest that of the thirty-one states carried in the tabulation, many—but not all—use the "unit rule" in railroad assessment. Under this approach, the individual state assigns a value to the entirety of a carrier's property, then allocates or apportions a fraction of the total to its own jurisdiction if the carrier operates interstate. The unit rule, as is well known, has a long history, having won the approval of the courts in a number of key decisions in the latter half of the nineteenth century.

It seems quite evident that impetus was given to adoption of the unit rule in the assessment of railroad properties and of other utility properties by strong indications that the common practice of piecemeal, "brick and mortar" valuation failed to reach enterprise value by neglecting to include the "corporate excess" of a going concern. Corporate excess is, of course, every bit as liable for assessment and taxation under the *ad valorem* tax as any other species of property.

It was, doubtless, typical of an era of aggressive railroad construction and expansion that the total worth of the carriers—or at least the most successful of them—was greater than the simple sum of the full values that could be imputed separately to their tangible components. By using the unit rule and relying on such evidences of enterprise value as capitalized earnings and the market value of outstanding stock and debt—which reflect the results of the totality of a carrier's operations and relate to all of its property—the assessment authorities could reach the intangible corporate excess that would otherwise elude their jurisdiction.

Over the years, corporate excesses in the railroad industry have been supplanted almost without exception by corporate deficiencies. To illustrate, during the past ten years the Class I carriers have generated net railway operating income (which is after-tax return on capital) that has averaged $810,000,000 annually. Capitalizing this at the time-honored and widely used (if questionable) rate of 6 percent yields an aggregate "earnings" value for the Class I sector of something like $13,500,000,000. While it has not been possible to compile stock-and-debt aggregates for the Class I roads, chances are that, despite the buoyancy of the stock market in recent years, such a compilation would add up to something *less* than the level of capitalized net railway operating income. The $13,500,000,000 value "evidence" suggested by net earnings is a great deal lower than the findings of value by the Interstate Commerce Commission (I.C.C.), and the difference strongly suggests the presence in the industry of a huge *negative* corporate excess.[3] At the end of 1962, the I.C.C. estimated the elements of value after depreciation and amortization for the Class I line-haul roads as $26,200,000,000. This figure, however, is based upon original cost at 1910–14 prices for road and equipment, less a substantial allowance for depreciation and amortization, plus the present value of land and rights. Substituting reproduction cost for original cost would raise the total to more than $48,000,000,000— more than three and one-half times the valuation inferred from net earnings alone.

In the relatively fluid and competitive markets within which ordinary sales transactions occur, market values tend to remain close to reproduction costs, after allowance for capital consumed. In short, the full market values that underlie the assessment ratios found by the Census Bureau are probably related closely to reproduction costs minus depreciation. Any substantial divergence would tend to set in motion its own corrective, because it would either stimulate or slow new construction activity. It seems to follow that, if the property of the Class I rail carriers were dealt with in the assessment process in the same manner as other property, the aggregate of railroad assessments might come close to equaling the $48,000,000,000 level that measures depreciated reproduction cost of rail plant and equipment, including the present value of land and rights. The fact that the sum total of capitalized earnings for the industry as a whole works out to be less than a third as much as this—combined with the likelihood that the stock and debt valuation is smaller still—serves to suggest that the valuation of railroad property upon which the industry's *ad valorem* tax liabilities rest must be substantially lower in relation to reproduction cost than the level of value measured by selling prices in the case of non-carrier property.

This is not to suggest, of course, that the full valuations set by the assessment authorities for rail-carrier property are indefensibly low, because the uncomfortable fact of large corporate deficiencies remains. The point is, however, that *because* the unit rule is used in railroad assessment, in conjunction with capitalized earnings and stock-and-debt along with reproduction cost as evidences of value, the rail carriers ordinarily bear assessments that reflect the presence of corporate deficiencies. Other enterprises are not similarly treated by the assessment authorities and may, therefore, fare much differently. A declining manufacturing firm, for example, will normally be confronted with a "brick and mortar," piecemeal valuation of its tangible property that will become the full valuation subject only to debasement in accordance with the statute, or simply with customary practice. Its poor and declining earnings performance will register no effect beyond supporting a finding of "no assessment" for its corporate excess, if, indeed, this class of property is expressly assessed in the first place.

The $13,500,000,000 earnings capitalization for the Class I carriers as a whole is misleading in one critical respect. In any one year, the aggregate net railway operating income *for the industry* will, of course, be the algebraic sum of positive figures shown for certain of the carriers and negative figures (net railway operating losses) reported for others. For example, in 1964, estimated net railway operating income for all Class I carriers combined was $819,000,000—very close, incidentally, to the $810,000,000 average for the 10 years ending in 1964. During 1964, 82 of the 101 Class I line-haul roads reported positive net railway operating incomes, which totaled something over $868,000,000. Another 19 carriers, however—including such well-known roads as the New Haven, Grand Trunk Western, Long Island, Jersey Central, Erie-Lackawanna, and Missouri-Kansas-Texas—reported net railway operating losses aggregating more than $49,000,000. In capitalizing the industry's net railway operating income, the losses sustained by a minority of the carriers, of course, exert their influence. Operating losses that enter into the earnings evidence of value, generally used in unit appraisal, constitute the source of negative corporate excesses that would call for "no assessment" if they were reported for non-carrier firms not subject to assessment in the same manner as the railroads. That is, within the framework of a statute explicitly specifying corporate excess or capital-stock assessment, the assessment levied against any taxpayer will be either some positive sum or else zero; it will never be a negative amount, however, as it may be, in effect, when the corporate excess is commingled with the valuations assigned to tangible properties.

Nor is this the end of the story. It may be noted that, while some of the best-known carriers reported substantial net railway operating incomes in relation to total operating revenues, others reporting substantial gross earnings were able to carry through only modest amounts to net. For example, the Norfolk and Western (inclusive of the Nickel Plate and Wabash) produced net railway operating income in 1964 totaling almost $104,000,000 out of operating revenues of $558,000,000. The New York Central, however, reported net railway operating income of only $34,000,000—one-third of the Norfolk's—out of operating revenues of $642,000,000, 15 percent more than the Norfolk and Western's operating revenues. Other examples could be readily found to illustrate the wide divergence in earning power among the roads. All this is strongly suggestive of the presence of some measure of deficiency as well as excess within the accounts of virtually all the carriers, including, no doubt, even the profitable Norfolk and Western.

Relatively few Class I carriers consistently operate in the red, and it is plausible to suppose that a state employing a capitalization-of-earnings value estimate within the framework of the unit rule would ignore a negative earnings capitalization, or—at the least—assign it an arbitrary value of zero for the sake of a *pro forma* valuation determination. Let a carrier consistently in deficit status merge with another road that regularly reports positive net railway operating income, however, and the negative earnings record of the one road will be a partial or, conceivably, full offset to the positive earnings capability of the other. This, perhaps, is simply another way of saying that the larger the area of aggregation, the greater the influence upon the earnings capitalization figure of segments of lines and classes of service that constitute drains upon carrier net revenue. The most significant meaning of all this is that the railroads, in effect, receive allowances in the normal course of assessment in the form of *de facto* credits or deductions that are not customarily available to non-carrier properties.

These considerations would seem to merit recognition in any evaluation of the discrimination that imperfections in the assessment equalization process are held to inflict upon the rail-carrier industry. Undoubtedly, the rail assessment authorities in the states are correct when they maintain that the determination made in the rail-assessment process is a *bona fide* estimate of full, fair cash value, or something closely resembling the market value sought by the assessor of non-carrier property. Marked differences between estimates for tax purposes of carrier full values and the sums ultimately realized in the liquidation of roads that are abandoned may be explained by the fact that the enterprise value of an operating carrier regularly sustaining losses will be lower, because of those losses—which continue until cessation of operation is finally authorized—than the sum of the values of its piecemeal tangibles. The presumption is that any buyer of such a property would assume the obligation to continue operations even in the face of persistent operating losses, so that the price he offers for the property would amount to less than the sum that might be realized if the individual physical assets of the carrier were separately liquidated.

One further implication deserves mention. The incentive to hold speculatively segments of property that are of marginal usefulness from the standpoint of rail operations and revenue may be much stronger if a rail carrier is subject to assessment under the unit rule— with substantial weight being placed upon earnings and the stock-and-debt value—than would be the case if the severity of the *ad valorem* tax were not mitigated by explicit recognition of earnings performance and the market value of stock and debt. In particular, rail carriers with substantial amounts of unutilized or appreciably underutilized passenger terminals and trackage may have little pressing incentive to dispose of such holdings or to reduce them, inasmuch as the tax liability marginally ascribable to them may be slight. The possibility that this factor is serving to retard the reclamation and renewal of rail-owned land located in the downtown sections of some of our larger cities may well be worth study.

The thrust of these comments would seem to be in the direction of questioning the carriers' contention that they have suffered discrimination under the property tax vis-à-vis other property, or at least of suggesting that the extent of the discrimination inflicted upon them remains to be precisely measured. It seems appropriate, therefore, to conclude with an expression of strong skepticism concerning the appropriateness of *ad valorem* taxation of railroads in the first place. By and large, the *ad valorem* taxes borne by the rail carriers are levied for the support of local governments. These units are largely engaged in mobilizing economic resources for the purpose of providing public services of a narrowly definable nature and of a sort that, in concept at least, should be appropriate for user charge or proxy-user charge financing as an alternative to present arrangements. Education, of course, is a striking exception to this generalization, but we appear to be witnessing the emergence of supra-local communities in respect to this important governmental function.

It is difficult to develop a persuasive rationalization for the manner in which business property generally is called upon to support local public services. It frequently is contended that railroads and other business firms must provide support for the schools, for example, because they are direct beneficiaries of school services. The better the quality of local schools, the better trained, more proficient, and more productive will be the manpower upon which business firms depend. This is unquestionably true, but it must be clear that the individual employer registers his preferences with respect to the comparative skills of the manpower available to him through the pattern of wage payments that emerges in the labor market. If a local school system provides above-average services and thereby equips its students with special skills, these people will be able to command wage premiums. There seems, in principle, no reason why these additions to earning power do not provide a suitable base upon which to levy school costs. Businesses have a stake in the quality of the medical care available to their employees, in the variety, cost, and quality of foodstuffs offered them, in the adequacy of their housing, clothing, and so on, but seldom is it urged that direct financial support of the purveyors of these services and goods is an appropriate charge upon business property or, for that matter, upon property in general.

Although there is a great deal more to be said about the property tax and its proper place, if any, in the scheme of things and about the impact of property taxation on resource use, it perhaps suffices in the present context to assert that it is no foregone conclusion that present methods of *ad valorem* taxation of businesses—and particularly of railroads—are economically defensible. Nor, as once it was argued, would the achievement of "uniformity" (assuming that goal were possible) set everything straight.[4]

Notes

1 U.S. Senate Committee on Commerce, Special Study Group on Transportation Policies in the United States (John P. Doyle, Staff Director), *National Transportation Policy* (Washington, D.C.: U.S. Government Printing Office, 1961), p. 487.

2 U.S. Bureau of the Census, *Taxable Property Values in the United States,* Vol. 5 in *U.S. Census of Governments: 1957* (Washington, D.C.: U.S. Government Printing Office, 1959), esp. Table 12, p. 81.

3 Interstate Commerce Commission, *Elements of Value of Class I Railroads, December 31, 1962* (mimeo.; Washington, D.C.: U.S. Government Printing Office, 1963).

4 The author is Senior Economist at the Federal Reserve Bank of Chicago, and was formerly (1943–49) railroad assessor for the State of Illinois. Opinions expressed are personal, bearing no endorsement by the Bank. Thanks are due to Eugene L. Maynard, of the Illinois Department of Revenue, for many constructive comments over the years on the subject matter of the forepart of this statement. He bears no responsibility, however, for the material here presented.

9. Paul E. Alyea

Property-Tax Inducements
to Attract Industry

The use of tax incentives to encourage investment decisions violates a cardinal principle of economic allocation of resources. Nevertheless, Jens P. Jensen, the great property-taxation economist, refrained from taking a doctrinaire position. In discussing this aspect of property taxation, he wrote: "Tax exemption for industrial encouragement, like a protective tariff, is a device of local, mercantilist commercial policy. It must be justified or opposed on the same grounds as a tariff. On economic grounds the presumption is against both. The principal claim for exemption must be the infant industry argument. In the industrially developing southern states, there are probably valid bases for exemption on that ground, despite the hazard that such a policy, adopted in one state, must tend to lead others in self-defense to adopt it also." [1]

Jensen, careful student that he was, did not adopt an uncompromising, doctrinaire position in support of laissez faire. In an earlier publication he stated: "There is no general principle of taxation that inexorably demands identical forms, equal rates, and complete inclusiveness of property for taxation. *A tax system must be justified by its results.*" [2]

The ultimate issue in this paper is the soundness of public policy concerning property-tax inducements to industry, and my particular concern is local (or state) policy rather than national or global practice. It would be unrealistic to assume that state or local attitudes regarding the subsidizing of industry will not be governed by what is thought to be good for the local economy whether it is also good for the national economy or not. This must be the case, for how else can we understand the persistence of the high incidence of local inducements to industry throughout our history, when such practices have been almost universally condemned by economists and other specialists in the field of taxation?

History of Property-Tax Exemptions

The granting of industrial subsidies through tax exemption is a practice that is, in the words of Mabel Walker, "hoary with antiquity." [3] The first specific exemption of property for commercial reasons was granted by the General Court of Connecticut in 1649. By 1783 the practice became more general, e.g., a ten-year exemption was given in Connecticut for manufacturing oil from flax seed. The stated purpose was "to furnish employment for poor persons, to achieve a happy influence over the balance of trade and to contribute to wealth." Exemptions of iron and steel works were thought to be desirable because such local industries would prevent large sums of money from being drawn out of the state to foreign countries. Not all exemptions were based on purely mercantilistic grounds. Manufacturers of malt liquor were to be encouraged, partly through exemptions, to diminish the use of ardent spirits and to preserve the health and morals of the people.[4]

In the Southern Colonies, the tendency was to encourage industry more often by direct subsidies than through tax exemptions. A summary of the development of industrial inducements in South Carolina will illustrate the relevance of time and place considerations.[5]

In 1707, a subsidy was provided for encouraging the making of potash and saltpeter. Manufacturing of these products started on a small scale before the Revolutionary War and was encouraged by the government after the end of hostilities. This encouragement took the form of direct subsidies. South Carolina first tried to encourage industry through tax exemption in 1823, when an act was passed exempting flour production, iron works, public salt works, and public nitre works, as well as individuals manufacturing gun powder. This 1823 Act also exempted "the products of this State or the unmanufactured products of any of the United States" from the tax on stock in trade.[6] According to Stimson, "This encouragement of general home manufacturing was the first of its kind in South Carolina to take the form of tax exemption; it was a part of the wave of governmental encouragement that was sweeping over the United States in an effort to retain manufacturing that had started during the War of 1812." [7]

The period following the Civil War brought significant policy changes with regard to exemptions for industry. Apparently there was little evidence that the previous minor exemptions had achieved their purposes. Stimson explains this failure as follows: "A slave economy was suited to the plantation form of agriculture; and the cotton, rice, indigo and other products found a ready market especially in England. Manufactured goods were obtained more economically by exchanging the staple plantation products for them. In the 1870's, the obstacle of slavery having been eliminated and the effects of war having begun to fade into the background with the restoration of civil government, industrial development became noticeable." [8] It is noteworthy that this renewal of governmental encouragement to industry (1873) explicitly recognized a subsidy as the equivalent of a tax exemption. Anyone who employed capital in the manufacture of cotton, wool, or paper fabrics, iron, lime, or agricultural implements was entitled to receive, from the state treasury, a subsidy equal to his total state taxes (except the 2-mill school tax) for a period of ten years. Counties and municipalities were authorized to grant similar bounties for investments made after the passage of the enabling act.

Present Extent of Property-Tax Incentives and Other Inducements to Attract Industry

No two states have precisely the same legal basis or identical practice with respect to any one aspect of property taxation in the United States, and the granting of tax favors to industry is no exception to this general rule. A few states favor semi-comprehensive exemptions available to any industry qualified under the law. Most states have laws permitting flexibility. In Alabama and Kentucky, the option to grant tax exemptions is in the hands of the governmental units affected. In Arkansas and Louisiana, exemptions are provided for by individual contract. In Alaska, there must be a central administrative certification that the legislative purpose will be served thereby. The constitutions of some states explicitly prohibit tax exemptions other than those specifically enumerated. In the absence of constitutional barriers, the general rule is that the legislature, as the repository of the state's taxing power, has implied power to grant exemptions even without express constitutional enablement. State constitutional requirements of uniformity and equality may impose some limits upon the implicit power of the legislature; to be effective, however, cases must be brought before the courts.

In the absence of effective constitutional prohibitions, exemptions are likely to be upheld.

While the grant of a tax exemption is in many respects similar to an absolute gift of tax revenues that would otherwise have accrued, and is thus arguably subject to public purpose and credit clause limitations, industrial exemptions have been sustained with few exceptions. This apparent anomaly may be explained on two grounds. First, the power to exempt can not realistically be limited by a concept of public purpose because of the very nature of that power. "The right to make exemptions is involved in the right to select the subjects of taxation. . . . To some extent it must exist always, for the selection of subjects of taxation is of itself an exemption of what is not selected. . . ." Second, because the public purpose and credit clause limitations were designed primarily to prevent the creation of public financial liability for the benefit of private industry, they would seem more properly applicable to an outlay of funds in the form of a gift than to a tax exemption.[9]

As of 1964, the following states provided by law for direct property-tax exemptions to new or expanded industry:[10] Alabama allows a ten-year exemption except from school taxes. Alaska gives a five- to ten-year exemption, the period varying directly with the size of the investment. Arkansas grants a seven-year exemption which is limited to textile mills. Hawaii's five-year exemption applies only to pulp and paper mills, but personal property of all taxpayers is exempted. Kentucky gives a five-year exemption from municipal taxes only. Louisiana's ten-year exemption (actually five years with privilege of renewal) does not include school taxes. Mississippi allows a ten-year exemption period, with liberal exemption of finished goods inventories in the hand of manufacturers and in transit. Oklahoma's five-year exemption privilege is limited to municipalities, but textile mills may also choose an in-lieu tax of .1 percent of the value of products manufactured. Oregon's two-year exemption applies only to buildings under construction, but there is also a liberal free-port law. Rhode Island grants a ten-year exemption. South Carolina has a five-year exemption (which does not extend to school taxes) and also a liberal free-port law. Vermont allows a ten-year exemption; in addition, all manufacturers' inventories are totally exempt from local taxation but are taxed by the state at a low rate.

The fact that only fifteen states make legal provision for direct exemption of industrial improvements and equipment from property taxes does not mean that the issue of local subsidies for industry is of interest in only a minority of our states. Industrial development and location may be affected by many other property-tax features or practices, including: (a) Exemption or liberal treatment under classification of personal property in some states and not in others; (b) persistently low effective rates in some states favoring industry; (c) effective long-term stability in assessed valuation (whether by contract or by practice), adding certainty to future tax bills; (d) the current practice of issuing bonds to finance industrial facilities, for lease at low cost, which is more widespread than the practice of direct tax exemption; (e) sub-rosa tax exemptions, i.e., areas where new industries obtain local tax exemptions not authorized by law; and (f) many other forms of financial assistance such as cash donations, payment of moving expenses, state insurance of mortgages, loans to community-development corporations, sales of land or buildings at low prices, payment of repair and installation costs, and advance agreements on utility rates or on services.

Of the states which give no "legal" direct exemptions to industry, fifteen are actively providing for local bond issues to finance the construction of facilities. All but a small minority of these states provide for the exemption of such facilities from the property tax— in fact, the exemption of the government-owned facility may be extended for periods longer than those commonly accorded industries occupying their own plants. In total, twenty-five states have laws permitting local bond issues to finance facilities. The low cost of capital because of the exemption of interest on these bonds from the federal income tax, together with the property-tax exemption, permits quite favorable terms to lessees. Fifteen states which do not grant direct tax exemptions practice sub-rosa tax concessions. Fourteen states offer other types of financial assistance. It appears that only a small minority of our fifty states are innocent of granting concessions of some type.

Property-tax inducements to attract industry must be considered as simply one device among many to speed industrialization. The larger issue concerns the merit of the entire complex of governmental inducements to industry, and the relative efficacy of tax concessions as one of the alternative devices. It is difficult to achieve a balanced judgment on this issue. One extreme position would be to assume that an almost universal practice is sufficient proof of its desirability. Ernest G. Miller expresses an alternative view, based upon a deep conviction that:

It is one thing to enact policies that are congenial to business activity, or to enact policies that are favorable to a *general* category of the population. It is quite another matter to bestow, through public channels, a special favor upon business that would apparently not be attracted to a community otherwise. To be sure, this is an old practice. But age and honor do not necessarily go together, and the newer and sharper distinction between public purpose and private interest is a development that is honorable and defensible in a society committed to fair treatment in law.[11]

The Case for Local Inducements to Industry

This paper opened with a quotation from Jensen, who recognized merit as well as danger in using the infant-industry argument in defense of local commercial policies. Jensen favored the principle of universal taxation, a view that led him to suggest certain restrictions on the practice of tax exemption. These were: "(a) The exemption should not be perpetual. That is a part of the infant industry argument. (b) The exemption should be limited in area, should perhaps be a matter of local option, and should be confined to the taxes of the areas that are to benefit. (c) Exemptions should apply only to the operative property used by enterprises whose encouragement is economically justified." [12] Clearly, this case for tax exemption is a quite limited one.

A controlled program of tax exemption may be necessary to neutralize a state and local tax system which is comparatively more onerous to industry than the systems of competing areas are. This rationalization has been advanced in support of the program in Louisiana. William D. Ross, whose study of the effects of tax exemptions in Louisiana is widely regarded as basic, reacts to this argument, stating that " a better solution to the problem would seem to be a complete renovation of the entire tax system." [13]

Local inducements to industry can be used effectively to achieve a reduction in unemployment and an increase in the level of prosperity at the local level.

The two principal reasons for seeking industry are *(a)* to promote the general welfare and *(b)* to broaden the property-tax base. It has been argued that the second of these purposes should be downgraded. Mabel Walker, whose opinion is highly respected among tax economists, has made a strong case for this argument:

Sometimes I think we should downgrade taxes. If a locality is considering whether to attract or permit industry, or whether to plan an urban renewal project, the effect on the tax rate should *not* be the predominant consideration—perhaps it should not even rank a major consideration. I realize that this is rank heresy. Having gone so far out on a limb, I am tempted to venture a little further and say that even the total fiscal effects—including expenditures as well as taxes—resulting from the proposed industry should not be the predominant consideration.

Just exactly *why* does a community need an industry? To give jobs, of course. That is the big reason and we should not lose sight of it. Visit any declining industry area and the jobless people, the relief workers, the retailers, and the small service enterprises will have an emphatic answer.

We want industry to give jobs. So eager are some of the depressed areas for job-giving enterprises that they would probably be glad to have them even if such industries did not pay any taxes. I do not mean to imply that the industry should not pay taxes.

The taxes that the industry is likely to pay and the expenses it will cause the community are of far less significance than the measure of prosperity it will bring to the area.[14]

The unemployment situation or the depressed conditions may be such as to constitute an emergency. To paraphrase a current slogan used in another area of human aspirations, what is wanted is: *"Jobs Now."* The number of jobs created and the ratio of new payroll to the cost of the subsidy are the sole tests of success. Niceties of finance tend to be ignored. A study of subsidization programs in forty Wisconsin cities provides some evidence of the success of such programs. W. D. Knight says such programs " . . . have largely achieved the amount of employment and payroll which was their original objective. It may be assumed, although it cannot be conclusively demonstrated, that the communities studied would not have obtained an equivalent amount of employment and payroll without the use of subsidization." [15]

A typical objection from the point of view of more lasting effects is voiced by Joe S. Floyd, Jr.: "The long run results of such competition can only be to produce an uneconomic distribution of industry, to subsidize inefficient enterprises at the expense of more efficient ones, and to disturb the equity and productivity of state and local tax systems."[16]

Quite the opposite is true according to John E. Moes, who holds that:

When circumstances make the subsidization of industry attractive to a local community, conditions are also such that this type of action will bring the economy as a whole closer to the social welfare optimum as usually defined. Thus the case is analagous to that in favor of competition between individuals and enterprises. . . . Competition between local groups or municipalities arises as a result of imperfections in the labor market and tends to mitigate the effect of wage rigidities.[17]

The circumstances to which he refers are (*a*) the existence of such a degree of unemployment or of under employment (or of disguised unemployment) that the marginal productivity of labor in a given area is extremely low and (*b*) a rigid wage system.

Moes explains that, in the South, "The effective wage minimum in industry impedes further industrial expansion long before the marginal productivity has fallen to anywhere near that in agriculture.

This then may well cause a situation in which the bottleneck to the transfer of labor from agriculture to industry is lack of employment opportunity, not a lack of capable workers willing to transfer at the existing level." In his view, a general case in favor of subsidization exists, whenever: "One, there is a discrepancy between the marginal productivity of transferable labor in different occupations as a result of restricted employment opportunity in the relatively highly paid occupations at the then prevailing wage level; and two, whenever there is involuntary idleness as a result of restricted employment opportunity at the prevailing wage level in any occupation that qualified un- or underemployed workers are desirous to enter." [18]

It should, perhaps, be stressed that Moes limits his case for subsidization to localities where the market price of labor is above its opportunity cost. He believes that this limitation will, in fact, prevail: "Both a priori reasoning based upon an assumption of rational behavior by local governments and existing practice lead us to maintain that the inducement to engage in this practice exists only when local employment opportunity is deficient." [19]

Moes' thesis has had only narrow acceptance. One reason may be that it is difficult for those who hold fast to a faith in competition within a purely private enterprise system to be receptive to his view that community competition (with direct governmental participation) is an analagous situation. Moes does seem to ask too much in the acceptance of this analogy. His assumption of "rational behavior of local governments" and his questionable assertion that "existing practice" universally is such as to confine community inducements to certain conditions, tax our credulity. The work, nonetheless, is a substantial one and deserves more consideration than it has received.

Assuming conditions of high employment and a satisfactory rate of economic growth elsewhere, one might accept as relatively harmless (as well as inevitable) local-government inducements to speed industrialization. But this assumption is scarcely warranted under conditions of persistent nation-wide unemployment of upwards of 4.5 to 5 percent and when the consensus is that this rate can be appreciably reduced (by monetary and fiscal policies) only at the risk of an uncomfortable rise in the price level. Involuntary unemployment exists primarily because of inadequate employment opportunity within an area reasonably accessible to those without jobs. Increases in employment opportunity depends upon additional investment. To the extent that involuntary unemployment is general throughout the economy, the problem of stimulating investment also is a general one.

To the extent that investment lags are due to inadequate net earnings, direct subsidies or tax reductions may be effective devices for the improvement of earnings.

The Case Against Local Inducements to Industry

If one were to judge by the number of objections voiced against local inducements to attract industry, one would be forced to conclude that the case against these practices is overwhelming. The positive aspects of the case against special inducements is not unrelated to Adam Smith's "unseen hand." William A. Johnson states, for example, that "In our capitalistic system the only sound industrial growth is that based on free competitive enterprise and sound location factors." This could very well be so. At least those of us nurtured on the liberal tenets of laissez-faire economics are predisposed to accept such a statement as sound in principle. We are inclined to the view that such a principle is self-evident, and rest content to stress evidence and reasons why governmental inducements may be wasteful, unethical, abortive, insidious, unnecessary, destructive of the tax base, of questionable legality, short-sighted, conducive to suicidal inter-community competition, and a handicap to sustainable economic growth and the maximization of national income. The following statement by Johnson illustrates the strategy usually employed in an argument against governmental inducements to industrialization.

Accordingly, it is incumbent upon all of us, irrespective of our present philosophies and current policies, to join in a serious, realistic and severely critical re-examination and re-appraisal of the use of tax exemptions as a vehicle for transporting new industry into a given state or community. To do this it is necessary to bring into focus and proper perspective some of the most fundamental precepts of our democratic form of government and several of the irrefutable economic facts of life. And we must view these factors with a clear, sharp eye and judge their relative value with fair-minded objectivity.[20]

There is, of course, nothing wrong with such a call to arms. Nor is it unreasonable to approach the issue by attempting to contrast the costs of inducement programs with their benefits. There have been many efforts to resolve the problem through empirical studies of the significance of tax favors in inducing the development of an industry and in influencing its location. Most of these studies conclude that the tax bill is a secondary factor, of insignificant importance in comparison with such items as raw materials, markets, transportation, power, and labor.

On the other hand, these empirical studies have not proved that, *ceteris paribus,* tax incentives or other inducement considerations are not significant *marginal* factors in attracting business to a community. There is evidence that subsidies have been the deciding factor in a small percentage of location decisions. The most nearly definitive factual study of an industrial-tax-exemption program is the one made by Ross in Louisiana, in 1953. Only in Louisiana is the direction of the program entirely central, and only there are complete records of the action taken available.

Certain results of Ross's study have enjoyed frequent mention, for example, his conclusion that only 7 percent of industrial investments made in that state during the period studied would not have been made without tax exemptions ($24,422,564.09 out of $355,121,753.60). Ross estimated that the ten-year tax loss would be over $51,000,000, a sum which clearly raises the question whether the new employment, additional payrolls, and added tax base will offset the tax costs eliminated by the exemption program. He grants that they might, but that "It must be remembered, however, that only if the exemption can be regarded as responsible for the location of the new industry within the State, can there be any justification for giving the industry the free ride. The evidence presented . . . indicates that this has seldom been the case in Louisiana." [21]

In another publication Ross concludes that "the cost of the program in terms of lost revenue is out of proportion to the direct results obtained." [22] This is, of course, a value judgment; it raises the issue of the validity of the comparison. Moes contends that this conclusion is valid only if the state and local units would have used the $50,-000,000 for new commercial investment. The conclusion should be different, Moes believes, if the revenue foregone would not have been used for direct investment. Before coming to any conclusions, he would like to know the size of the payrolls brought into the state as a result of the exemption. His calculations are based on the assumption that an investment of $9,000 would employ another worker who would receive between $2,000 and $3,000 in wages annually (an investment-wage ratio of between 3:1 and 4:1). If this assumption is correct, the new investment would have yielded an annual payroll of about $7,-000,000, or $70,000,000 for the ten-year period, which, even disregarding any multiplier effects, would more than offset the total revenue loss. If the enterprises to which the exemption means most experience a more unfavorable ratio, however, "the state program may be adversely discriminatory, yet even with all the objections that can be raised against them it is hard to condemn tax exemption programs outright under present conditions." [23]

Most attempts to determine the effectiveness of tax inducements on the localization of industry have relied exclusively on questionnaires and interviews, without benefit of the factual information available to Ross. Closely allied with the questionnaire and interview technique is an attempt to measure comparative industrial tax burdens in selected states or localities by estimating the tax bills on hypothetical corporations. The extent of these attempts bear witness to the belief that inquiry concerning the "tax burden" and the "tax image" of a given state goes beyond mere academic interest.[24] Generally speaking, the results of these studies have not been entirely convincing, and the common implication that the importance of tax considerations is relatively insignificant may be misleading.

An examination of the importance of property-tax administrative practices as a factor in the locational decisions of South Carolina firms may be revealing. Until 1964, the South Carolina State Tax Commission assessed manufacturing firms on the basis of the "productive" gross plant account. Beginning in 1964, the assessment ratio was fixed at approximately 9.5 percent of the gross plant account (land, buildings, and equipment) of new investments as determined from balance sheet data. This assessment is continued from year to year, changing only when new investments are added. Replacements are permitted without a change in assessment, because depreciation is not taken into account. Manufacturers meeting certain minimum requirements regarding size of investment or number of jobs provided are exempt in those counties which have obtained special enabling legislation. Municipalities may exempt manufacturers from all levies except school taxes if the exemption is ratified by referendum. Because most manufacturing is located outside city limits, however, this exemption is of little practical significance. The dollar value of the exemption varies with the total millage, other than for schools, levied among the forty-six counties. Several counties levy less than 20 mills. A few levy up to about 35 mills. The effective rate of exemptions seldom exceeds .2 percent and extends for only five years. Clearly, the money saved could scarcely be considered significant.

In 1963, the Bureau of Business Research, University of South Carolina, conducted a study of industrial location. The procedure used was the familiar one of mailing a confidential questionnaire to fifty-five firms which had recently located in South Carolina. Thirty-two firms (58 percent) responded. One part of the questionnaire listed ten categories (fifty-nine items) which management was asked to designate as "very important," "important," "unimportant," or "not considered." The responses were reduced to weighted averages: if a firm stated it did not consider an item in its decision, a weight of one was given; a response of "unimportant" was given the weight of two; items checked "important" were weighted three; and those checked "very important" were weighted four. The maximum weighted average would be four—the minimum, one.

As might be expected, the firms responding indicated that various manpower considerations were of predominant significance. The item with the highest weighted average was "labor relations" (history of and list of work stoppages), with 3.710, and the next-highest weighted average of 3.700 was for "extent of unionization in the proposed area." The results belie the common impression that the tax structure is unimportant, however. The weighted average of the item, "assessment bases" was 3.593; that of "property tax rates and fees," 3.625; "trends in tax legislation," 3.586; and "special tax inducements to industry," 3.172. Most of these weighted averages are significantly higher than those for many other items. Weighted averages in the major categories of Raw Material Supply (2.626); Finished Goods Market (2.831); Industrial Sites (3.165); Transportation (2.735); Community Distributing Services (1.948); Money (1.978); and Miscellaneous (2.815); were considerably below the averages for the categories of Manpower Considerations (3.279); Local Government (3.582); and Legal Aspects, including the tax structure (3.335).[25] Quite clearly, the tax structure of South Carolina was viewed as of *greater than average significance* by firms who had located there recently.

One of the incontrovertible arguments against tax exemptions is based on the fact that subsidies can be effective only if they are not universal. Harold Groves once stated that "Exemption tends to provoke retaliation and further exemption in an unending cycle." [26] Perhaps the practice of granting inducements of all forms, including tax exemptions, has already reached a point of no return. This seems to be the opinion of Joe S. Floyd, Jr. In discussing the use of local industrial bonds, he recently estimated that the total amount of such securities is in excess of *two billion dollars*. They are even in use in states which have not provided for them through state statutes.

I believe they can be found in every state east of the Mississippi and in other states as well. They may be hidden under a Port or Airport Authority or simply without any shadow of statutory authorization. . . . Does such a financing plan help a state to get new industry? If all states have such plans the answer would be unqualifiedly no for the advantage in one state would be offset by similar advantages elsewhere. And the fact that firms use the plans is not conclusive proof that they help get industry since much of the industry probably is coming for other reasons. Yet a small residual remains.

And if your state does not have some sort of financing program, it is going to be difficult to avoid adopting some sort of program within the near future."[27]

The case against tax exemptions (and other inducements) has not been successful in the only meaningful sense of the term—that of convincing state and local governments to cease and desist such practice. Exhortations and appeals to fiscal virtue have not prevented a proliferation of inducement devices. Some areas are sorely in need of jobs—others are vitally concerned with keeping existing industry or maintaining a desirable rate of expansion.

If such inducements were not important to industry, it is difficult to believe the practice would have become so general. Direct tax exemption may not lower costs to an appreciable extent, but the total complex of property taxation—including exemption of personal property, underassessment, or a favorable classified property-tax system—may. Favorable utility contracts and liberal services such as access roads and sewer lines may—when coupled with governmental financing—add up to considerable savings, thus inducing additional development and influencing localization.

Increased employment opportunity does depend on additional investment. A decision to invest is affected by costs as well as by hoped-for gross revenues. Since the dollar investment needed to create a new job is large and continues to increase, cost-reducing governmental inducements are of interest to the credit-worthy, efficient, and successful firms, as well as to those characterized as fly-by-night. The alacrity with which corporations are taking advantage of the more liberal rules governing depreciation and the tax credits for investment suggests that the volume of additional investment is not unrelated to tax savings. It may be assumed that these recent changes in the federal income tax have had some influence on increased investment, however difficult it might be to determine the precise effect.

"Pro" or "Con"?

Because there is merit on either side of the foregoing dialogue, it is difficult to reach any firm conclusion. A decision is, nonetheless, required. After weighing all arguments, the conclusion reached is that well-conceived local inducements to attract industry are both inevitable and justifiable. Ill-conceived programs should be avoided. The basic problem is one of making wise selections. There is nothing inherently "wrong" and much that is "right" in sound community efforts to strengthen a local economy.

The general case for organized community efforts to induce industrialization is similar to the case for the conpensatory tariff or to the infant-industry argument. An area with an industrial potential but with little or no industrial experience can benefit from an extra lift. Such an area may ultimately be industrialized without benefit of an organized effort; this result is highly uncertain, however, and, in any event, industrialization may be delayed for generations. In the interim, the area may suffer both from emigration of its more aggressive young people and from extreme under employment of those who remain.

One may retain considerable faith in neo-classical economic doctrine without losing touch with reality. There are many barriers to overcome before an under-developed region can achieve a satisfactory economic position. Some of these are: (*a*) inertia on the part of those who make developmental and locational decisions; (*b*) ignorance of the industrial potential of the industrially backward areas; (*c*) a desire to safeguard sources of raw materials; (*d*) a desire to avoid the time and expense involved in training industrially inexperienced labor; and (*e*) a desire to protect vested interests, e.g., employment at a higher wage scale than can be sustained in developing areas.

One of the better-known and more highly successful "bootstrap" operations is the developmental program of the government of Puerto Rico. In less than twenty years "Puerto Rico has undergone a dramatic transformation from a stagnant, predominantly agricultural area to a more fully diversified and rapidly growing economy." The developmental program was not a simple one, but it did include specific measures to promote private investment, including a comprehensive tax-exemption program, which played an important role. "These extended tax holidays resulted in a substantial increase in net profits and thereby sharply reduced the payback period and thus the initial risk inherent in the investment. At the same time *tax incentives focused attention on investment opportunities that might otherwise have gone unnoticed* and also aided in the internal financing of the expansion of the exempt enterprise." [28]

Other features of "operation bootstrap," such as low corporate-income-tax rates and complete management discretion in depreciation policy, have reduced the incidence of firms retrenching in their operations once the exemption period expires. The most compelling reason for expecting the development to continue lies, however, in the relatively high pre-tax profits of the new firms. The potential was there all the while but remained undiscovered until the government gave it a persistent and successful push.[29]

On the other hand, some inducement programs have failed. It will be recalled that, in 1933, the State of Florida rushed through a constitutional amendment authorizing a tax-exemption program for the express purpose of luring the motion-picture industry from California. The anticipated result was not achieved, and the program was repealed in 1948.

Another aspect of the argument that local subsidies are unsound is based on distress suffered by communities losing plants. Indeed, it does sometimes happen that a community will directly pirate a plant from another area (e.g., the Village of Deming, New Mexico) but the more numerous cases relate to decisions concerning the location of new plants or the rebuilding of obsolete and depreciated facilities.

This argument can be overemphasized, however. If a general economy is healthy, the results of diversification may, in the long run, be advantageous to all areas involved. One effect is to stimulate thought and energy which may lead to the development of even more profitable activities. This has happened in some New England communities following the loss of textile plants. The situation is not unlike that experienced by labor following successive nineteenth-century waves of immigration. The result was that much of the labor displaced by immigrants was "freed" to accept higher level jobs. Any development which lowers cost or increases the effective buying power of workers will expand markets to the benefit of areas initially damaged. As a general proposition, it remains true that, while wants are insatiable, productive resources remain scarce. We should, therefore, welcome soundly conceived programs which will enhance the productivity of our scarce productive agents.

The task, and it is not an easy one, is to choose wisely among the available industrial inducement devices. The balance of this paper concerns an alternative to general property taxation. In essence, the thesis is that property-tax differentials, as we now know them, are not suitable inducement devices. Moreover, general property taxation, as practiced in the United States, handicaps rather than assists in arriving at sound industrial expansion and locational decisions. The alternative suggested would both minimize the need for developmental programs and simplify decision-making in this area.

An Alternative

Taxes on improvements and tangible personal property are far from uniform throughout the United States. Diversity in state legal provisions relating to the scope of the base, assessment standards and practices, and classification create differential burdens on industrialization which may be as significant as direct exemptions, if not more so. Legal provisions governing direct exemption vary widely among the states. To focus exclusive attention upon direct exemptions as an attraction to industry is grossly inadequate. The competitive influence of the property tax as a device to encourage industry cannot be removed except as property-tax laws and administration become uniform throughout the country, a goal which will never be reached as long as *ad valorem* taxes are imposed on improvements and personal property.

The only way to remove all competitive influences of property taxation would be to confine the tax base to land—the only productive factor which is fixed in a physical sense. Variation in the effective tax rate on land—such as that between jurisdictions—would not be an influence in the same sense as differences in the effective rates applied to improvements would be. In fact, that jurisdiction with the highest rate on land would probably have a competitive advantage, i.e., the tax would be capitalized, thus reducing the cost of land acquisition.

The point that might be emphasized, however, is that the taxes saved by those owning improvements and personal property could be sufficient to induce additional investment. The value of such tax savings would vary with the effective tax rate, the length of life of the improvement, and the rate of discount reasonably applied to such investments. Mason Gaffney recently illustrated the tax burden on improvements by calculating its equivalent as a lump sum at the time of building. He estimated that an annual tax payment of $1.00, continued for 60 years and discounted at 5 percent, would have a present value of $19. An effective tax rate of 1 percent would thus be the equivalent of a 19 percent tax, payable at time of building. Since few localities have an effective rate this low (abstracting out exemptions or favorable taxation *via* classification), the taxes levied could be quite a deterrent to the investment decision.[30]

There would, of course, be a revenue replacement problem, the size of which would depend on the proportion of economic rent (or future increments) which was taxed away. At the very least, the taxes on land should be sufficiently high to make land readily available for higher uses at reasonable prices. Land taxes ideally should go as high above this limit as local political sentiment would permit, perhaps stopping short of taking all economic rent.

Current assessment experience in Richland County, South Carolina, demonstrates that it is politically possible to increase land taxes rather sharply as a component of an equalization program. In the course of a reassessment program, the Richland County Assessor was strict in basing his assessments on market value. He has raised assessments of suburban "fringe" lands as much as seventy-fold by basing them on market value, as opposed to the value of the lands in their present use (e.g., farming).

Even if higher land taxes would not offset the taxes foregone on improvements, additional productive investment, with more jobs and larger payrolls, would certainly increase the productivity of other, more broadly based state and local taxes.

Developing areas would do well to give serious consideration to a property tax confined to land. Those first to adopt such a practice would have a temporary advantage. The fallacy of composition teaches that the relative local advantage would disappear in the unlikely event the practice became universal. Even if all states should conform, not all gain would be lost to those first to practice such a program. The effect should be larger total investment throughout the country. Assuming such an effect, confining periodic *ad valorem* taxation to land should reduce the extent to which fiscal and monetary policy are used to reduce underemployment.

Restricting the base of the property tax to land probably would not end interarea competition. Areas lagging in economic development would continue to experiment with programs designed to compensate for deficiencies in the factors which influence industrialization. Some of the more affluent communities would continue their attempts to supplement their environmental advantages for the purpose of achieving an even greater prosperity. Our federal form of government and our commitment to the sentiments of states' rights and local self-government permit widespread differentiation in state-local commercial policies.

Competition among organized communities is an established practice, and this fact has not been given sufficient attention by economists. Organized efforts of communities to further local self-interest will not be discouraged by essentially negative attacks. Although expedient and opportunistic in origin, the economic policies and programs of local areas must be judged on pragmatic grounds.

Property-tax inducements to attract industry have become outmoded. It has been well said that the most successful form of inducement will be that which provides the greatest financial benefit. Local industrial bond plans clearly offer more than do tax exemptions. The real challenge lies in trying to determine the "public purpose" inherent in the administration of such plans or in other effective inducements.

In our fluid society the concept "public purpose" is affected by time and place considerations. One legal opinion suggests that the doctrine should be related to "the threatened abuses and intended benefits" of a given governmental action, thus serving "as a constitutional check on exuberant or corruptly motivated exercise of governmental powers without restricting the use of these powers only to means and ends considered proper at a given point in time." [31]

The thesis of this paper is that many features of property taxation exert divergent effects upon industrialization but that "the threatened abuses and intended benefits" simply cannot be determined. Restricting property taxation to land would neutralize these effects and would make it easier to appraise other local commercial policies and practices.

Confining the property-tax base to land would not only simplify the problem but would assure a tax climate of *general* benefit. A reform that would assist the managers of the "little" economies (and the state courts) to choose more wisely between the alternatives of stimulative and inducement devices; would reduce the pressure for federal restrictions; and would tend to promote a better accommodation among local, regional, and national interests deserves a trial.

Notes

1 Jens P. Jensen, *Property Taxation in the United States* (Chicago: University of Chicago Press, 1931), p. 158.
2 Jens P. Jensen, *Tax Exemption as a Means of Encouragement to Industry* (Kansas Studies in Business; Lawrence: University of Kansas, May, 1929), p. 10. (Emphasis supplied.)
3 Mabel Walker, "The Plant, the Office and the City, Part II: Industrial Location Impacts," *Tax Policy*, 23, Nos. 2–3 (February-March, 1956), 15.
4 Jensen, *Tax Exemption*, pp. 13–14.
5 Claude W. Stimson, "Development of Tax Exemption in South Carolina," *South Carolina Law Quarterly*, 4 (1951–52), 396–419, esp. 398–407.
6 *Ibid.*, citing 5 Stat. 424.
7 *Ibid.*, p. 406.
8 *Ibid.*, p. 412.
9 "Inducements to Industrial Location," *Columbia Law Review*, 50 (1959), 628–29.
10 The principal source for the factual information in the three following paragraphs is William A. Johnson, "Industrial Tax Exemptions: Sound Investment or Foolish Giveaway?" in National Tax Association, *1962 Proceedings of the Fifty-Fifth Annual Conference on Taxation*, ed.

Walter J. Kress (Harrisburg, 1963), pp. 433–35. A more recent compilation and description of state and local development incentive is Benjamin Bridges, Jr., "State and Local Inducements for Industry, Part 1," *National Tax Journal*, Vol. 18, No. 1 (March, 1965).

11 Ernest G. Miller, "Municipal Financial Inducements to Industry: Policy Consequences," in *Occasional Paper Series*, No. 3 (Davis: Institute of Governmental Affairs, University of California, September, 1964), p. 12.

12 Jensen, *Property Taxation*, p. 101.

13 William D. Ross, "Louisiana's Industrial Tax Exemption Program," *Louisiana Business Bulletin*, 15, No. 2 (December, 1953), 50.

14 Mabel Walker, "Fiscal Considerations Involved in Patterns of Industrial Development," in National Tax Association, *1962 Proceedings*, p. 455. In this paper Miss Walker is not arguing for industrial subsidization. Her principal point is that the large number of small local governments and the numerous tax shelters distort the fiscal importance of industrialization. She offers sensible suggestions for minimizing this imperative.

15 W. D. Knight, *Subsidization of Industry in Forty Selected Cities in Wisconsin* (Wisconsin Commerce Series, Vol. 1, No. 2; Madison: University of Wisconsin, Bureau of Business Research and Service, 1947), p. 25.

16 Joe S. Floyd, Jr., *Effects of Taxation on Industrial Location* (Chapel Hill: University of North Carolina Press, 1952), p. 113.

17 John E. Moes, *Local Subsidies for Industry* (Chapel Hill: University of North Carolina Press, 1962), p. 5.

18 *Ibid.*, pp. 10, 17.

19 *Ibid.*, pp. 108–9.

20 Johnson, "Industrial Tax Exemptions," pp. 425, 423–24.

21 Ross, "Louisiana's Industrial Tax Exemption Program," p. 46.

22 William D. Ross, "Tax Exemptions in Louisiana as a Device for Encouraging Industrial Development," *The Southwestern Social Science Quarterly*, 34 (June, 1953), 22.

23 Moes, *Local Subsidies for Industry*, Appendix II, pp. 215–17.

24 See Reuben A. Zubrow, "Some Difficulties with the Measurement of Comparative Tax Burdens," in National Tax Association, *1961 Proceedings of the Fifty-Fourth Annual Conference on Taxation*, ed. Walter J. Kress (Harrisburg, 1962), pp. 151–60; Henry J. Frank, "Measuring State Tax Burdens," *National Tax Journal*, 12, No. 2 (June, 1959), 179–85; Don M. Soule, *Comparative Total Tax Loads of Selected Manufacturing Corporations with Alternative Locations in Kentucky, Indiana, Ohio and Tennessee* (Lexington: Bureau of Business Research, University of Kentucky, 1960); *Alabama Goes Industry Hunting* (Alabama Business Research Council and the University of Alabama School of Commerce and Business Administration; University, Alabama: University of Alabama Press, 1957); and a great many others. James S. Currie reminds us that the concept of "tax image," like beauty, lies in

the eye of the beholder; the factors motivating people making business location decisions vary with their personality. "Among a certain type of companies if your tax image is not a reflection of the true feeling of equal treatment, fairness, lack of under the table deals and that sort of thing they do not consider your state for location if there are other equally desirable locations under normal factors elsewhere." (National Tax Association, *1962 Proceedings,* p. 463.) William Carmil, attorney for several California cities, is convinced that industry is telling the truth about what it wants. "They aren't looking primarily for 'free' this and 'free' that, or preferential treatment or tax favoritism." ("Industry into California Cities," in *Occasional Paper Series,* No. 3 [Davis: Institute of Governmental Affairs, University of California, September, 1964], p. 19.)

25 A. C. Flora, Jr., "Industrial Location in South Carolina," *The University of South Carolina Business and Economic Review,* Vol. 10, No. 4 (January, 1964).

26 Harold M. Groves, "Effects of Tax Exemptions and Tax Differentials on the Location of Business," in National Tax Association, *Proceedings of the Thirty-First Annual Conference on Taxation,* ed. W. G. Query (Columbia, South Carolina, 1939), p. 565.

27 Joe S. Floyd, Jr., "Federal, State and Local Government Programs for Financing Industrial Development," in National Tax Association, *1962 Proceedings,* pp. 453–54.

28 "The Puerto Rican Economy in Transition," *Monthly Review* (The Federal Reserve Bank of New York; May, 1965), pp. 108–9. (Emphasis supplied.) Advantages from property-tax inducements were minor, however, in comparison with federal-income-tax and shipping-rate benefits.

29 To meet another standard objection, it is assumed that the areas striving for an industrial development will somehow finance the social overhead services which are both a prerequisite and a result of industrialization. This was a part of the Puerto Rican program.

30 Mason Gaffney, "Property Taxes and the Frequency of Urban Renewal," in National Tax Association, *1964 Proceedings of the Fifty-Seventh Annual Conference on Taxation,* ed. Walter J. Kress (Harrisburg, 1965), pp. 272–85.

31 "Legal Notes," *Columbia Law Review,* 50 (1959), 647.

Part III Special Problems

Introduction

In the first paper of this group, Irving Howards tries to determine the relationship between the effectiveness of systems of property taxation in the United States and the political power of the various levels of local government. Dr. Howards concludes that major defects in the methods by which property is taxed can be attributed to the fact that "government," in the true sense of the word, exists only at the federal level and that governmental bodies at the local and state levels are "communities" rather than "governments." The elected officials of state and local governments, he maintains, do not set policy and cannot effectively control progress toward the solution of state and local problems. At the local level, he suggests, private interest groups are often more influential than elected officials in determining policy. To illustrate this theory, Dr. Howards examines in detail the operation of property-tax-rate limitations in Illinois.

The federal government's exercise of its government powers and the impact of private pressure groups on the quantities of property exempt from taxation are considered by Joan E. O'Bannon. Her analysis is comprehensive, but the emphasis is on the exemption of federal-government property from property taxation. Dr. O'Bannon concludes that a property-tax exemption is a hidden subsidy and that there is much need for reform in the treatment of the real estate holdings of the federal government.

If an analysis of property-tax exemption is limited to the removal of land from the property-tax rolls, it becomes a rather straight-forward consideration of how the use of a scarce resource can be best maximized. In a price-income society, efficient allocation is assisted if costs are uniform. Because land was largely a free good originally, and because certain benefits continue to arise without additional input, it is appropriate that a portion of the annual cost of land consists of land-value taxes.

If all land were subject without exception to taxation based on value, then all users of land could make land-use decisions by comparing benefit with a cost consideration which was identical in all cases. This situation is very far from realization, however, and perhaps the concept is much too simple to be workable. It is, nevertheless, a basic economic principle against which land-tax exemption, to whomever granted, should be measured.

Undoubtedly there is a temptation for governments and exempt organizations to be much more lavish in their use of land than land users who pay taxes annually can afford to be. The impact of this situation is very difficult to evaluate. Perhaps the best that can be done within a mixed public and private economy is to continue to press for the reduction of the types of land holdings exempt from the land tax.

Bernard E. Sliger and Yung-Ping Chen in the next two chapters discuss different facets of a common problem. They have under consideration the legislative political temptation to use the property tax to provide benefits better distributed through government payments. Dr. Sliger describes how the exemption of veterans' homes from the property tax has developed since its introduction in 1932. In the following paper, Dr. Chen discusses a new development in the adjustment of the property tax on homesteads: he describes what is happening in the application of property taxes to homesteads of the aged. Dean Sliger demonstrates through indifference curve analysis that, in order to provide the same satisfactions, the government must sacrifice more revenues through the exemption of veterans from the property tax than it would lose if it paid them subsidies. Professor Chen does not conclude that the aged would be better off with a subsidy than with an equal tax exemption. He considers instead the possibility of setting up a plan to liquidate the principal asset of many aged—their homes. Dr. Chen's paper also includes a summary of current legislation in this new area of property taxation in the United States.

Hitherto, the problem associated with using the property-tax exemption to favor certain politically popular groups has not been realistically approached by academic tax specialists. Both Dr. Sliger and Dr. Chen outline politically realistic ways of meeting pressures for the exemption of certain homesteads from the property tax.

The final paper by Clarence W. Nelson is a careful examination of what can happen when the property tax is applied to a mineral resource. The mineral deposits in the case examined are concentrated in a rather small area and are owned largely by non-residents. This resource, vital to the total economy of the region, can be exploited by district residents only through tax programs. The effort to develop a workable concept of technical surplus in this paper is a contribution to land-rent theory which could be usefully applied by those who frame tax legislation in the developing areas around the world which are rich in resources. The study of the taxation of minerals in the past would seem to support the idea that the administration of the property tax should be moved to the state level. The lessons to be learned from the past also lend support to the theory that property taxes should be levied by the state. The revenue collected could then be distributed to local communities on the basis of a formula determined by need and could be expended on state-wide and state-initiated programs, as appropriate.

Richard W. Lindholm

10. Irving Howards

Property-Tax-Rate Limits:
A View of Local Government

As the activities of the United States Supreme Court suggest, the concept of federalism in this country is one which has been the subject of immense interpretation. Although this complex relationship between governments in one geographical entity has been defined in a variety of ways, it is, nevertheless, still acceptable to indicate that federalism implies a theory that the values of our society can best be assured by a division of governmental powers among the various levels of government.[1]

It is a well-known fact, however, that the question of how to allocate governmental powers to the various levels in order to best assure the retention of these values has long been in dispute. On the federal-state level, the predominant view now is that powers are best divided when they are, for the most part, concurrently assigned, but with major responsibility for the broad issues affecting our entire society placed with the federal government. The question of further division of powers to a third level, i.e., local government, has usually been the subject of even more diverse opinion. One view is that the basic values of our society can especially be preserved if this level of government is assigned powers to govern which, in truth, enable it to meet whatever governmental problems it might face. A contrary view is that the local level of government exists only because of powers delegated to it by the state.[2]

It is the position of the author that much of the confusion regarding the powers to be held by local government exists because the view is still popular that the political process at all levels of government is effectuated by the marriage of that amorphous entity called "government" to those elected or appointed to serve in its name. This view usually recognizes that a multitude of factors affect the decision-making process, but it implicitly assumes that the official holding the power of government in his hands is the primary variable influencing the governmental process.

Local Government—A Theoretical Definition

It is apparent that the special kind of mystique, awe, and authority inherent in any entity with potentially infinite powers over its constituents is still associated with the national government.[3] It should also be noted that, to a degree varying with position and personality, those who represent this level of government carry with them some of this same deification. This, in turn, suggests that the attention of the general public is intimately intertwined, albeit not necessary on specific issues,[4] with the machinations of the federal government.

Because of the importance and scope of national government, a number of groups are involved in the decision-making process at the federal level.[5] One can point, for instance, to cases in which non-governmental groups have been the predominant factor in determining the final direction of particular decisions.[6] Nevertheless, the ultimate power and prestige of government at this level is such that, even in such instances, non-governmental groups must exercise extraordinary effort to overcome the influence of the political elite officially representing the "general will" as expressed through national government. In short, the existence of an almost Hegelian concept of government at the national level makes it more difficult for non-governmental groups to assume ascendancy in the decision-making process.

As one moves downward (in a hierarchical categorization rather than on the basis of any normative judgment concerning the relative importance of each level of government) it becomes increasingly difficult to maintain the view that "government" exists in this unusual sense. One of the most severe criticisms directed at the state is that it is not a government at all. Indeed, some feel that, if present trends continue, the state will ultimately exist only as an administrative appendage of the central government.[7]

Without passing judgment on this charge, one can, at least, agree that the characteristics of state government can only be delineated in terms which lack the specificity of detail and exactness of any definition of the central government. Decisions of the United States Supreme Court and the corresponding movement of the central government into areas thought originally to be the province of state governments are eloquent testimony to this view. The degree to which the state—by satisfactorily meeting problem areas besetting our society—is able to retain viable corporate powers of its own determines, to a large extent, whether one can identify with the state as a governmental entity in the same manner as that described above for the federal government.

It is at the local level, however, that it becomes most difficult to maintain that government, as the term is defined above, exists in any real sense, whereby decisions are made predominantly by the elected and appointed political representatives and their authority is virtually unquestioned. The legal position of local government as a creature of the state suggests, in itself, that there is no inherent justification for the existence of this level of government and that its powers flow, not from the fact that *it* exists, but from the purpose for its creation at the state level. It is, of course, possible to point to many municipalities, some counties, and a few special-purpose districts as exceptions to this rule. They are exceptions, however, only to the extent that the particular needs of the constituencies involved are being met in a true "governmental" fashion.

Most local communities, however, have been unsuccessful in assuming this appearance of governmental distinction. Norton Long believes that, as a result, one is forced to think of government on the local level as a "highly limited affair in which office holders respond to demands and mediate conflicts. They play politics, and politics is vastly different from government if the latter is conceived as the rational, responsible ordering of the community." In such a situation, the political elite cannot "assume any such confident pose as top community leaders. The latter position is reserved for a rather varying group . . . of holders for the most part of positions of private power, economic, social, and ecclesiastical." They, instead, consider themselves "largely as mediators or players in a particular game that makes use of other inhabitants." [8]

If this view is correct, then one must analyze the local-government process in terms of the *groups* which are actively engaged in trying to influence the decision on each issue—and one must be prepared to recognize the probability that the most influential group will frequently have no official status in the government (as that word is commonly used).

This approach suggests a serious methodological problem. If one cannot look to the official representatives of local government as the indicator of political power in a community, how then is it possible to determine the distribution of power which does exist?

The answer to this query is presently the subject of intense debate among social scientists.[9] In examining the question, one astute analyst, Robert Dahl, finds that at least seven different properties of a power relationship have been isolated by various writers and that these properties in turn have a number of specifications. He notes that if " . . . you make a table of these 7 properties and the alternative requirements . . . it turns out that there are some 856 theoretically possible ways of specifying the essential characteristics of power . . . if we add 4 more properties . . . frequently suggested, there are some 14,000 logical possibilities. And you still have not disposed of the staggering question of what you mean by differences in the *amount* of power. . . ." [10]

Any approach, therefore, which attempts to consider all the nuances of power is doomed to failure. The alternative to this approach and the method pursued here, is to focus on a specific power relationship, assuming that it will illustrate and illuminate other power relationships which exist. In this instance, the particular focus will be on the limitations placed upon one presumably basic local-government power, the property tax.

Such an approach obviously makes one vulnerable to the charge that the choice is arbitrary and unenlightening. Because no satisfactory method has yet been devised for analyzing the total distribution of power, however, it seems the only alternative, if for no other reason than "because it is the sole strategy that is realistically possible." [11]

When using this approach, it may be hypothesized that the property tax and its use is an issue which should be of fundamental concern to at least two groups: the political elite of the local government (since it has been demonstrated that the property tax remains a significant source of revenue for local government and is one of the few remaining powers over which local government is supposed to have significant control) [12] and the non-governmental groups representing real estate interests.

Hopefully, this assumption, and the theory that non-governmental groups play the primary role in the ultimate decision concerning the use of property-tax-rate limits, will be verified by a brief survey of these limits in the United States to indicate their nature and by a more intensive view of rate limits as they exist and have been implemented in the state of Illinois.

Property-Tax-Rate Limits in the United States

The fact that property taxation remains the primary source of locally collected revenue for local governments has been well documented. The Advisory Commission on Intergovernmental Relations noted, for example, that "if one considers *local* tax revenue alone, the proportion borne by property taxes was almost the same in 1961 as in 1902—87.7% and 88.6% respectively. Local governments other than municipalities rely almost entirely on the property tax for their locally raised revenue." [13] This dependence on property-tax revenue has not altered in the years since this study. It is clear, therefore, that any limit designed to prescribe the maximum rate which may be applied against an assessed valuation should be a matter of serious concern to those representing local government.

Types of Rate Limits in Existence

The phenomenon of property-tax-rate limits has been the subject of a vast number of critiques.[14] Although these studies have revealed a great variety of rate limits,[15] the ways in which these limits are used throughout the country can generally be divided into three broad categories: (*a*) overall property-tax limits restricting the aggregate rates of all local governments to a certain amount prescribed in the state constitution or by statute—Michigan, Nevada, Ohio, Oklahoma, and Washington have such overall rate limits in their constitutions, while Indiana, New Mexico, Rhode Island, and West Virginia make similar provisions by statute; (*b*) specific constitutional or statutory limits restricting rates of certain funds of a governmental unit or limiting the total rate which can be levied by a particular type of local government—Alabama, Arizona, Arkansas, Florida, Illinois, Kentucky, Louisiana, Missouri, New York, Texas, and Wyoming have such limits in their constitutions, while Georgia, Idaho, Iowa, Kansas, Minnesota, Mississippi, Montana, Nebraska, North Carolina, North Dakota, Pennsylvania, South Carolina, Utah, and Wisconsin make similar provisions by statute; (*c*) (a relatively recent development) rate limits restricting increases in levies to a percentage of the increases in the previous year, unless additional changes are approved by local election—Colorado and Oregon make such provisions.[16]

A Brief Historical Survey of the Development of Tax-Rate Limits

Much of the early impetus for the establishment of rate limits stemmed from the reaction against the tremendous expansion of local debt and the resulting defaults which occurred immediately after the Civil War and again from 1903 to 1932. This increase in local debt, incurred primarily to finance local improvements and to help subsidize the extension of railroads, was hastened by restrictions already placed on state governments. Thus, by 1870 municipal debt totaled

$516,000,000; by 1880, approximately $821,000,000; by 1893, $925,-000,000; and by 1900 the billion dollar mark had been reached. The expansion of municipal debt was so great from 1903 to 1932 that, at the end of this period, the figure had ballooned to slightly over $16,-000,000,000.[17]

Many attempts were made to curb this exuberant expansion of debt by restricting the power of local government officials to incur debt. Limitations were frequently imposed prescribing the amount of the issue, the interest rate, and the general procedure for selling and retiring the bond issue. Another procedure was to restrict the tax rates which could be levied by local government officials. Such action was based on the common assumption that such restrictions would generally inhibit their use of the property tax in an unwarranted fashion. In 1870 and 1895, for example, overall statutory tax-rate limits were adopted in Rhode Island and Nevada respectively. In 1875 and 1884, Alabama and New York restricted by constitutional mandate the rates which could be used by certain local governments. Oklahoma adopted, in 1907, the first overall constitutional rate limitation and Ohio followed this example four years later.

Further impetus was given the movement to establish rate limits during the Depression of the 1930's, when the overexpansion of local debt again revealed the extent of overextended borrowing by local government, augmenting the feeling of distrust which already existed about local-government fiscal practices. The Advisory Commission on Intergovernmental Relations states, for example, that "at the worst of this period some 3,200 local governments fell behind in paying interest or principal on debt." [18] An additional problem was caused by the fact that, early in the depression, property values declined more sharply than property taxes did. As a result, "a drive was begun largely through the efforts of organized real estate groups, to convince state legislatures and the electorate that property was carrying an inordinate share of the tax burden. To relieve the pressure . . . it was urged that stringent over-all tax limitations be written into state constitutions." [19]

As a result of this situation, Indiana and Washington enacted overall statutory limitations in 1932, and Michigan, New Mexico, and West Virginia adopted overall constitutional rate limits in 1933. In the same year, Ohio and Oklahoma further reduced the limits already in their constitutions. Nevada, in 1936, and Washington, in 1945, made their statutory restrictions constitutional.

These rate limits, albeit with some changes, have continued to the present time. The Advisory Commission on Intergovernmental Relations noted in its recent study that, as of 1962, forty-three states still "have constitutional and statutory restrictions which limit in varying degrees the power of local governments to raise property tax revenue." [20]

Property-Tax-Rate Limits in Illinois—A View in Depth

After abortive attempts from 1901 to 1929 to place a statutory limit on the aggregate tax rates which could be used by local governments, Illinois has turned to placing property-tax-rate limits on individual funds as one means of controlling local government expenditures. Since 1945, however, Illinois statutes have reflected an interesting variation from the common pattern which persists in the United States. At least two sets of rate limits have, in effect, been established for the same fund—the normal statutory limit and a rate, usually lower, determined by a complicated formula spelled out in the statutes. Additional statutory provisions have specified the means by which a local governmental unit could move from the lower, formula rate to the higher, statutory rate.

The Development of Property-Tax-Rate Limits in Illinois After 1945

It is a truism that the rate limitations become increasingly restrictive as property is assessed at a decreasing percentage of full value. Presumably this means that, prior to 1945, the many individual rates in effect in Illinois were less restrictive than their full potential, because a 1927 Illinois statute required that all property be assessed at its true full value. The full-value program was never really enforced, however. As a result, property throughout the state was assessed at values varying from 14 percent to 68 percent of full value. This policy naturally caused considerable anguish to the property owners who suffered from the inequities implicit in this situation. Local governmental units were also placed in a difficult position, because tax-rate limits inevitably had more restrictive effects when applied against a property-tax base assessed far below true value. In an attempt to rectify this situation, a so-called full-value-assessment program was passed during the 1945 session of the Illinois General Assembly and became effective in 1946. As a corollary to the full-value program, maximum tax-rate limits were reduced by one-half.[21]

Rates were halved on the theory that the state-wide assessment average was about 50 percent and that, consequently, increasing this average to 100 percent would double the taxes of most citizens. It was assumed that the 50 percent reduction in rates would keep the taxpayer's obligations about the same, but that both the taxpayer and the governmental unit would receive added benefits from the uniform assessment which was implicit in a full-value program guarded by an equalization policy supervised by the Property Tax Division of the State Department of Revenue. But the end result of the full-value assessment program when coupled with the one-half reduction in rate limits was to give counties with assessment ratios below 50 percent increases in their tax revenue, while at the same time reducing the amount of taxes receivable by counties with assessment ratios above 50 percent.[22]

To meet this problem, a formula was devised by the Illinois General Assembly for the purpose of obligating local government units to adopt limits which would, for the most part, return tax rates to their effective pre-1946 level.[23] The formula was to be used to determine rates until January 1, 1951, at which time the prerogative of determining rates according to other statutory provisions would be returned to local government officials.

Almost as soon as the formula went into effect, dispute arose as to its meaning. Two provisions were questioned in particular. One stated that "unless changed by referendum, 15 per cent was the largest proportion by which any tax rate might exceed the product of the 1942 ratio of assessed to full fair cash value times the maximum tax rate limit effective for the levy and assessment year 1942." [24] The second attempted to restrict any tax extension increase (a tax extension is the act of applying the tax rate against the value of the property involved) in any one year to 5 percent of the maximum extendible in 1942. Some people contended that the 5 percent limitation meant that the 1942 rate times assessed value of the same year could not be increased more than 5 percent each year, up to the maximum of 15 percent.[25] Others took a more liberal view and suggested that 5 percent each year was added to the total of the 1942 rate times the assessed value of the same year *plus* any increase up to 15 percent. The issue was ultimately decided in 1947 when the Illinois Supreme Court in *Grace Anderson* v. *the City of Park Ridge* (396 Ill. 235) declared in favor of the more liberal view. In the same year, however, the 65th Illinois General Assembly authorized a more restrictive formula by which rates were to be prescribed until December 31, 1952. Local governments would then be free to move to the higher statutory rates established in 1945.[26]

Once again, controversy arose concerning the answers to two major, interrelated questions: Were the rates as prescribed by the formula unrealistic in view of increased needs of local government, and how long could the General Assembly prescribe formula rates for local governments? Regarding the first issue, many agreed with the view expressed by Vernon Morrison that ". . . as the need for government revenues rose, numerous units and funds reached their tax limits. Many jurisdictions where demands for services increased but property values lagged found the new limits restrictive." [27] Regarding the second point, the statutes, as indicated above, called for a termination of local governments' obligations to compute rates by formula on December 31, 1952. Formula termination, therefore, became a crucial question. One group was anxious for the end of the prescribed formula in order to free local governments from its rates; the other, epitomized by the Taxpayers Federation of Illinois, was perturbed that unless "some new protections for the property taxpayers . . . [are] enacted by the General Assembly . . . the lid will be off in taxing power. . . ." [28]

The two divergent views were clearly illustrated in 1950 when the issue was brought before the State Supreme Court in *Kremers* v. *The City of West Chicago* (406 Ill. 546). This case concerned a city-library rate determined by formula which was made permanent by statute— apparently as a deliberate test. If the act had been allowed, all formula rates might have become permanent, and abandoning the formula on December 31, 1952, would, consequently, have been a meaningless process. The court did declare this rate unconstitutional, however, and some feel that this decision raised a serious question concerning the constitutionality of all rates determined by the formula.[29]

Whatever the implications of the Kremers' case, the Illinois General Assembly in 1951 passed legislation (commonly referred to as the Hodge-Downing Amendments) which called for the abrogation of the *formula provisions* by December 31, 1953, and for most governmental units to establish, by means of a resolution or an ordinance to be passed by December 31, 1951, what will be the "maximum tax rate limit in effect." [30]

Two major interpretations again developed. One view was that abandonment of the formula also implied abandonment of the rates determined by its provisions. According to this interpretation, statutory provisions which required governing bodies to move to the "tax rate limit in effect" by a resolution or ordinance passed by December 31, 1951, could only mean that local governments could now adopt any rate up to the maximum statutory rate established by the General Assembly in 1945. Any other interpretation, it was argued, would have the effect of binding local governments to the formula provisions even though such provisions were stricken from the statutes. Furthermore, it was maintained, any interpretation of the provisions which did not permit local governments to move beyond the formula rates and had the effect of making the formula rate permanent was unconstitutional in view of the State Supreme Court's declaration in *Kremers* v. *The City of West Chicago.* In spite of these arguments, others declared flatly that "those rate limitations determined by formula became permanent on December 31, 1951, unless taxing bodies by that date increased them by referenda." [31]

As a result, the tax-rate-limit picture since 1951 has been one of immense confusion with most governmental units operating under formula rates,[32] but with some utilizing the higher, statutory rates. A number of Illinois Supreme Court decisions on the issue did little to clarify the situation [33] until the case of *People* v. *New York City Railroad Company* (22 Ill.2d 266) in March of 1961. In this decision, the Court reaffirmed, first, that rates in existence on January 1, 1946, and not increased by referenda, "should be computed according to the formula . . . even though the formula provisions themselves expired," and, second, that formula provisions, at least for the county, are constitutional.

Thus, after sixteen years of doubt, some grounds exist for determining the property-tax rates legally applicable to local governments, i.e., unless exceptions are provided, rates are to be set at a pre-1946 level as determined by a formula.

An Analysis of Property-Tax Rates Determined by Formula

As noted above, the basic purpose of determining rates by the various formulae was to maintain rates at the same amount as before the full-value legislation of 1945, although small increases were permitted by the formula and additional rate increments could be obtained by referenda.[34] This policy was based on the supposition that the combination of limited local rate adjustments and of uniform assessment at full value as enforced by state and local equalization programs would permit local governments adequate revenue. An important corollary assumption must have been that increased property values throughout the years would provide the base for any additional property-tax revenues needed by the local governments.

The primary questions to be raised, therefore, concerning the existence of rates determined by formula are, first, whether such rates are actually equivalent to the rates before the full-value program of 1945 (as was purportedly the design of the statutes), and, second, whether state equalization and natural increase in property values have been sufficient to provide additional revenues to local governments bound by formula rates. An examination of the corporate

rate (the general "housekeeping" fund which the county uses for a variety of purposes including salaries and maintenance of county facilities) of Illinois counties is helpful in obtaining answers to these queries.

Regarding the first point, the Illinois Department of Revenue noted that comparison of the county corporate rate determined by formula to the 25-cent rate permitted before 1945 (counties could levy taxes before 1945 in an amount not to exceed 25 cents for every $100 of assessed value) would be misleading "since no account . . . would be taken of year-to-year variation in the ratio of assessed to full or market valuation of property." [35] One acceptable method of determining the effective rate before the full-value program is to measure the 25-cent rate in each county according to the assessment ratio (assessed value as compared to full value) which existed before the full-value program.[36]

As Table 10.1 indicates, assessment ratios for counties presently subject to the county corporate formula rate varied from 14 percent to 47 percent. Table 10.2 illustrates that, in all instances, the effective 1945 county corporate rate was far below the actual 25-cent rate permitted. As the third column of this table shows, the effective county corporate rates are similar to the rates presently prescribed for the county corporate fund by formula. Indeed, a comparison of the specific effective corporate rates to the formula rates revealed that the formula rate in 35 counties is substantially the same as the effective county corporate in 1945; and the formula rate in 39 counties is

Table 10.1—1945 Assessment Ratios in Selected Illinois Counties [a]

Number of Counties	Ratio of assessed value to full value
1	47–45
9	44–40
10	39–35
15	34–30
21	29–25
15	24–20
2	19–15
1	14

[a] Eighteen Illinois counties whose county corporate rates are excepted from the formula provisions are not included in this table or those which follow.

Source: The 1945 assessment ratios were obtained from the Illinois Department of Revenue, *Illinois Property Tax News Letter, No. 6* (Springfield, July, 1949), pp. A1–A3.

Table 10.2—Illinois County Corporate Rates in 1945
Compared with Present Formula Corporate Rates

Tax Rate in Cents [a]	1945 Effective Rate—No. of Counties [b]	Existing Formula Rate—No. of Counties
11.5 to 12.0	1	1
11.0 to 11.5	3	3
10.5 to 11.0	4	2
10.0 to 10.5	2	6
9.5 to 10.0	5	7
9.0 to 9.5	3	4
8.5 to 9.0	1	5
8.0 to 8.5	6	10
7.5 to 8.0	7	11
7.0 to 7.5	8	4
6.5 to 7.0	7	10
6.0 to 6.5	11	4
5.5 to 6.0	7	4
5.0 to 5.5	3	—
4.5 to 5.0	2	3
4.0 to 4.5	—	—
3.5 to 4.0	1	—

[a] Rate figures are given in cents per $100 of assessed valuation.

[b] The statutory county corporate rate in 1945 from which the effective rate is derived was 25 cents. The effective rate was determined by multiplying the statutory rate against the 1945 assessment ratios.

somewhat higher than the effective county corporate rate in 1945.[37] According to these figures, then, one announced purpose of the formula-rate program, i.e., maintaining rates at approximately their 1945 levels, was apparently achieved.

The second part of the original query—i.e., whether state equalization and increased property values have provided significant increases in the revenue available from formula rates—is still unanswered, however. A comparison of the amount of revenue available to county corporate funds from the formula rate with the amount of revenue available from the effective rates existing in 1945 is one obvious method of determining the maximum county corporate extension possible under the applicable rates when applied against the existing assessed valuations. Table 10.3 indicates that, in 1960, the maximum county corporate rate in 16 counties could have yielded over $100,000 more in revenue than the 1945 maximum effective county corporate rate; $50,000 to $100,000 in additional revenue was

Table 10.3—Dollar Increase in Illinois Corporate Revenue from 1945 to 1960 [a]

Number of counties	Dollars
16	100,000 and over
15	50,000 to 100,000
16	25,000 to 50,000
24	10,000 to 25,000
3	5,000 to 10,000

[a] This data was obtained by multiplying the formula rate against the 1960 assessed valuations of the selected counties.

available in 15 counties; $25,000 to $50,000 more in 16 counties; $10,000 to $25,000 more in 24 counties; and $5,000 to $10,000 more in 3 counties. These figures do not tell us whether, along with the additional revenue available in 1960, there was also an increase in the uses to which this revenue was committed or what the additional cost of this expanded obligation would be, but they do at least suggest that a combination of changing valuations since 1945 and the program of state property-tax equalization has provided an absolute increase in the total revenue available from rates established according to a 1945 base.

Table 10.4 suggests, however, that any conclusions drawn from this absolute increase in revenue must be drastically modified after a comparison is made of the value of the dollar in 1960 and in 1945. The Bureau of Labor Statistics found that, using 1947–49 as the base, a consumer price index of all items indicates that the dollar was worth 79.1 cents in 1960 compared to $1.30 in 1945.[38] This means, in effect, that the value of the dollar in 1960 was approximately 60.85 percent of the value of the dollar in 1945. When the maximum amount of increased revenue permitted in 1960 is multiplied by this percentage

Table 10.4—Actual Increase in Value of Illinois Corporate Revenue from 1945 to 1960

Number of counties	Dollars
1	100,000 and over
2	100,000 to 50,000
3	50,000 to 25,000
4	25,000 to 10,000
17	10,000 to 0
46	*Less in 1960 than in 1945*

to obtain the actual value of this increase, one receives a very different impression of how effective the formula rates have actually been in providing these counties with additional revenues. Table 10.4 reveals that, if the value of the dollar in 1960 is compared with the value in 1945, the money obtained in 1960 from the county corporate rate has actually decreased in value in forty-six counties. In seventeen counties, there were only very moderate revenue increases of up to $10,000, while four counties received from $10,000 to $25,000 more in 1960 than they did in 1945. Three counties increased their revenue from the county corporate rate from $25,000 to $50,000; two counties increased their revenue from $50,000 to $100,000; and only one county increased its revenue by more than $100,000. It is significant that all the counties obtaining more than a $25,000 increase are considered metropolitan in nature and that four of these six counties are located in the Cook County–Chicago area. In each of these counties, population and assessed valuation have also increased substantially.

Thus, if one can use the county corporate rate as the standard for other rates, one must conclude that the formula rates set on a 1945 base and applied against existing assessed valuations have, in most instances, restricted local-government revenues to an amount equal to, or less than, the amount they received in 1945.[39]

An Evaluation

The Validity of Rate Limits

The debate over the validity of rate limits has raged ever since this device was first employed to restrict the use of the property tax. Essentially, proponents of the property-tax rate suggest that it is an acceptable technique for the following reasons:[40]

a) By limiting the amount of revenue which can be obtained from the property tax, the local government is forced to seek other sources of non-property revenue, thereby lessening the tax load on the beleaguered property owner.

b) Lower rate limits can be an inducement to attract industry into a community.

c) The use of tax-rate limitations will mean that the local governmental unit will have to take a new look at the various services it provides in order to determine whether they should be offered locally or by the state with its broader tax base.

d) The use of tax-rate limitations can mean that there will be an enlargement of state aid in order to provide adequate finances for the services provided locally.

e) The limited amount of property-tax revenue available because of rate limits will force local governments to be more exacting in their budget practices.

f) A limitation of particular funds by the state legislature will ultimately aid in providing greater uniformity in the various services offered.

g) The limitation on property-tax revenue, in combination with the demands of competing local governments for the tax dollar, will ultimately hasten the simplification and reduction of local governments.

On the other hand, those who oppose the rate limit as a revenue-control device suggest that:

a) The history of tax-rate-limit legislation clearly demonstrates that there are so many exceptions to and outright violations of the limits that they are really ineffective.

b) Whenever a governmental unit does adopt a non-property tax to supplement its property-tax revenue, it is very difficult to determine whether such adoptions represented a natural development in taxing powers or were a result of the tax-rate limitations.

c) There is disagreement over whether new sources of local revenue, usually regressive in nature, lessen the tax load on the majority of those who pay property taxes, the owners of single-family dwellings.

d) There must be some doubt that the transfer of local government services to the state is a desirable trend, not only because of the added costs for the state, but because of the implications in terms of local government autonomy.

e) Although additional subsidization by the state may be welcome locally, the added expense may place a serious drain on the state's fiscal resources.

f) The entire tax-rate-limit concept implies state control over a very fundamental local government prerogative—local budget-making.

g) There is no evidence to suggest that local government reorganization, where it has occurred, is related to the existence of tax-rate limits.

h) The major contention of proponents of property-tax-rate limitations is that they benefit those who pay property taxes. Implicit in this major argument is the assumption that owners pay all of the taxes levied against their property. Macy argues, however, that, while taxes on owner-occupied homes are not easily shifted, levies on income-producing properties "are costs which . . . enter into the pricing process and are shifted to the consumers. . . . It is apparent [then] that the ultimate beneficiaries of property tax limitations are difficult to determine, a circumstance which weakens the case of those who contend that property owners are the parties who should be given tax relief and that limitations on property taxes will accomplish this objective." [41]

It seems to me that this highly legalistic debate is for the most part uninformative. There seems little point in analyzing whether rate limits which are already in existence are economically justifiable or whether they accomplish their announced goals. It was suggested above that local "governments" represent, for the most part, a community of interest groups which are activated in response to the prevailing issues of the moment. Accordingly, an analysis of rate limits in terms of this theoretical framework would seem to be the most fruitful approach.

If the concept of "local government" can be defined in this fashion, one no longer need visualize the interests of political officials and of other, non-governmental groups as being incompatible or in opposition to each other. One may recognize, for example, that a basic area of local government such as the taxation of property concerns both the political elite and groups of property owners to an equal degree.

If this view is proper, there is no particular reason for suggesting that a limit upon the use of the property tax is detrimental to the local community. That is to say, interests representing property owners need not be concerned with the effect of such limits upon the local government as represented by the political elite, because that elite is merely considered as another group within the community. The history of rate-limit implementation in the United States and in Illinois can best be understood using this analytical tool.

Thus, as indicated in the historical survey above, elected and appointed elites of the local community, using the powers given to them as political representatives, heavily indebted their communities after the Civil War. Since such a course severely affected property interests, and since property owners existed as a co-equal group within the local community, the reaction (i.e., restriction of the ability of the political elite to assume ascendancy in this area of activity) was to be anticipated. Limitations on debt and on tax rates inevitably followed as a result of the successful efforts of such interest groups at another level of political community—the state legislatures. The chain of events during the Great Depression can be similarly explained as the necessary reaction by the property groups to a situation resulting from the activities of the political elites. The present existence of rate limits, albeit with less stringent provisions, indicates the continued vigilance of property interests within the community of local interests.

A detailed examination of the Illinois experience illustrates the sort of interplay between the political representatives of the community and the property-interest groups which seems to have occurred all over the nation throughout history.

It is common knowledge that the first establishment of the formula rates in 1945 was primarily the result of the activities of allied property interests in the State. Indeed, the very interpretation of these complicated rates was the responsibility of the spokesmen of this group.[42]

It is, furthermore, not improper to view each of the court tests described as a contest (or "game" to use Norton Long's terminology) [43] between the political representatives of the local and the state communities and the groups representing the combined interests of property owners. Court decisions upholding the use of formula rate limits, despite their restrictive nature, are sufficient proof of how effectively property groups have argued their case.

It is interesting to note that, where the formula rates have been eliminated or eased in Illinois, this modification has been the result of direct negotiations between the representatives of the political and the property-tax groups. During the 1965 legislative session, for example, the Illinois County Problems Commission obtained an agreement from the property-tax groups to support an increase in the county corporate rate; only after this agreement was reached did the Illinois General Assembly approve the bill allowing the additional rate.[44] It will be recalled from the preceding analysis of the Illinois situation, however, that the ability of the county representatives to raise adequate revenue from the property tax has been severely restricted for years by the formula rate as applied to the county corporate fund.

Conclusions

The analysis presented is not intended as a normative judgment of how local political processes *ought* to operate. It has been offered instead as a preliminary evaluation of how the process does operate—at least so far as this particular issue is concerned.

Long has indicated that the situation in which the local-government office holder in effect responds to demands and mediates conflicts is encouraged by the fact that, although local politicians "have the formal governmental office that might give them responsible governing roles . . . their lack of status makes it both absurd and presumptuous that they should take themselves so seriously." [45] Under these circumstances, therefore, only an increase in the prestige of local politicians can significantly augment their relationship vis-à-vis the other groups in the community. And increased prestige, in turn, can only come, if the analysis presented here is accurate, to the extent that the local community becomes a local "government." It is no accident that rate limits in Illinois were applied most severely to the county.

The status of the local community and its political representatives will improve, however, only when the other groups of the community are persuaded that the political elite can meet the needs of the local community with adeptness, sophistication, talent, and perception. Such recognition should also bring from non-governmental groups a willingness to expand the powers of the political elite to meet the traditional governmental problems affecting the geographical areas contained within their communities.

Until this transition from local communities to local governments occurs, one must continue to view the political process at the local level as an "ecology of games."

Notes

1 For example, note the emphasis upon liberty, equality, and welfare as the basic values to be preserved by such a division of powers in Arthur Maass, ed., *Area and Power: A Theory of Local Government* (Glencoe, Ill.: The Free Press, 1959), *passim*.

2 See, for example, Paul Ylvisaker, "Some Criteria for a 'Proper' Areal Division of Governmental Powers," in *ibid.*, pp. 27–49.

3 Note the following literature as illustrative of this view: Frank J. Goodnow, "The Work of the American Political Science Association," *Proceedings of the American Political Science Association*, 1 (Lancaster, Pa.: Wickersham Press, 1905), 45–54; and W. W. Willoughby, *The Nature of the State* (New York: Macmillan, 1896).

4 See Warren Miller and Donald E. Stokes, "Constituency Influence in Congress," *American Political Science Review*, 62 (1963), 45–56 *passim*.

5 The literature on "group" activity is abundant. It is still proper, however, to cite Arthur Bentley, *The Process of Government* (San Antonio: Principia Press of Trinity University, 1949), and David Truman, *The Governmental Process* (New York: Alfred A. Knopf, 1951). For an

excellent review of such literature see Harmon Zeigler, *Interest Groups in American Society* (Englewood Cliffs, N.J.: Prentice-Hall, 1964), Chap. 1; and *American Political Science Review*, Vol. 54 (1960): R. E. Dowling, "Pressure Group Theory: Its Methodological Range," 944–54 *passim;* Myran Q. Hale, "The Cosmology of Arthur F. Bentley," 955–61 *passim;* Robert T. Golembiewski, "The Group Basis of Politics: Notes on Analysis and Development," 962–71 *passim.* (These articles appear under the general title "Bentley Revisited.")

6 As classic illustrations of this fact, see Peter H. Odegard, *Pressure Politics: The Story of the Anti-Saloon League* (New York: Columbia University Press, 1928); E. Pendleton Herring, *Group Representation before Congress* (Baltimore, Md.: The Johns Hopkins Press, 1929); and E. E. Schattschneider, *Politics, Pressures and the Tariff* (Englewood Cliffs, N.J.: Prentice-Hall, 1935).

7 See, for example, Leonard D. White, *The States and the Nation* (Baton Rouge: Louisiana State University Press, 1953), p. 3.

8 Norton Long, "The Local Community as an Ecology of Games," in *The Polity* (Chicago: Rand McNally, 1962), pp. 146–47.

9 See, for example, Floyd Hunter, *Community Power Structure: A Study of Decision Makers* (Chapel Hill: University of North Carolina Press, 1958); Robert Dahl, *Who Governs?* (New Haven, Conn.: Yale University Press, 1961); Robert Presthus, *Men at the Top* (New York: Oxford University Press, 1964); and Robert E. Agger, Daniel Goldrich, and Bert E. Swanson, *The Rulers and the Ruled* (New York: John Wiley and Sons, 1964).

10 Robert Dahl, "Power, Pluralism and Democracy: A Modest Proposal," an unpublished paper delivered at the 1964 annual meeting of the American Political Science Association, Chicago, September, 1964.

11 *Ibid.*

12 See, for example, Advisory Commission on Intergovernmental Relations, *State Constitutional and Statutory Restrictions on Local Taxing Powers* (Washington, D.C.: U.S. Government Printing Office, 1962).

13 *Ibid.,* p. 19.

14 For example, see A. Miller Hillhouse and Ronald B. Welch, *Tax Limits Appraised* (Public Administrative Service, No. 55; Chicago, 1937); Glen Leet and Robert Paige, eds., *Property Tax Limitation Laws* (Public Administration Service, No. 36; Chicago, 1936); C. Ward Macy, "Property Tax Limitations Re-examined," National Tax Association, *1961 Proceedings of the Fifty-Fourth Annual Conference on Taxation,* ed. Walter J. Kress (Harrisburg, 1962) pp. 50–99; Irving Howards, "Property Tax Rate Limits in Illinois and Their Effect upon Local Government," *National Tax Journal,* 16 (September, 1963), 285–93; and Advisory Commission on Intergovernmental Relations, *State Constitutional and Statutory Restrictions on Local Taxing Powers.*

15 See, for example, Rodney L. Mott and W. O. Suiter, "The Types and Extent of Existing Tax Limitations," in Leet and Paige, eds., *Property*

Tax Limitation Laws, pp. 41–45; and Advisory Commission on Inter-governmental Relations, *State Constitutional and Statutory Restrictions on Local Taxing Powers.*

16 Irving Howards, *Selected Aspects of State Supervision over Local Government in Illinois* (Carbondale: Public Affairs Research Bureau, Southern Illinois University, 1964), p. 26.

17 *Ibid.,* pp. 52–53, 61. See also Advisory Commission on Intergovernmental Relations, *State Constitutional and Statutory Restrictions on Local Government Debt* (Washington, D.C.: U.S. Government Printing Office, 1961); Francis L. Starner, *General Obligation Bond Financing by Local Governments: A Survey of State Controls* (Berkeley: Bureau of Public Administration, University of California, 1961); A. U. Millhouse, *Municipal Bonds, A Century of Experience* (New York: Prentice Hall, 1936); and Leroy A. Shattuck, Jr., *Municipal Indebtedness, A Study of Debt-to-Property Ratio* (Baltimore, Md.: The Johns Hopkins Press, 1940).

18 Advisory Commission on Intergovernmental Relations, *State Constitutional and Statutory Restrictions on Local Government Debt,* p. 20.

19 Advisory Commission on Intergovernmental Relations, *State Constitutional and Statutory Restrictions on Local Taxing Powers,* pp. 29–30.

20 *Ibid.,* p. 39.

21 Ill. Rev. Stats. (1945), c. 120, §§ 627, 643a.

22 Irving Howards, "The Tax Rate Limit Controversy in Illinois," *Current Economic Comment,* 19 (February, 1957), 25.

23 "Effective rate," as used here, suggests the revenue obtained when the statutory rate was applied to the assessed valuation.

24 Ill. Rev. Stats. (1945), c. 120, § 643a.

25 Maurice Scott, "The ABC's of Illinois' Most Serious Tax Problems," *The Illinois Taxpayer,* 6, No. 7 (August–September, 1946), 5.

26 Ill. Rev. Stats. (1949), c. 120, § 643a.

27 Vernon Morrison, "Property Tax Limitations," *Report of the Revenue Laws Commission of the State of Illinois* (Springfield: State of Illinois, 1947), p. 126.

28 Taxpayers Federation of Illinois, *Taxpayers Federation of Illinois Tax Clinic—Proceedings,* ed. Maurice Scott (Springfield, 1958), p. 11.

29 Howards, "The Tax Rate Limit Controversy in Illinois," p. 28.

30 Ill. Rev. Stats. (1953), c. 120, § 643b. Taxing districts with a population of more than 500,000 and town-fund and bond statutes were exempted. Rates could not be lower than the amount necessary to qualify for state aid.

31 Taxpayers Federation of Illinois, *Tax Clinic—Proceedings,* p. 10.

32 As will be noted, a variety of rates have been excepted from the provisions of the formula.

33 For example, note *People* v. *Touchette,* 5 Ill.2d 303 (1955); *People* v. *Chicago, Burlington and Quincy Railroad,* 8 Ill.2d 257 (1956).

34 More liberal provisions were ultimately made for districts created after

1945, or for funds being used for the first time after that date, on the theory that the property owner involved was being taxed for these purposes *after* the full-value program. Accordingly, there was no need for determining these rates by a formula geared to taxes as they were before 1945.

35 Illinois Department of Revenue, *Illinois Property Tax Statistics* (Springfield: State of Illinois, May, 1946), p. 2.

36 Illinois Department of Revenue, *Illinois Property Tax Statistics*. The year 1945 was used as a base for determining the effective rate since it was the last year before the full-value program.

37 A formula rate was considered higher than the effective county corporate rate existing in 1945 if it varied from the 1945 effective rate by .5 cent or more.

38 U.S. Department of Labor, Bureau of Labor Statistics, *Monthly Labor Review*, Vol. 83, 1960 Statistical Supplement, Part 1 (1961), Table IV–1, p. 19; and Vol. 78, No. 6 (June, 1955), Table D–4.

39 The analysis in this section is abstracted from Howards, "Property Tax Rate Limits in Illinois."

40 The following summary of views is taken from Howards, *Selected Aspects*, pp. 24–26.

41 C. Ward Macy, "Property Tax Limitations Re-examined."

42 As consultant to the Illinois Commission on County Government, this author has had abundant opportunity to view this situation and, indeed, to seek advice from this interest group about the meaning of the formula-rate provisions.

43 Long, "The Local Community."

44 See Illinois Senate Bill 1058, *Legislative Synopsis and Digest of the Seventy-Fourth General Assembly* (Springfield: State of Illinois, Legislative Reference Bureau, May, 1965), p. 288. It should be noted that the Commission had been unsuccessful in making a similar recommendation without agreement from the property-tax groups. See, for example, County Problems Commission, *Report to Governor Otto Kerner and the 73rd General Assembly of Illinois* (Springfield: State of Illinois, 1963), pp. 11–12.

45 Long, "The Local Community," p. 146.

11. Joan E. O'Bannon

Payments from Tax-Exempt Property

Various properties, both private and government owned, are exempt from the property tax. Exemptions of private property and state- and local-government property differ from state to state, but exemptions for federal property are uniform. In some instances, substitute payments have been instituted to remunerate governments for properties exempt from the tax. This paper will first explore the types of exemptions and the reasons for exempting private property and federal-, state-, and local-government property from taxation. Next, the types and reasons for substitute payments made on the exempt properties will be discussed, and a concluding section will attempt to evaluate these substitute arrangements.

Exempt Property

Federal Lands

Although the United States Constitution does not specifically forbid the taxation of federal properties by state and local governments, the court's interpretation of this document has been that it exempts federal property from state and local taxation except as authorized by Congress. The immunity of federal properties was first declared in 1819 by the Supreme Court in the case of *McCulloch* v. *Maryland*.[1] In this case, the Supreme Court held that Maryland could not tax a bank which was United States property and engaged in business for the federal government and that no state could impede the operation of constitutional laws, which are the supreme laws of the land. It was ruled that taxation by the states of the property of the federal government would be an interference with the latter's sovereignty. If states were allowed to impose taxes on the exercise of power granted to the federal government by the Constitution, it would be possible to prevent the proper use of such federal powers. Chief Justice John Marshall stated in this case his oft-quoted dictum, "The power to tax involves the power to destroy." [2]

Since 1819, many cases have upheld this doctrine of immunity,[3] and, for a time, the decisions of the Supreme Court expanded the area of intergovernmental immunity to include public securities, public employees' salaries, patent royalties, and even public contractors' purchases.[4] About 1930, a trend toward limiting the application of intergovernmental immunity to cases which involved an actual or direct burden on the governmental unit gradually became discernible. For example, the immunity of patent royalties was reversed on the grounds that exemption from state taxation would benefit only the patentee, not the federal government.[5] Similar decisions reversed immunity of salaries.[6] The Court overruled earlier cases granting immunity to lessees of government land and sustained state taxes on income derived by independent contractors from work done for the federal government.[7]

Although the first court case dealing with the doctrine of immunity was in 1819, earlier examples of the immunity doctrine can be found. In Louisiana, the first territory acquired from a foreign country by the United States, an act on March 26, 1804, not only established territorial government but also stated that, "the Governor or legislative Council shall have no power over the primary disposal of the soil, nor to tax the lands of the United States." [8]

On April 28, 1806, Attorney General John Breckenbridge stated that there was no power in the council or the departments of Orleans territory to tax property of the United States. Exercise of this power had never been tried before in the United States, and he did not think that the principle should now be admitted. The levying of the tax would be harmless, he thought, for there was no way payment could be enforced.[9] This is the earliest known legal opinion on the question.

By the acts of 1811 and 1912, which admitted Louisiana to the union, the people of the territory disclaimed any right to waste or unappropriated lands and agreed, furthermore, that each and every tract of land sold by the United States would be exempt from taxation for five years after the sale and that no taxes would be levied on the property of the United States.[10] Other states admitted to the union also have similar provisions in their admission acts. A study of the proceedings by which the states became members of the union shows, in fact, that the states were expressly forbidden to tax United States lands.[11]

Private, State-Government, and Local-Government Lands

Exemption of private property, and of state-government and local-government property varies from state to state. Because of the multiplicity of such laws, it is inexpedient to enumerate the exemptions on a state-by-state basis. Nevertheless, certain generalizations can be drawn.

The major reason that state and local governments do not tax their own property is because this, in effect, would mean the transfer of money from one pocket to another; to save on bookkeeping, it is, therefore, advisable to exempt this property. Nor are local units usually allowed to tax state-government property or other local-government property. This prohibition may exist because of the difficulties involved in assessing such property or because it is believed that local units would compete for new buildings and improved property to be paid for by the other governmental unit.

Non-profit institutions—institutions for educational, religious, or charitable purposes—have traditionally been exempt from the property tax. These institutions generally serve a function which the government would have to perform in their absence or which are socially desirable but not the proper function of government, such as religion. Rather than tax them and reapportion the money, the state contributes to the institution an amount of money equal to the value of its property tax.[12] Exemptions for religious institutions can be traced to an earlier period when the state undertook to support the church. The practice has continued since the separation of church and state, although the obligation no longer exists.

In the twentieth century, the property tax has been increasingly criticized for the relatively heavy burden it places on real estate in comparison with the lighter tax burden on other objects. As a result of these criticisms, state legislatures have exempted numerous and varied real estate properties from the tax. Discrimination against real estate still exists, however. For example, some states, such as New York, have completely abolished the personal-property tax, but retain a real estate tax, while others have exempted only intangibles.[13] Some states discriminate by placing a lower tax rate or assessment value on intangibles (and sometimes on tangibles) than on real property.

Homestead exemptions are found in about 20 percent of the states. This exemption was granted to encourage home ownership as well as to provide relief from the burdensome property tax. The exemption was first granted by Texas in 1932 and had spread by 1938 to thirteen states. It resulted from a basic need to reform the property tax but has instead increased inequities by redistributing the tax burden to individuals still subject to the tax payment.[14] Farm properties are frequently exempted from the tax, and veterans and widows are often granted special homestead exemptions. Our gratitude to veterans, however, is quite uneven, since the amount of exemption varies directly with variations in state taxes and assessment rates.

As an inducement to home building, housing projects are exempted or given special, favorable treatment in some states. This exemption favors low-income groups and places an increased burden on other home builders and owners. Likewise, a number of states grant five- to ten-year exemptions to new industries as an inducement to locate in their state. Other properties that are sometimes exempt include municipally owned utilities, fraternal orders, business and professional associations (such as dental and medical societies), and groups which are considered to serve the public good rather than just the good of their members (such as the Girl Scouts and the Young Men's Christian Association).[15]

Substitute Payment Arrangements

Types of Federal Payments

The immunity from taxation legally granted to all federal property is fully maintained in many instances, and no payment is made to the areas where this property is located. Among these properties are those which provide services to the local area, for example: post offices, courthouses, customhouses, weather stations, hospitals, cemeteries, and most reclamation projects. Other property—such as river and harbor projects, lighthouses, and radio stations—is exempt because its facilities are designed to promote commerce. Still other lands are exempt because they are used for such traditional governmental functions as mints, immigration stations, penal institutions, national parks, and national defense properties. Finally, the various federal office buildings devoted to the general administration of government are exempt. Congress has authorized certain payments to be made on some types of federal property, however. Three types of arrangements —in-lieu payments, *ad valorem* taxation, and shared revenues—exist for making these payments, and the method used varies with the type of property involved.

In-Lieu Payments.—Congress has, in some cases, authorized pay-

ments to state or local units based on the value of the federal property
or on the cost of local service rendered to it or to the persons occupying the property. In others, it has based the payments on tax equivalents, making adjustments for burdens and benefits conferred on the
locality by the federal holding. These are known as in-lieu payments.
Specific provisions for in-lieu tax payments vary—some require payment; others merely permit payment. In-lieu payments to state and
local units have been utilized primarily for housing properties of the
Housing and Home Finance Agency. They have also been extended,
however, to Atomic Energy Commission properties, surplus properties,
lands acquired for certain public works, some forest lands, some
properties of the Farmers Home Administration, "Case Wheeler Act"
lands, and land for resettlement and rehabilitation purposes.

Ad Valorem Taxation.—Congress has also consented to a second
method of remunerating state and local units, allowing the application of *ad valorem* taxes to some types of federal property. Congressional consent to full *ad valorem* taxation of federal property by
state and local governments has been limited to the taxation of
property owned by the federal banking or credit agencies. Much of
this property was acquired principally as a result of foreclosures in
the process of lending operations and is temporarily being held by
federal agencies, pending disposition to private persons.

Shared Revenues.—The third and final method of remunerating
state and local governments for federally owned property is shared
revenues. The largest portion of the lands in federal ownership are
covered by this arrangement. Shared revenues are historically the
oldest type of federal payment to state and local units for federal
holdings and are currently the most important in terms of amounts
paid for these holdings. Payments are based on a percentage of the
revenue derived from activities on certain federal lands, with percentages paid ranging from 5 percent to 75 percent depending on the
type of land.[16] In general, the lands are large, little-improved tracts
lying in rural areas. Moreover, the great bulk of them are part of the
public domain and have never been on the local property-tax rolls.

Reasons for Federal Payments

Sharing of revenue is the oldest type of payment on federal property to states. The initial reason for shared-revenue payments can be
traced back to the act which admitted Ohio to the union in 1803.
This act provided, in part, that the state should receive 3 percent of
the net proceeds from the sale within the state of public lands for the
construction of roads and that 5 percent of the net proceeds was to

be used by Congress for the construction of roads leading to and through the state. In return, Ohio agreed to exempt from taxation all land sold by the government for five years from the date of sale.[17] Similar provisions became quite common in subsequent statutes admitting other states.

Toward the end of the nineteenth century, the emphasis of federal policy shifted from disposing of public lands to conserving them. With this conservation policy came the withdrawal of the public domain and a rift in federal-state relations which has not been entirely mended to this day. Withdrawal meant less land for settlers and, consequently, a slowed rate of state development. As a result, sharing revenue became a method used by the federal government to compensate the states for loss of potential tax revenue. A more detailed description of the change in conservation policy and the consequent agitation for substitute payments follows.

Reservation of Public Land.—Before 1891, reservation of the public domain was limited. In 1817, the President had been given power by Congress to reserve public lands from entry for certain purposes.[18] The main purpose for reserving the public domain was to secure supplies of timber for the navy. This power was exercised for a second purpose, the creation of national parks, for the first time in 1832, at Hot Springs, Arkansas, but none of the reservations at this time were very large.[19] Not until 1871 was there an attempt to develop a comprehensive conservation policy. It appeared as a forestry bill.[20] The debate of this bill (H.R. 2197) indicated one of the grounds for the opposition between East and West which flourished in subsequent years on conservation topics. The East, which began to recognize its own folly in the destruction of forests, now hoped to preserve certain irreplaceable natural resources and spots of scenic beauty in the West. The West felt, on the other hand, that it should not be hampered in its quest for settlement and development. The bill was not passed.[21]

Agitation for forestry legislation continued, and, in 1891, an amendment (later known as the Forest Reserve Act) to the land act of that year authorized the President to withdraw public forest lands from entry and to establish forest reserves by proclamation.[22] President Cleveland subsequently reserved about 39,000,000 acres of forest land in the West, and President Roosevelt reserved all the remaining federal forest lands, about 44,000,000 acres, in Washington, Oregon, Montana, Idaho, Wyoming, and Colorado, causing much protest from the West, which felt it was entitled to these lands.[23]

Agitation for Shared Revenues.—Agitation for remuneration to states for public lands held in forest reserves began in 1906, when

Senator Heyburn of Idaho introduced a bill (S. 1661) calling for payment to states of the minimum value of lands previously granted to them for schools and now withdrawn into forest reserves.[24] Two bills (S. 5744 and H.R. 19575) proposing that states and counties be granted 10 percent of the money received from the sale of products from the forest reserves were also introduced at this time. The proposal for a 10 percent payment finally appeared as an amendment to the Agricultural Appropriations Act of 1906 which, after some debate, was passed into law.[25] In 1908, the amount of the payment was amended to 25 percent.[26] It has been said that if the provision for a sharing of revenues had not been adopted, some of the forestry programs could not have been enacted.[27]

Agitation for Payment Revision.—Because of the unprecedented acquisition of taxable lands for various federal projects in the 1930's, agitation broke out anew in this decade for a revision of payment arrangements. As the traditional functions of government expanded, more land was necessary to support increased departmental activities. Added to these new government land acquisitions were those of newly created agencies such as lending agencies and corporations engaged in quasi-business activities, in the production of power, and in urban housing and rural resettlement. Large acquisitions were made for defense purposes: forts, camps, firing ranges, docks, airfields, housing, and national defense plants. Even more significant was the expansion of government lands for conservation purposes. Conservation aims were coupled at this time with the desire to increase employment through extensive development work on the land, and increased employment was, in fact, stipulated as a purpose of the emergency funds made available for conservation.[28]

By 1940, some 65 percent of the approximately 34,000,000 acres of land obtained for conservation purposes had been acquired between 1933 and 1940. Slightly more than half of the forest lands and almost four-fifths of the Fish and Wildlife Service lands acquired were purchased in this period. Lands acquired for conservation amounted to 85 percent of the total land acquired for all purposes by 1940.[29]

This unprecedented acquisition of lands caused protests from local units throughout the nation. Senators from Arizona and North Dakota introduced a bill in 1935 to require payment of taxes on federal acquired lands, and, in 1936, four more bills were introduced by southern representatives for the same purpose.[30] Flocks of bills appeared in subsequent years. Acquisition of land stirred up the old western fight against federal retention of the public domain. Ironically, much of the land was purchased in the same western states in which public domain holdings were large. The western states again contended that withdrawal and purchase impaired the future growth of the tax base. These states had argued for years that Congress was required to dispose of these lands to private owners as rapidly as possible. They argued that failure to do so meant that they had not been admitted on an equal basis with the other states and that their state sovereignty was impaired.[31] Once again, speeches were made in Congress against these holdings.[32] The 1941 American National Livestock Association meeting adopted a resolution not to sell any more land to the United States in the eleven western states. Taxpayer associations registered protests. Attempts were made to deny public services to exempt federal properties and to their occupants.[33]

Congressional Studies.—The stir created in the early 1930's led President Roosevelt to appoint a committee in 1935 to undertake a study of federal ownership of real estate and its bearing on state and local taxation. This was the first of nine studies to be made in the next twenty years.[34]

Out of the reports of the various committees, many bills were presented to Congress, but little action was taken.[35] In general, the reports summarize the various payment arrangements for federal land and review the sources of discontent with these arrangements. All of the reports indicate a need for further study, and many of them recommend the establishment of some federal-state fiscal authority to review in-lieu problems for individual communities. All agree that no single solution is possible because of the range and technical complexities of the problems involved and their long, controversial history. Two different approaches to solutions are proposed in these reports. One set of proposals suggests that individual communities that are adversely affected by the present program be treated separately, in an attempt to find solutions for each community's individual problem. The other set of proposals recommends that each type of property under the present arrangements be considered separately and that a single solution be found for each type, regardless of its location.

These reports all recommend continuing the general policy of exempting federal property from state and local taxation. They also recommend that some type of payment arrangement be continued for most of these lands but that no payments be made for property which is primarily used to serve a local interest or which would be exempt from taxation if it were privately owned. Most of the reports consider some minimum payment necessary for lands under the shared-revenue program on which, for some reason, no revenue payments are made. Most of the reports state that the type of federal contribution made should take into account, not only the extent of the tax loss, but also the extent of benefits which the localities receive from federal ownership. In general, the suggested payment arrangements are designed for more careful and consistent treatment of exempt property.

Substitute Payments for Private, State-Government,
and Local-Government Property

Where the loss of money to a local government unit because of the exemption of state property or of property of other local governments produces a serious revenue problem, such properties may be subjected to the tax of the local unit in which it is located. More often, however, specific intergovernmental payments are made as substitutes for the tax.

In a few states which allow homestead and/or veterans exemptions, the state government provides funds to reimburse the taxing unit for the loss. In Louisiana, for example, homesteads in Orleans Parish are exempted from numerous taxes, and the State Treasurer is authorized to reimburse from a special fund any agency which loses revenue as a result of the exemption. Similar arrangements also exist for veterans. Maine reimburses municipalities for taxes lost from veterans' exemptions.

Substitute payments, in lieu of property taxes, are sometimes imposed on private businesses, since many are relatively permanent corporations with a great deal of property which is no longer bought and sold frequently enough to establish current market values. Office buildings, steel mills, railroad equipment, and even real estate, for example, are difficult to assess, and many states try to solve this problem by levying a tax on gross earnings rather than on capital values. Transportation companies, such as express agencies, pay a similar tax on gross earnings because the nature of their business makes the value of the property used in any one state a variable quantity.

Other in-lieu taxes on property include motor-vehicle license taxes and gross-production taxes, which are measured by value but are not direct property taxes. Growing crops are assessed in some states as part of the value of the land on which they are growing. In other states, these crops are exempted from the land assessment but are subject to a severance tax when harvested. In the majority of cases, however, no substitute payment arrangement exists for property that is exempt from the property tax.

Evaluation of Federal Payment Arrangements

Up to this point, the types of exempt properties and the substitute payments made for them have been noted. In this section federal payment arrangements will be evaluated. The nature and value of federal lands and the estimated taxes on them must be discussed, however, before the effect of these payment arrangements can be fully appreciated. Objections to shared revenues will then be noted, and these arguments will be evaluated in terms of a study made for national forest lands and wildlife refuges in the State of Louisiana. Finally, objections to in-lieu payments and to *ad valorem* taxation will be examined.

Nature of Federal Holdings

Total federal land holdings in the United States amount to about 770,000,000 acres, approximately one-third of the total area of the United States. These lands vary greatly in physical features, value, use, and significance to their locality. Their distribution is quite uneven. Table 11.1 shows that federal land area in five states amounts to more than 50 percent of the state's total area, while in six others federal ownership is less than 1 percent of total state land area. Even

Table 11.1—Percentage of Land Area in Federal Holdings in Each State: 1963

State	Percent
Alabama	3.3
Alaska	99.9*
Arizona	44.6
Arkansas	9.1
California	44.9
Colorado	36.1
Connecticut	0.2
Delaware	2.6
District of Columbia	28.9
Florida	9.6
Georgia	5.5
Hawaii	5.7
Idaho	63.8
Illinois	1.2
Indiana	1.5
Iowa	0.4
Kansas	0.9
Kentucky	4.2
Louisiana	3.6

(Table continued on following page)

Table 11.1 (continued)

State	Percent
Maine	0.6
Maryland	2.9
Massachusetts	1.3
Michigan	8.9
Minnesota	6.5
Mississippi	5.0
Missouri	3.8
Montana	29.7
Nebraska	1.4
Nevada	85.5
New Hampshire	12.2
New Jersey	2.1
New Mexico	34.9
New York	0.7
North Carolina	6.1
North Dakota	4.6
Ohio	0.8
Oklahoma	2.9
Oregon	52.1
Pennsylvania	2.0
Rhode Island	1.1
South Carolina	5.8
South Dakota	6.5
Tennessee	5.8
Texas	1.7
Utah	66.2
Vermont	4.3
Virginia	8.4
Washington	29.3
West Virginia	6.2
Wisconsin	5.1
Wyoming	48.3

[a] Figure based on 1962 estimate.

Source: U.S. General Services Administration, *Inventory Report on Real Property Owned by the United States Throughout the World,* as cited in U.S. Bureau of the Census, *Statistical Abstract of the United States* (Washington, D.C.: U.S. Government Printing Office, 1964), p. 195, Table 258.

more revealing is the fact that, excluding federal land holdings in Alaska, eleven of the western states—Arizona, California, Colorado, Idaho, Montana, Nevada, New Mexico, Oregon, Utah, Washington, and Wyoming—contain about 90 percent of federal land holdings within their boundaries, and that Alaska alone contains about 47 percent of all federal holdings.

While the acreage of federal holdings is fairly well established, the value of these lands is not. A study in 1937 placed the value of federal real property at 2.89 percent of the total assessed value of private assessed lands.[36] This figure is biased, as it omits many categories of federal property. In 1948, an estimate for the eleven western states mentioned above placed the ratio at 12.83 percent.[37] Although these states contain about 90 percent of federal land holdings, the value of this land is not 90 percent of the total value of federal holdings throughout the country because more federal rural land and fewer federal urban holdings of high value are to be found in these states than in many other states.

Estimates of the value of donated lands and public domain lands total approximately $16,000,000,000,[38] which is 6 percent of the total assessments made by local governments in 1961 on all taxable real estate. The $16,000,000,000 figure is very restricted since it does not include acquired lands; nor is it known how much of the public domain or donated lands would be subject to taxation.

Table 11.2 shows the value of tax-exempt government land in those nine states where these values have been estimated. These values have then been expressed as percentages of the total assessed value of

Table 11.2—Value of Exempt Property by Type of Government Ownership and Total Assessed Value of Taxable Land in Selected States

			Exempt Lands					
			Federal		State		Local	
State	Year	Total assessed value of taxable land (billions)	Value (billions)	Percent of total assessed value of taxable land	Value (billions)	Percent of total assessed value of taxable land	Value (billions)	Percent of total assessed value of taxable land
California	1964	36.74	6.25	17.01	3.34	9.09	9.94	27.05
Colorado	1964	3.92	.38	9.69	.04	1.02	.22	5.61
Connecticut	1961	9.80	.20	2.04	.28	2.86	.81	8.27
Massachusetts	1963	11.57	.30	2.59	.50	4.32	1.67	14.43
New York	1963	46.27	1.14	2.46	1.01	2.18	12.56	27.15
Ohio	1963	19.97	.41	2.05	.25	1.25	1.38	6.91
Oregon	1964	3.11	3.25	104.50	.43	13.83	1.02	32.80
Pennsylvania	1957	12.50	.29	2.32	.26	2.08	1.01	8.08
Washington	1964	3.84	.30	7.81	.10	2.60	.40	10.42

Source: Based on tax reports from the various states.

land subject to the property tax in each state to give an indication of the erosion of the property-tax base. Unfortunately, not all estimates were available for the same year. This is not a serious problem, however, since the years are sufficiently close together for meaningful comparisons to be made (with the possible exception of the data for Pennsylvania which were available only for 1957).

The largest estimated dollar exemption of federal land, $6,250,000,-000, was in California. The lowest estimate, $2,000,000, was in Connecticut. Connecticut also had the lowest estimate for the value of exempt land as a percentage of total assessed value—2.04 percent. At the other extreme, the value of exempt federal land in Oregon exceeded the value of land that was assessed: exempt property was 104.50 percent of total assessed property. Five of the nine states had exemptions which amounted to less than 3 percent of total assessed value, but the percentage of exemptions was larger in the other four states—17.01 percent in California, 9.69 percent in Colorado, 104.5 percent in Oregon, and 7.81 percent in Washington. It is noteworthy that these four states all contain fairly large holdings of federal lands.

Because no complete inventory of federal property exists, it is impossible to accurately estimate the theoretical taxes on this property. A general estimate made in 1949, however, placed them at $200,000,000 to $300,000,000 a year. In 1948, an estimate of taxes on federal real property, excluding river dam projects, in the eleven western states amounted to $93,500,000. The value of defense production facilities was estimated in 1954 at $115,000,000 to $127,000,000.[39]

In contrast to these estimates, federal compensation to states in the form of shared revenue amounted to only $19,000,000 in 1949.[40] Even the 1964 payments—the highest shared-revenue payments ever made—amounted to only $106,000,000.[41] Expenditures by the federal government for in-lieu payments and *ad valorem* taxation amount to less than shared revenues.[42]

Shared Revenues

Although the question of whether or not payments made by the federal government wholly compensate local governments for the loss of property-tax revenue cannot be answered with any certainty, complaints concerning federal payment arrangements usually center on their inadequacy. Dissatisfaction is also expressed for other reasons, however.[43]

Dissatisfaction with the shared-revenue program can arise for several reasons. First, no payment is made unless income is derived from the use of the land. If the use yields no income, then states or local units are not compensated at all for loss of property-tax revenue. Even when the lands yield some income, the percentage payment may not be sufficient to equal potential tax revenue.

Some of these properties, such as flood-control lands and wildlife refuges, may yield no direct monetary benefits. These lands are managed, not with a view to providing monetary returns, but in order to provide non-monetary benefits to the communities in which they are located or to communities remote from their location. For instance, building a dam prevents flooding of adjacent areas, but the dam itself yields no revenue. The protection and conservation of wildlife may yield no monetary return, but they yield benefits for aesthetic and recreational purposes.

In cases where payments are forthcoming, many of the counties concerned have been dissatisfied because the amount of payment fluctuates from year to year so that they are unable to depend on it for long-range financial planning. It has been charged that, under this arrangement, the largest contributions from the lands are received during periods of greatest general economic activity when they are least needed by the counties, whereas the smallest contributions are made when income from other sources is also at its lowest. If federal lands are in a depleted condition when they are acquired, many years may be required to restore them to productive use, and they will yield no revenue during this time.

A further problem with the shared-revenue program is that, in many instances, expenditure of contribution funds is limited to public schools and public roads. Because these two activities are presently financed by special taxes or allotments in many states, this limitation handicaps the counties' ability to use the funds in the most beneficial manner. Most counties argue that contributions could be used more effectively if they were a part of the general funds of the county.

These objections were substantiated in a previous study which compared shared-revenue payments with potential tax revenues over a period of years.[44] The study dealt with national forest lands and wildlife refuges in Louisiana. The nature of wildlife refuges is such that little or no revenue-producing activity is found on them. Marketable products, for the most part, are not produced on wildlife refuges, although small amounts of revenue are obtained as a by-product of conservation management—e.g., from the sale of sand or gravel from the refuge. Large revenues do result sometimes, however, from activities totally unconnected with conservation, such as the discovery of oil on the refuge.

It was found that no revenue was produced on some of the refuges studied. In these cases, the local government received no shared revenue, and potential tax revenues were, therefore, greater than federal payments. The local government did receive some shared revenues for other refuges, but federal payments for revenue derived from *conservation* activities on these lands have never exceeded potential tax revenues.[45] In addition, federal payments in any given year differed from refuge to refuge and also fluctuated widely from year to year on any given refuge.

In contrast to wildlife refuge lands, forest lands could be expected to produce a high income through the sale of forest products. The study showed that, in the early years of federal ownership, a smaller amount was paid to the state in the form of shared revenue than would have been received from potential tax revenue but that, in later years, shared-revenue payments exceeded potential tax revenue. This pattern of payments is characteristic of forest lands which were in a depleted, cutover condition when acquired by the Forest Service. Years of management were required before newly planted trees matured enough to provide valuable marketable products and, thus, large shared-revenue payments.

The study tried to determine whether the excesses of shared revenues over potential tax revenues in later years offset surpluses of potential tax revenues over shared revenues in the early years of the forest. A comparison showed that, up to 1961 at least, the local governments would have been better off if potential tax revenues had been collected. The surplus, however, was such that cumulative shared revenues would exceed cumulative potential tax revenues within a few years if the trend of increases in shared revenues continued. It was also noted that shared revenues did tend to fluctuate widely from year to year.

The tax structure of the local government seems to determine whether shared revenues exceed potential tax revenues. If the area is growing and developing quite rapidly, then it is possible that potential tax revenues might equal or surpass shared revenues. If, on the other hand, the area is not growing and developing rapidly, then shared revenues will most likely exceed potential tax revenues. Moreover, the fact that the forest exists could be a contributing factor to slow growth and development, since forest lands may take up the major portion of land in the county or may be scattered in such a way that private plots which exist are too small for any major development. In this case, shared revenues would compare favorably to potential tax revenues. Even when the local government does eventually receive more total revenue from shared revenues than it would have obtained in property-tax revenue, this usually occurs only after a number of years—in Louisiana, it was more than thirty years.

The objection to restrictions imposed on the local government's use of shared-revenue funds also seems valid. When general property taxes are collected, they go into a general fund to be used where the government finds the greatest need for them. When shared revenues replace these taxes, the government no longer has control over their use.

Other Federal Arrangements

Other federal arrangements for compensating local governments consist of direct payments in lieu of taxes and the relaxation of the exemption rule by consenting to pay the tax on certain properties. Some dissatisfaction has been expressed because—for fear of discrimination—in-lieu payments are determined by the federal government instead of by the local government. The critics of in-lieu payments feel that, if federal-government property were subject to full taxation, the government could protect its interests in the same way as any other taxpayer—through legal action. These critics also protest the practice of taking into account any benefits the local area might receive from federal ownership in determining the amount of in-lieu payments. For example, federal installations often supply their own water, fire protection, and so forth. Because these services are not required of the local unit, their value is often deducted from the tax-equivalent payment. Critics argue that local governments maintain these services anyway in case the federal services are withdrawn or inadequate. They also point out that some privately owned enterprises furnish their own services but still must pay taxes, and they contend that the value of federal services would be taken into account by local officials when the tax was computed wherever this practice was consistent with local policy regarding private property. Offsets for general economic benefits to the community, such as increased employment, are criticized because these benefits do not differ from those accruing from private industry. Furthermore, increases in employment and payrolls do not necessarily increase the value of the local property on which the local government is dependent for revenue.

A consent by the federal government to payment of property taxes would involve no problem for the local units except in those cases where only the real property of the federal government is taxable, and no taxes are paid on federal personal property. If local units levy a personal-property tax, non-exempt taxpayers bear a greater tax burden in proportion to the loss of tax revenue from property on which no payments are made. Although dissatisfaction with this arrangement is most severe where federal ownership results in the removal of existing property from the tax rolls, it occurs even when the federal government builds new industrial installations. Critics contend that this type of property is virtually identical to private installations engaged in the same type of production—the private installation is subject to property taxes, however.

Removal of property from the tax rolls can result either from acquisition of private lands by the federal government or from the transfer of public property from one federal agency that makes in-lieu payments to another federal agency that does not. In either case, the community is subjected to a deflated tax base rather suddenly and, in some cases, is rather severely affected. A payments problem is caused by the uneven distribution of land holdings rather than by the totality of holdings, and no urgent problem would arise from federal tax immunity if federal lands were uniformly distributed among all the local taxing units. Under these circumstances, the loss of tax revenue from federal property not required to pay its share of the cost of local government must still be met by a larger property-tax burden for the local taxpayer rather than by an increase in federal tax levies. According to the Commission on Intergovernmental Relations, however, this would present no problem because "the equality of [the] federal load on all communities and the general distribution of federal taxpayers would presumably mute local dissatisfaction and agitation for change in the tax status of federal property." [46]

Evaluation of Private, State Government, and Local Government Arrangements

The property tax is the chief source of revenue for local governments, and there is often no other major source of tax revenue available to them. In 1962, for example, 87.7 percent of local revenue came from the property tax.[47] As additional property has been exempted from taxation, local-government discontent has increased, and the already strained fiscal positions of local governments have become even more difficult.

Since property taxes provide the major tax revenue for the local government, any substitute payment arrangement for the tax is important. This section will evaluate private, state-government, and local-government substitute-payment arrangements. First, the value of exemptions from the property tax will be noted, and then non-federal in-lieu arrangements will be evaluated. Finally, arrangements which permit either full or partial exemption of payments will be discussed.

Value of Exempt Property

The total value of all exempt property in approximately three-fourths of the states is unknown. Tables 11.2 and 11.3 show the value of exempt property in those states where either partial or full value is known. Of the twenty-three states which have estimated the value of any exempt property within their boundaries, only thirteen have made an estimate of the total value of all exemptions—the other ten have made only partial estimates. As in Table 11.2, the estimates in Table 11.3 were not all available for the same year. Again, however, the years for which the estimates were made are sufficiently close together to permit meaningful comparisons. The estimates in these tables show how severely the property-tax base has been eroded by exemptions. The estimates shown most likely understate the true burden of exemption, since assessors do not change the evaluation as often on exempt property as on taxable property. Little, if any, effort is made to revise the original value placed on the exempt property.

In the thirteen states where estimates have been made of the total values of exemptions, these exemptions vary from 168.81 percent of the value of taxable property in Oregon to 15.37 percent in Ohio (Table 11.3). As noted above, the high percentage in Oregon is attributable to the large exemption of federal property, amounting to 104.5 percent of the total value of property subject to taxation. The value of exemptions for state-government property ranged from 13.83 percent in Oregon to 1.02 percent in Colorado, and the range for local-government property was from 32.80 percent in Oregon to 5.61 percent in Colorado (Table 11.2).

Private-property exemptions range from a high of 74.58 percent in Louisiana to a low of .53 percent in Idaho (Table 11.3). In both of these states, however, only partial information was available for the value of private property. The high rate in Louisiana is caused by the exemption of industrial plants. In some parishes in Louisiana the value of the plant exemptions exceeds the total assessed value of property for tax purposes—in Iberville Parish, for example, the value of plant exemptions is almost seven times greater than the total assessed value of non-exempt property. The value of private-property exemptions in states where complete data are available varies from a high of 19.38 percent in California to a low of 2.37 percent in Mississippi. The 19.38 percent figure is misleading, however, since four

Table 11.3—Total Assessed Value of Taxable Property in Selected States in Relation to Value of All Tax-Exempt Property and of Tax-Exempt Private Property

State	Year	Total assessed value (billions)	Total exempt lands (including government property)		Exempt private property	
			Value (billions)	Percent of total assessed value	Value (billions)	Percent of total assessed value
Alabama	1964	3.59	n.a.	—	.79 [a]	22.01
Arizona	1964	2.19	.12	5.48	n.a.	—
California	1964	36.74	26.65 [b]	72.54	7.12	19.38
Colorado	1964	3.92	.76 [b]	19.39	.12	3.06
Connecticut	1961	9.80	2.30 [b]	23.47	1.01	10.31
Florida	1964	13.83	n.a.	—	4.95 [c]	35.79
Georgia	1964	5.02	n.a.	—	1.18 [d]	23.51
Idaho	1964	.76	n.a.	—	.004 [e]	.53
Indiana	1964	6.26	n.a.	—	1.03	16.45
Louisiana	1964	4.13	n.a.	—	3.08 [f]	74.58
Maine	1963	2.34	1.02	43.59	.21	8.97
Maryland	1964	12.50	2.50	20.00	n.a.	—
Massachusetts	1963	11.57	n.a. [b]	—	1.78 [g]	15.38
Minnesota	1962	7.32	1.37	18.72	n.a.	—
Mississippi	1963	1.69	n.a.	—	.04	2.37
Nevada	1964	1.30	n.a.	—	.07	5.38
New Jersey	1963	24.10	4.00	16.60	n.a.	—
New York	1963	46.27	18.10 [b,h]	38.12	3.30	7.20
Ohio	1963	19.97	3.07 [b]	15.37	1.03	5.16
Oklahoma	1964	3.34	n.a.	—	.53 [i]	15.87
Oregon	1964	3.11	5.25 [b]	168.81	.55	17.68
Pennsylvania	1957	12.50	2.80 [b]	22.40	1.24	9.92
Washington	1964	3.84	1.00 [b]	26.04	.20	5.21

n.a.—Not available.

[a] Includes only homesteads and industrial factories and plants.

[b] See Table 11.2 for exempt government property in this state.

[c] Includes only homesteads.

[d] Includes only homesteads and personal property.

[e] Includes only the real property for veterans, the blind, and widows.

[f] Includes only homesteads and manufacturing plants.

[g] Includes only some private non-profit, district, and county property.

[h] Includes Indian and foreign lands also.

[i] Includes only homesteads and personal property.

Source: Based on tax reports from the various states.

other states with only partial estimates have exemptions which exceed this figure.

Data in nine states—California, Colorado, Connecticut, Massachusetts, New York, Ohio, Oregon, Pennsylvania, and Washington—are complete enough to compare the categories of land exemption. In four of these states—California, New York, Ohio, and Washington—the largest exemption is granted to local-government property, while in two of them—Colorado and Oregon—the largest exemption is for federal-government property. In the other three states—Connecticut, Massachusetts, and Pennsylvania—the largest exemption is for private property.

In-Lieu Payments

When in-lieu payments are made instead of property taxes, their fairness can be said to depend on how closely they approximate potential tax revenue and on the source from which the revenue is raised to make these payments. Unfortunately, for comparative purposes, no estimates exist of potential tax revenues from the properties involved.

The incidence of in-lieu payments by one government to another would be the same as the incidence of tax payments if both payments were raised in the same manner, and the fairness of the in-lieu method would, therefore, be unquestionable. The fairness of payments made by the state to reimburse local governments for exemptions granted to veterans or on homesteads, for example, depends on the method used by the state to raise the revenue for these payments. To the extent that the revenue is raised from individuals other than those receiving veterans or homestead exemptions, the property-tax burden has simply been shifted and subsidies are, in effect, being granted to those receiving the exemptions. Taxes levied on gross earnings and severance taxes can be shifted to the consumer in the same manner as a property tax. In-lieu taxes such as motor vehicle licenses are paid by the owner of the automobile in the same manner as a direct property tax and are therefore fair because the property-tax burden has not been shifted.

Complete or Partial Exemption

When private, state, or local property is exempted from part or all of the property tax, this property is, in effect, subsidized except when the property belongs to the unit levying the tax. It has been argued, moreover, that exemptions tend to increase faster than taxable values.[48] When this happens, the additional tax burden placed on those properties still subject to the tax would be eased if local governments were allowed to tax the property of other governments, although an exception can be noted when the property is used primarily to serve the local area. In this case, the cost should be borne by those who benefit the most from its existence. This would be analogous to justifying the exemption of certain federal property, such as post offices, which are primarily for use by the local populace.

A strong case can be made for subsidizing some organizations that perform desirable government services. In such cases, however, it could be argued that the subsidy should be by direct appropriation of the legislature and not concealed from public view by a property-tax exemption. The desirability of subsidizing such institutions would then be a matter of legislative debate and not an automatic grant under a property-tax-exemption law. The cost of maintaining these institutions would then be known to the public, and, if the value of these activities did not measure up to the expenditure, the subsidy could then be eliminated. As the needs of the public changed, the allocation of public funds would change *pari passu*.[49]

Under the present arrangements, non-profit institutions are sometimes subsidized for activities which are not in the nature of a governmental service: for example, colleges and universities often own houses which they rent cheaply to faculty and staff members, and churches may own property—such as radio stations or hotels—which competes with privately-owned property.[50]

Institutions which teach morality, respect for law, good health practices, and so forth, do much good for society, but they do not necessarily have any greater claim to a state property-tax exemption than do parents who teach their children such things. The exemption of institutions such as churches (insofar as they are subsidized for such teachings and not just for providing educational institutions, orphanages, and other governmental services), the Girl Scouts, and the Young Men's Christian Association promotes further inequities in the property tax. It is not the function of the state to pay individuals or groups of individuals to do good. This is not to deny the validity of the theory that communal teaching of these virtues may be commendable or necessary and should, therefore, be rewarded, but any subsidy in such a case should be direct and in accordance with the wishes of the public.

Subsidization of low-rent housing projects (and thus low-income groups), veterans, and widows may be desirable, but better machinery than the property tax exists for this purpose. Because the amount of exemption varies with local tax rates and assessment values, individuals in the same category of exemption may be treated differently. Exemption of fraternal organizations and of business and professional associations is indefensible because the services of such an organization are extended only to its members and are governed by the economic or social interests of this group. Exemption provided to induce industries to locate within a given area may result in a distortion of resources. The exemption introduces an artificial advantage over those properties still subject to the tax or to a higher rate of tax.

Conclusion

The exemption of property from the property tax is, in effect, a subsidy. To the extent that substitute payments arise from these lands the amount of the subsidy is reduced. The substitute payment may, at times, offset the loss of potential tax revenues, but the payment arrangement may be inadequate in many instances. If the arrangement is inadequate, the tax burden is increased for those still subject to the tax. The reduction of the property-tax base and inadequate compensation for exempt lands at a time when local governments are in great need of increasing funds indicate that reform is needed. More studies should be undertaken estimating the values of exempt lands, the intensity of exempt-land use, and potential tax revenues, and comparing these potential tax revenues with substitute payment arrangements.

Notes

1 17 U.S. 579 (1819).
2 A century later Justice Holmes, dissenting on another case, qualified Marshall's statement by observing, "The power to tax is not the power to destroy while this court sits"—*Panhandle Oil Co.* v. *Mississippi,* 277 U.S. 218 (1928), in which the court declared void a state tax on the sale of gasoline to the federal government.
3 Cf. *Van Brocklin* v. *Anderson,* 117 U.S. 151 (1885), which held that the federal government was immune from taxes by the states because of its sovereignty, something which had only been a general belief before that time. See also *S.R.A., Inc.* v. *State of Minnesota,* 327 U.S. 558 (1946). The court ruled in this case that the state had no territorial jurisdiction and thus could not enforce payment of the tax. Moreover, state laws were ineffective in taxing other property or persons upon that real estate.

4 National bonds: *Weston* v. *Charleston,* 2 Peters 449 (1829); state and municipal bonds: *Mercantile Bank* v. *New York,* 121 U.S. 138 (1887) and *Pollack* v. *Farmers Loan & Trust Co.,* 158 U.S. 601 (1885); national salaries: *Dobbins* v. *Commissioners of Erie County,* 16 Peters 435 (1842); state salaries: *Collector* v. *Day,* 11 Wall. 113 (1871); royalties: *Long* v. *Lockwood,* 277 U.S. 142 (1928); national purchases of goods: *Panhandle;* state and local purchases: *Indian Motorcycle Co.* v. *U.S.,* 283 U.S. 570 (1931).

5 *Fox Film Corp.* v. *Doyal,* 286 U.S. 123 (1932).

6 *Helvering* v. *Gerhardt,* 304 U.S. 405 (1938), held that salaries of the employees of the Port of New York Authority were subject to the national income tax. *Graves* v. *N.Y. ex. rel. O'Keefe,* 306 U.S. 466 (1939), held that employees of the Home Owners' Loan Corp., a national government agency, were not exempt from state taxation.

7 Leases: *Helvering* v. *Mt. Products Corp.,* 303 U.S. 376 (1938); income: *James* v. *Dravo Contracting Co.,* 302 U.S. 134 (1937); *Silas Mason Co.* v. *Tax Commission,* 302 U.S. 189 (1937); and *Atkinson* v. *State Tax Commission,* 303 U.S. 20 (1938). For a general discussion of the McCulloch case and cases narrowing the concept of immunity see B. U. Ratchford, "Intergovernmental Tax Immunities in the U.S.," *National Tax Journal,* 6 (December, 1953), 305–32. For a summary of general rules defined by the court on intergovernmental tax immunity see Robert E. Cushman, *Leading Constitutional Decisions* (New York: F. S. Crofts, 1946), pp. 352–54. Also, for a discussion of an important decade of court decisions in this area see David Fellman, "10 Years of the Supreme Court," *American Political Science Review,* 61 (December, 1947), 1153–60.

8 2 Stat. 277.

9 1 Ops. Att'y. Gen. 157.

10 2 Stat. 641 and 2 Stat. 701.

11 *Van Brocklin,* 25.

12 For a discussion of exemptions for non-profit institutions see Farwell Knapp, "Tax Exemptions," *Proceedings of the Twenty-Eighth Annual Conference of the National Tax Association,* ed. A. E. Holcomb (New York: National Tax Association, 1935), pp. 74–84.

13 For a list of states taxing tangibles and intangibles see U.S. Bureau of the Census, "Property Tax Assessments in the United States," Advance Release No. 5 of *Census of Governments: 1957* (Washington, D.C.: U.S. Government Printing Office, December 16, 1957).

14 For the early history of homestead exemptions see Alonzo B. May, "The Status of Homestead Tax Exemptions in the United States," *Land Economics,* 13 (May, 1953), 130–37.

15 For a discussion of these and other exemptions, see M. Slade Kendrick, "Property Tax Exemptions and Exemption Policies," in National Tax Association, *1957 Proceedings of the Fiftieth Annual Conference on Taxation,* ed. Walter J. Kress (Harrisburg, 1958), pp. 84–98.

16 A recent amendment pertaining only to wildlife refuges provides the government with the alternative of paying .75 percent of the purchase price of these lands. The provision does not, therefore, apply to public domain lands used as wildlife refuges. 78 Stat. 701.

17 2 Stat. 226, § 2.

18 3 Stat. 347.

19 4 Stat. 5050.

20 U.S. Department of the Interior, *Annual Report* (Washington, D.C.: U.S. Government Printing Office, 1900), p. 111.

21 *Congressional Globe,* 42nd Cong., 2nd Sess. (1872), 17, Part 3, 2367–68, and Part 4, 2925–29.

22 26 Stat. 1095, § 24. For the Senate discussion of this act see *Congressional Record,* 51st Cong., 2nd Sess. (1891), 29, Part 6, 3546–47, 3614.

23 For further discussion, see Roy M. Robbins, *Our Landed Heritage* (Princeton: Princeton University Press, 1942), Chap. 19; and E. Louise Peffer, *The Closing of the Public Domain* (Stanford: Stanford University Press, 1951).

24 *Congressional Record,* 59th Cong., 1st Sess. (1906), 40, Part 2, 1677.

25 *Ibid.,* Part 8, 7416; and 34 Stat. 684.

26 *Congressional Record,* 60th Cong., 1st Sess. (1908), 42, Part 6, 5722, 5724, 5925; Part 7, 6058, 6062. Another attempt was made to increase the payment to 35 percent, but this effort failed. See *Congressional Record* debates on H.R. 18162, 61st Cong., 2nd Sess. (1911).

27 *Congressional Record,* 66th Cong., 1st Sess. (1919), 58, Part 8, 7772. Since the initial act, provisions for revenue sharing have been enacted for other purposes. These include: mineral leasing act lands, Oregon and California revested lands, Corps of (Army) Engineers flood-control lands, Boulder Canyon project lands, submarginal lands, Taylor Grazing Act lands, Grand Teton National Park acquired lands, reconveyed Coos Bay wagon road grant lands, Columbia Basin project lands, certain oil and gas lands, Indian lands, properties of the TVA, revenues from sales of public lands and timber, and revenues from the sale of Federal Power Commission licenses.

28 See, for example, 48 Stat. 22.

29 Derived from a table in Peffer, *The Closing of the Public Domain,* p. 300.

30 S. 2052, 74th Cong., 1st Sess. (1935), and H.R. 10551, H.R. 10554, H.R. 11184, and H.R. 11667, 74th Cong., 2nd Sess. (1936).

31 Subcommittee of the Senate Committee on Public Lands and Surveys, *Hearings, Administration and Use of Public Lands,* 76th Cong., 1st Sess. (1941).

32 See, for example, the statement of Mr. Winter, ex-representative of Wyoming, *Congressional Record,* 73rd Cong., 2nd Sess. (1934), 78, Part 1, 1050.

33 For a list of various protests, see Senate Committee on Intergovernmental Fiscal Relations, *Federal, State, and Local Government Fiscal*

Relations (prepared by Treasury Department), S. Doc. 69, 78th Cong., 1st Sess. (1943), pp. 277–78.

34 For a list of these reports, see Senate Committee on Government Operations, *Authorizing the Payment to Local Governments of Sums in Lieu of Taxes and Special Assessments with Respect to Certain Federal Real Property,* S. Rept. 2424, 84th Cong., 2nd Sess. (1956). There is now a permanent committee, the Advisory Commission on Intergovernmental Relations, which was established to study continually problems arising from federal-state-local government relations.

35 *Ibid.*

36 Message of the President, *Federal Ownership of Real Estate and its Bearing on State and Local Taxation,* H.R. Doc. 111, 76th Cong., 1st Sess. (January 16, 1939).

37 Committee on Tax Education and School Finance, *Status and Fiscal Significance of Federal Lands in the Eleven Western States* (Washington, D.C.: National Education Association, 1950), p. 144.

38 House Committee on Government Operations, *Federal Real and Personal Property Inventory Report of the United States Government,* 87th Cong., 1st Sess. (December, 1961).

39 Study Committee of the Advisory Commission on Intergovernmental Relations, *Payments in Lieu of Taxes and Shared Revenues* (Washington, D.C.: U.S. Government Printing Office, 1955), p. 25.

40 U.S. Department of the Treasury, *Annual Report* (Washington, D.C.: U.S. Government Printing Office, 1949), pp. 567–75, Table 98.

41 U.S. Bureau of the Budget, *Budget of the United States Government,* as cited in U.S. Bureau of the Census, *Statistical Abstract of the United States* (Washington, D.C.: U.S. Government Printing Office, 1964), p. 418, Table 554.

42 Advisory Commission on Intergovernmental Relations, *Payments in Lieu,* p. 83.

43 See, for instance, M. M. Kelso, "Current Issues in Federal Land Management in the Western U.S.," *Journal of Farm Economics,* 29 (November, 1947), 1295–1318.

44 Joan E. O'Bannon, "A Comparison of Federal Shared Revenues and Local Potential Tax Revenues on National Forest Lands and National Wildlife Refuges in the State of Louisiana" (Ph.D. dissertation, University of Virginia, 1963).

45 The lands which currently receive no shared revenues will still not receive any revenue under the new law, which allows a payment of .75 percent of the cost of acquiring the refuge to be made when shared revenues are less than this amount (see Note 16) because these refuges are public domain lands which are not included in this law. Of those refuges which do receive some shared revenue, some will benefit from the new law as they will now receive an amount of money from the federal government which is larger than the potential amount of tax revenue.

46 Advisory Commission on Intergovernmental Relations, *Payments in Lieu,* p. 24. A discussion of these criticisms can be found in chapter six of this report. No index of the tax burden exists for the uneven distribution of land, but some indication of the problem imposed on individual communities can be found in Appendix B, pp. 178–79. Other reports containing complaints of particular communities include: House Committee on the Public Lands, *Interim Report on Study of the Problems in Connection with Public Lands of the United States,* H.R. Rept. 1884, 78th Cong., 2nd Sess. (1944); Special Subcommittee of the House Committee on Government Operations, *Hearings,* 83rd Cong., 1st Sess. (1953); Senate Committee on Government Operations, *Hearings,* 83rd Cong., 1st Sess. (1953); Subcommittee on Legislative Program of the Congressional Committee on Government Operations, *Hearings on S. 2473 and H.R. 5605,* 83rd Cong., 2nd Sess. (1954); and Senate Committee on Government Operations, *Hearings,* 86th Cong., 1st Sess. (1959).

47 U.S. Bureau of the Census, *Census of Governments: 1962,* Vol. 6, No. 4 (Washington, D.C.: U.S. Government Printing Office, 1964), p. 44, Table 6.

48 See Mabel Newcomer, "The Growth of Property Tax Exemptions," *National Tax Journal,* 6 (June, 1953), 116–28.

49 It could be argued that direct subsidies could lead to more logrolling and graft in government. This is not denied, but it is felt that the possibility of this injustice does not destroy the case for eliminating the type of injustice which already exists and which is more difficult to detect.

50 In some instances, governments have not allowed the exemption of all property owned by a non-profit institution when part of the property is not in accordance with the main function of the institution. The State of Maryland, for example, declared illegal the exemption of a wharf owned by a church. *Baltimore* v. *Starr Methodist Protestant Church,* 106 Md. 281, 67 A. 261 (1907).

12. Bernard F. Sliger

Exemption of Veterans' Homesteads

The so-called veterans' homestead-tax exemption is one branch of the homestead-tax-exemption tree. Homestead-tax exemption in the United States developed from the three bases: (*a*) the encouragement and protection of home ownership; (*b*) the dissatisfaction with the general property tax; and (*c*) the idea of tax exemption for certain types of property, income, and wealth. With these bases serving as the underlying force, implemented and encouraged by the possibility of losing property caused by the Great Depression, the states passed numerous homestead-tax-exemption laws during the 30's.[1] The first state to pass a homestead law during the 30's (1932) was Texas. Minnesota and West Virginia quickly followed in 1933. By 1939, the homestead-tax-exemption movement had spread to Florida, Louisiana, Mississippi, Oklahoma, Wyoming, Iowa, Alabama, Arkansas, and Georgia.[2] This movement subsided nearly as quickly as it started, however. Since 1940, only two states, North Dakota and Wisconsin, have passed such legislation, and Wisconsin's law was soon repealed. Wyoming recently repealed its homestead-tax-exemption law also. There are, therefore, twelve states that presently have the general homestead feature as a part of their tax laws.

Veterans' Exemption

The new look in the homestead-tax-exemption picture came directly after World War II with the introduction of the special exemption for veterans. Since 1945, thirty-two states have granted some form of exemption for the property of veterans. The fact that thirty-two states have special provisions of this type makes this the most

213

widespread exemption in the nation, and there is no evidence that the exemption is losing its popularity.[3]

There is considerable historical precedent for special treatment, in taxes and in other ways, for United States military veterans. The federal Homestead Act of 1872 and its amendments stipulated that military service should be rewarded, and, in addition, veterans had been the beneficiaries of certain restricted tax exemptions from time to time prior to World War II. These precedents, in conjunction with popular sentiment in many states for homestead-tax exemption, brought about the wholesale passage of veterans' homestead-tax-exemption laws.

Provisions for property-tax exemption for veterans vary considerably. In approximately half the states, the exemption includes the real and the personal property of the veterans. Most of the other states having such a provision exempt only real property.

In approximately half the states, the exemption applies only to veterans who are partly or completely disabled. About one-quarter of the states extend the exemption equally to all eligible veterans, disabled or not, but, in the remaining states, the exemption is larger for disabled than for non-disabled veterans.

Several states require that, in order for a veteran to be eligible for the exemption, his property be valued at less than a stipulated amount and/or his income not exceed a certain amount. The property qualifications range from $3,600 to $8,000.

In most states, the tax exemption for veterans is applicable to all state and local property taxes. This is not always true, however; in Louisiana, for example, the exemption is not extended to municipal taxes. Special assessments apply to all taxpayers, however, even in the states which grant exemptions to veterans.

The maximum-exemption feature of the laws also varies considerably. As mentioned above, disabled veterans receive larger exemption grants in several states than non-disabled veterans. The maximum exemption for disabled veterans reaches as high as $10,000 in some states and as high as the total value of the homestead in others. The exemption for non-disabled veterans generally does not exceed $2,000 of assessed value of real and personal property, and, at the other end of the exemption spectrum, Oklahoma permits an exemption of only $200 of personal property.

Most of the exemption laws passed after World War II limited the property-tax exemptions to veterans of World War II; several states made their exemptions applicable to surviving veterans of previous wars, however. Many states have also revised their laws to include veterans of the Korean War.

In addition to having an honorable discharge, a veteran must meet two specific criteria in most states to be eligible for participation in the property-tax-exemption program. First, he must, in most states, have been in the service for a specified number of days during a period of "national emergency." This period is often defined rather narrowly. In Louisiana, for example, a World War II veteran must have served between December 7, 1941, and July 25, 1947, whereas a World War I veteran needs only to show his discharge papers. If the Louisiana veteran is claiming eligibility under the Korean War proviso, he must have served between June 27, 1950, and January 31, 1955. The corresponding dates in Nevada are December 8, 1941, to December 31, 1946; April 6, 1917, to July 2, 1921; and June 1, 1950, to February 1, 1955.

Second, to be eligible for the exemption, the veteran must be a "resident" of the state granting it. Many states are very specific in their definition of residency for veterans' tax-exemption purposes. Maine, for example, grants the exemption only to veterans—assuming they qualify otherwise—who were residents of the state at the time they entered the service or who resided in the state for ten years prior to their application for the exemption. Nevada has a three-year residence rule for eligibility. In Arizona, an eligible World War II veteran must have been a resident of Arizona before September 1, 1945. Thus, if a World War II Silver Star winner who had entered the service from Wisconsin were to move to Arizona for reasons of health, he would not be eligible for a veterans' property-tax exemption; on the other hand, a person who had entered the service from Arizona, but who might have worked during the period of "national emergency" as a commissioned officer in a Selective Service Battalion, would be eligible for the tax exemption. Similar, and equally questionable, residence requirements could be cited for other states.[4]

The Louisiana Case

Little published information is available on the veterans' homestead exemption in any particular state. An examination of a particular state's program would, therefore, seem desirable. Because Louisiana is my home base, and because its veterans' exemption law has some unique features, this state was a likely candidate for consideration.

Louisiana has a relatively long history of homestead-tax exemption and of veterans' property-tax exemption. The first attempt by any state to pass a general homestead-tax-exemption law was made by Louisiana in 1912. This attempt was unsuccessful when a constitutional amendment to effect the exemption was defeated by a 2 to 1 vote. The major opposition to the amendment came from the New Orleans area.

In 1934, Louisiana passed a homestead-exemption law. Interestingly enough, this law provided for an exemption of up to $2,000 of assessed value from state, parish, special district, *and New Orleans city taxes.* In order to vote the amendment in, it was necessary to grant a special privilege to the citizens of New Orleans. Thus, in Orleans Parish the exemption applies to state, parish, city, school, levee, and levee board taxes.

Louisiana, along with many other states, passed its first veterans' homestead-exemption law in 1946. Veterans of World War II or their dependents were granted homestead exemptions of up to $5,000 per year for five years. This provision was to expire in 1951. In 1952, action was taken to make veterans of the Korean Conflict or their dependents eligible for the exemption, and the deadline for the exemption for all eligible veterans was extended to 1959. In 1956, the deadline for taking advantage of the exemption was again extended, to 1964. In 1958, an additional five-year exemption was granted to veterans or dependents of veterans who had served in both World War II and the Korean War, and a "qualified" veteran of both conflicts was, therefore, eligible for the exemption from $5,000 of assessed valuation for a total of ten years. In the same year, the deadline was extended from 1964 to 1969. In 1964, veterans of World War I were made eligible for the exemption for the first time. An additional five-year exemption was also granted inadvertently to veterans who had already used up their exemption.

The Louisiana law exempting veterans from the property tax provides that the eligible veteran is excused from all parish-wide taxes, from taxes assessed by special districts which are not parish-wide but which were created prior to 1956, from general city taxes in New Orleans, and from all state *ad valorem* taxes. He is not exempt from municipal and city taxes (except in New Orleans) or from special district taxes when the special district was created after 1956.

As stated previously, honorably discharged veterans or the widow, children, or legal representatives of such veterans are eligible for the exemption under the following conditions:

a) World War I—Must show discharge papers.
b) World War II—Must have served between December 7, 1941, and

July 25, 1947, in any branch of the armed forces in any location.
c) Korean Conflict—Must have served between June 27, 1950, and January 31, 1955, in any branch of the armed services in any location.

The homestead exemption for a veteran in Louisiana covers 160 acres of land (or two or more tracts) with a *bona fide* residence on one tract and a field, pasture, or garden on the other tracts. Incidentally, the assessors in Louisiana, for obvious political reasons, have been very liberal in their interpretations of this aspect of the exemption law. A maximum of one homestead exemption is allowed for a husband and wife.

To complicate the Louisiana exemption program, the state has a property-tax relief or reimbursement system. The state reimburses parishes through the Property Tax Relief Fund for revenues lost because of any homestead exemptions; this reimbursement is provided for all exemptions—not just for those granted to veterans—and is based on the following calculations: The total exemption (T.H.E.) is multiplied times the millage rate of each parish-wide tax and each special district tax. For example, in Caddo Parish (Shreveport) the calculation is:

Parish-Wide Taxes

T.H.E. $\times$ the police jury plus the school board (millage rates)
T.H.E. $\times$ the special sanitation tax and the special juvenile court tax (millage rates)

Special District Taxes
(created prior to 1956)

T.H.E. $\times$ Levee District tax (millage rate)
T.H.E. $\times$ Caddo Water District No. 1 (millage rate).

The revenue sources of the Property Tax Relief Fund are the state income tax, the alcoholic-beverage tax, and the public-utilities tax. After refunds have been made to the police jury, the school board, the levee district, and the special districts, any surplus in the Property Tax Relief Fund remits to the General Fund of the state.

The effect of the $5,000 veterans' property-tax exemption in Louisiana is that, during the period of time that the exemption is applicable, very few veterans pay anything but city taxes (and not even those are paid in New Orleans). In most parishes in Louisiana, a veteran would, in fact, have to own a home valued on the market at over $30,000 before he would be obligated to pay any property tax during the period of his exemption.

Fiscal Effects of Veterans' Property-Tax Exemptions

Unfortunately, many states do not keep records of the amount of property that is subject to veterans' homestead-tax exemption. In 1961, only fifteen of the thirty-two states with veterans' exemptions reported the data to the Census Bureau in a form that made it possible for the researcher to determine the magnitude of the veterans' homestead-tax exemption. In a report of the Advisory Commission on Intergovernmental Relations, however, the amount of the exemption reported by the fifteen states ". . . represent[s] the bulk of the national total."[5] Based on available evidence, it is clear that veterans' exemption benefits are not on the wane. During the ten-year period 1946–56, tax-exempt property of veterans increased 15.6 percent in Arizona, 22.2 percent in California, 23.3 percent in New Jersey, and 24 percent in Oregon.[6] The fifteen states reporting in 1961 showed a total of $2,600,000,000 worth of exemptions. This figure represents an increase of 24 percent over the $2,100,000,000 that was reported from the same states in 1957. Only Wyoming showed a decrease in its exemption total during the four-year period in question, and, as mentioned previously, the number of states providing for veterans' homestead-tax exemptions has been increasing.

There are three primary reasons for the increase in the amount of veterans' exempt property since 1946: first, there has been an increase in the number of states granting property-tax exemptions to veterans; second, the value of real estate has increased considerably since the advent of veterans' homestead laws in 1946; and, third, ". . . population shifts and growth have increased at a particularly rapid rate in several of the states that have liberal exemptions."[7]

Using Spears' data again, one observes the following tax savings to veterans as a result of the property-tax exemption. In Arizona, the tax saving distributed among 42,810 veterans in 1956 was approximately $2,400,000. In Iowa, 186,732 veterans saved $5,800,000 in 1955. In 1956, California's eligible veterans saved $54,400,000. In New Jersey, the figure was $12,600,000 in 1956.[8]

These figures indicate that the tax loss because of the veterans' property-tax exemption is not too significant in any one state. Yet the loss may be quite heavy for a particular locality. In California, for example, it was estimated in 1958 that the ratio of veterans' exemption to the total state assessed valuation was 4 percent, but, among the state's counties, the ratio ranged from a low of 0.43 percent to a high of 6.5 percent.[9] In twenty-one counties in New Jersey, the range varied in 1956 from 1.1 percent to 7.4 percent, and the ranges within counties were even greater. Within one of the New Jersey counties, the ratio of veterans' exemptions to the total assessed valuation ranged from less than 1 percent in some taxing districts to over 9 percent in others.[10] The number of veterans receiving property-tax exemptions also varies by taxing districts. In 1958, less than 3 percent of the population in some California counties received veterans' exemptions, while over 10 percent of the population in other counties received exemptions.

It is obvious from the remarks above that the local level of government is the one that is hit hardest by the practice of exempting all or a portion of veterans' homesteads from the property tax. In an attempt to help correct this problem, some states have procedures for reimbursing local governments for revenues lost because of the veterans' tax exemption. As pointed out earlier, Louisiana has a procedure for compensating local government through what is called a Property Tax Relief Fund. Although new problems often arise with reimbursement procedures, it is generally agreed that reimbursement is better than letting local units go it alone.

Weaknesses of Veterans' Homestead-Tax Exemptions

There are four major defects in the system of granting homestead-tax exemptions to veterans. First, veterans' exemptions reduce the tax base of state and local governments—primarily the local government. Second, they are inequitable because they discriminate against the propertyless veteran. Third, the veterans' property-tax exemption is an inefficient method of rewarding veterans for public services. Fourth, the exemptions unduly complicate an already complicated property-tax system.

Because the veterans' exemption reduces the property-tax base of state and local governments, it is highly probable that these exemptions either impose a heavier burden on the non-exempt property owners or force a reduction of government services. In either case, such exemptions impose an unnecessary hardship on the governments concerned, because funds must still be found by these governments to finance many necessary public services, especially at the local level. Mabel Walker has stated categorically that, if exemptions are pushed too far, they will cause a resistance on the part of the taxpayers to the point where bond issues will be repudiated, school levies will be rejected, and pressure will be built up for the election of tax-slashing candidates.[11] In addition to causing an erosion of the overall tax base of a taxing jurisdiction, the exemption also discriminates among taxing districts, with the degree of discrimination depending on the number of veterans in the district and the value of their exemptions. A number of states have made some amends for these inequities by reimbursing local units from state coffers.

Veterans' homestead-tax exemptions are inequitable for two reasons. (a) Exemptions discriminate against the veteran without property. The previously cited report of the Advisory Commission on Intergovernmental Relations states: "If these benefits to veterans are socially desirable they should not be contingent on property ownership. Under the present dispensation the propertyless veteran gets nothing and the veteran whose sole taxable possession is an old automobile worth $300 does not fare nearly as well as his more affluent comrade." [12] (b) Exemptions differ among states and within states. The differences among states have been pointed out previously. Within the same state, there can be striking differences in the value of a given assessment among taxing districts that assess themselves independently. For example, if a state has a $2,000 exemption with a ten-mill state property tax, a county with an average assessment ratio of 20 percent gives a much larger "bonus" to its veterans than does a county that assesses at 50 percent of true value. To illustrate, if a veteran has a $10,000 home in a 20 percent county, he pays no property tax because of his veterans' exemption. If he should happen to live in a county with a 50 percent assessment ratio, however, he would be eligible for a state-property-tax payment of $30.

The system of granting homestead-tax exemptions to veterans is faulty because it is an inefficient means of providing bonuses and disability payments to veterans. Quoting again from *The Role of the States in Strengthening the Property Tax*—"Property tax exemption is the wrong way to finance veterans' continuing bonus and disability payments. This method, to be sure, politically, is a rather painless way of making big annual expenditures since it can be done without budgeting and without accounting." [13] If it is deemed advisable to award post war benefits to veterans, non-disabled and/or disabled, then the more efficient method is to issue cash subsidies to the beneficiaries. Figure 12.1 supports the conclusion that it would be better to give a veteran a cash payment and let him spend it as he thinks best than to force him to take his bonus in the form of a homestead exemption.

Finally, the exemption of veterans' homesteads complicates the administration of the property tax. The assessor has to keep a larger quantity of records than is otherwise necessary. He has to spend considerable time checking the eligibility of veterans, evaluating the degree of disability in some cases, and reviewing and auditing the

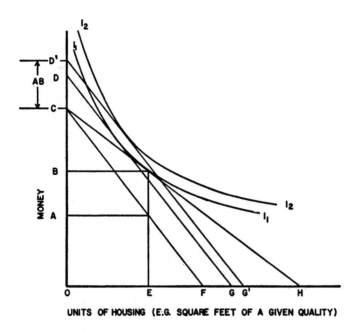

Figure 12.1—Indifference curve analysis of tax reduction and grant. Money has been placed on the vertical axis and home ownership on the horizontal axis. Line *CF* is the "market line" (the price of housing in terms of money) prior to the veterans' homestead exemption. Line *CH* is the market line after the introduction of the exemption. The slope of *CF* shows the market price of housing; the slope of *CH* shows the price paid by a person with the exemption. Line *DG* is the market line compensated for the income effect. Given indifference curve I_1 and market lines *CF* and *CH*, quantity *OE* of housing will be purchased, and the market value will be *CA*. With the exemption, however, the veteran spends only *CB* for quantity *OE*. This leaves *BA* as the cost to the subsidy-granting agency for the exemption; in other words, *BA* is the amount of the subsidy. To achieve the same level of satisfaction, a change of income in the form of a grant *equalling DC* is needed. *DC* is less than *AB*. As long as the indifference curve has a smooth curvature, *DC* can never exceed *AB*. Alternately, for a cash grant of amount *AB*, the level of satisfaction exceeds that given by the tangent of *CH* to I_1. It should be noted that I_2 represents a higher level of satisfaction than I_1. The line *D'G'* represents an income supplemented by cash grants equalling *AB* (or the cost to the state of the exemption subsidy) .

applications. Mr. Behrens, in his article "Property Tax Exemptions for Veterans," relates the following interesting account of a California assessor who upon taking office reviewed his veterans' exemption file: "He invalidated 31 exemptions as a result of legislation establishing a termination date for the Korean War. He removed 14 others where the taxpayer involved had never been in military service." [14] Presumably, if this kind of record-keeping exists in California, it exists in all states that have veterans' tax-exemption laws.

Concluding Remarks and a Suggestion

The practice of rewarding ex-servicemen for past services by granting them homestead-tax exemptions is detrimental to a state's fiscal system. Veterans' exemptions erode the property-tax base; they discriminate against the propertyless veteran; they are an inefficient means of subsidizing veterans; and they complicate the property-tax administrative process. What then should be done about exemptions?

The ideal solution to the problem of homestead exemptions for veterans would be to completely eliminate the exemptions—removing them gradually, however. A gradual elimination of the exemptions would not work an undue hardship on most veterans. Moreover, if an individual state concludes that its veterans should receive state bonuses or disability benefits, it should make these grants through cash payments from the state treasury, and not through property exemptions. The Advisory Commission on Intergovernmental Relations carried this suggestion one step further when it said: "All of the defects [of the veterans' exemptions] could be eliminated by replacing the granting of benefits to veterans through tax exemptions with a State administered benefit program based on merit and need instead of property ownership, and financed by general state revenues or by the levy of a state property tax. Use of the latter financing method would give official recognition to the present *de facto* use of property taxes for this purpose and divest it of its gross inequities." [15]

Notes

1 Two states, South Dakota and Wisconsin, had homestead-tax laws prior to the 1930's, but these laws were relatively short-lived.
2 For a history of the development of homestead-tax exemption in the United States, see the M.A. thesis by Joseph M. Bonin, "Homestead Tax Exemption in Louisiana" (Louisiana State University, 1952), pp. 7–24.
3 In 1952, there were 26 states providing for veterans' homestead exemp-

tions; in 1957, 28 states granted a property-tax exemption to veterans; and, in 1964, 32 states were granting the exemption.

4 For a more detailed resumé of the legal provisions pertaining to veterans' property-tax exemption, see M. H. Spears, "Veterans' Property Tax Exemptions," *National Tax Journal,* 11 (June, 1958), 130–33.

5 Advisory Commission on Intergovernmental Relations, *The Role of the States in Strengthening the Property Tax,* 1 (Washington, D.C.: U.S. Government Printing Office, 1963), 82. The staff work for the report was conducted by Frederick L. Bird and Edna T. Bird.

6. Spears, "Veterans' Property Tax Exemptions," p. 135.

7 *Ibid.*

8 *Ibid.*

9 California State Senate Subcommittee on Veterans' Tax Exemption, *The California Veterans' Tax Exemption* (Sacramento: State Office of Printing, 1958) pp. 44–45. See also John O. Behrens, "Property Tax Exemptions for Veterans," *Municipal Finance,* 32 (February, 1960), 125.

10 Spears, "Veterans' Property Tax Exemptions," p. 136.

11 Mabel Walker, "Increasing Clamor for Property Tax Exemptions," *Tax Policy,* 31 (October, 1964), 14.

12 Advisory Commission on Intergovernmental Relations, *The Role of the States,* pp. 82–83.

13 *Ibid.,* p. 82.

14 Behrens, "Property Tax Exemptions for Veterans," p. 128.

15 Advisory Commission on Intergovernmental Relations, *The Role of the States,* p. 83.

13. Yung-Ping Chen

Property-Tax Concessions
to the Aged

Since the 1950's, a new development can be observed in property taxation in the United States—property-tax concessions to the aged (generally defined as those persons 65 years of age or older) .[1] To date, three forms of concessions—tax exemption, tax credit, and tax deferment—are offered to the aged in 7 states. (See Appendix, pp. 234–35.) [2] In the last few years, similar measures have been considered in more than 25 states, with Michigan adopting an exemption law as recently as May, 1965. Widespread sentiment for and the active movement toward preferential tax treatment for this age group would seem to indicate the necessity for an examination of this new fiscal measure.

A critical review of this tax phenomenon requires an examination of the case for tax favors for the aged.[3] The central issue is the economic circumstances of the aged vis-à-vis those of other age groups. This paper summarizes a study of certain aspects of the economic status of the aged with particular reference to their taxpaying ability. In the light of the evidence examined, the case for favorable tax treatment of the aged appears tenuous. In addition, this paper provides initial thought on a proposal for a voluntary home-liquidation plan as a means to enable some aged homeowners to improve their financial position.

Relative Economic Status of the Aged

Some Arguments

Based on the assumption that the self-contained home is a preferred type of living arrangement, the arguments for property-tax concessions to the aged follow these main lines: (a) The aged have low incomes. (b) The aged spend a larger proportion of their incomes for housing and, thus, bear a special burden from a tax on housing. (c) The aged tend to oppose levies on their homes when they do not benefit directly from certain government expenditures, such as those for schools. Their political opposition would be lessened by offering them tax privileges.

These *ad hoc* arguments for preferential treatment of the aged ignore, however, that the taxpaying ability of a person (aged or otherwise) must be judged on the basis of budget needs and asset or wealth holdings as well as on the basis of income. In this light, the arguments on the grounds of income status and housing expenditures can be called to question. Moreover, a reassessment of the economic circumstances of the aged in comparison with those of the non-aged is imperative, if the issue of "tax favors for the aged" is to be placed in proper perspective.

Low Incomes of the Aged in Perspective

Aside from the fact that not all aged persons have low incomes, the income statistics used to show their low-income status may be misleading also. The income statistics from the 1960–61 *Survey of Consumer Expenditures* of the Bureau of Labor Statistics [4] have been used, for example, to support the low-income argument. The *Survey* reported average family incomes, both before and after taxes, for seven groups, classified according to the age of the head of family, in 66 urban places (in its urban sample). These income figures indicated that the older age groups (65–74 and 75 and over) often had incomes below those of younger age groups. In the interest of more meaningful comparisons in the present study, however, these figures for family incomes were converted into per-capita incomes according to the average size of families in each age group. The relative position of the older groups is more favorable when income is compared on the basis of per-capita figures. Although calculations were made for 20 selected cities, only the data for Los Angeles, California, are reported in Table 13.1 as an *illustration*.

As shown in this table, the 7 age groups in Los Angeles were ranked according to the average income of each group, with *1* indicating the highest income and *7* the lowest. The 65–74 age group, for example, ranked *5* in "before-tax average family income," but ranked *2* in "before-tax average per-capita income." After taxes, the same group ranked *5* also in average family income, but it ranked *1* in per-capita income. On the other hand, alterations in the rankings of

Table 13.1—Average Money Incomes of 7 Age-of-Head Groups, Ranked [a] by Total-Family, Per-Capita, Before-Tax, and After-Tax Incomes: Los Angeles, 1960

Age groups	Average before-tax family income [b]	Average before-tax per-capita income [c]	Average after-tax family income [d]	Average after-tax per-capita income
Under 25	$5,406	$2,079	$4,880	$1,877
	(4)	(6)	(4)	(6)
25–34	7,142	2,232	6,448	2,015
	(3)	(4)	(3)	(5)
35–44	8,388	1,997	7,636	1,818
	(2)	(7)	(2)	(7)
45–54	9,394	2,936	8,174	2,554
	(1)	(1)	(1)	(2)
55–64	4,804	2,669	4,385	2,436
	(6)	(3)	(6)	(3)
65–74	5,047	2,804	4,676	2,598
	(5)	(2)	(5)	(1)
75 and over	3,696	2,174	3,564	2,096
	(7)	(5)	(7)	(4)

[a] Ranking among 7 age groups is shown by figures in parentheses. These figures indicate income standings in decreasing order, with *1* representing the highest income and *7*, the lowest.

[b] Family income before taxes included total money income of all family members during the survey year from wages and salaries (after deductions for occupational expenses); net income from self-employment; net rents, interest, dividends, social security benefits, pension, and other public and private transfers. Food and housing received as pay were counted as money income and as expenditure.

[c] Per-capita figures were obtained by dividing family income by the average size of families in each age group.

[d] Money income after taxes represented income after deduction of personal taxes (federal, state, and local income taxes, poll taxes, and personal-property taxes).

Source: U.S. Department of Labor, Bureau of Labor Statistics, *Survey of Consumer Expenditures, 1960–61* (BLS Report Number 237–22 [for Los Angeles]; Washington, D.C.: U.S. Government Printing Office, May, 1963).

the younger groups were significantly less favorable. For example, the 35–44 age group ranked 2 in both before-tax and after-tax family income, but ranked 7 in per-capita income in both instances. Although the per-capita approach suffers from certain deficiencies, it is, nevertheless, a step in the right direction.

Expenditures for Shelter by the Aged in Perspective

The 1960–61 *Survey of Consumer Expenditures* included figures for the urban United States on the average expenditures for shelter

Table 13.2—Average Expenditures for Shelter as a Percent of Current Consumption, Ranked among 7 Age-of-Head Groups for Urban United States: 1960–61

	Under 25	25–34	35–44	45–54	55–64	65–74	75 and over
Percent	15.8	15.0	13.1	12.6	13.4	15.9	18.2
Ranking [a]	(5)	(4)	(2)	(1)	(3)	(6)	(7)

[a] Ranking among 7 age groups is given according to the magnitudes of percentages, with *1* indicating the lowest percentage and *7*, the highest.

Source: U.S. Department of Labor, Bureau of Labor Statistics, *Survey of Consumer Expenditures*, 1960–61 (BLS Report Number 237–38 [for urban United States]; Washington, D.C.: U.S. Government Printing Office, April, 1964).

by 7 age groups. Table 13.2 shows that, according to the *Survey* data, the older age groups (65–74 and 75 and over) spent a higher proportion of their current consumption budget on shelter than the middle age groups (35–44, 45–54, and 55–64) did. The younger groups (under 25 and 25–34) spent as high a percentage of current consumption for shelter as the 65–74 group, however. Further data for the individual cities not specifically quoted here also indicate that the two youngest groups and the oldest group spent similar proportions of their current consumption outlays for shelter. The oldest group most frequently spent the largest percentage of current consumption dollars for shelter, however.

In order to place the matter of shelter cost in proper perspective, recognition must be given to the fact that shelter is only one of many items comprising the entire budget. That is to say, even though shelter does constitute a larger percentage of the current consumption expenditures of the aged (as compared with the non-aged), their overall economic position must not be judged by this factor alone. There is some evidence that consumption patterns tend to differ among age groups. Using the 1950 BLS *Survey of Consumer Expenditures,* Jean Crockett recently published a study [5] which analyzed the age differences in consumption patterns in terms of (a) the percentages of total consumption assigned to food, housing, clothing, medical care, housefurnishings and equipment, and auto purchase, and (b) the percentages of income devoted to consumption. Table 13.3 shows the differences in consumption expenditures between families headed by persons 65 and over and those headed by younger persons (35–49 and under 35). The differences in dollars spent for the various items were calculated on the basis of multiple regressions for white em-

Table 13.3—Differences in Average Consumption Expenditures
between Families with Head over 65 and Younger Families [a]

Item	Differences in dollars [b] between families headed by persons 65 and over and those headed by persons	
	35–49	Under 35
Total consumption	$— 402	$— 340
Food [c]	$— 57	$+ 30
Housing [d]	— 27	— 12
Clothing	— 89	— 54
Medical expense	+ 27	+ 48
Housefurnishings and equipment	— 118	— 175
Automobile expense [e]	— 97	— 201
Personal care	— 16	— 9
Reading, recreation, and education	— 61	— 59

[a] Based on multiple regressions for white employee families in the after-tax income range $1,000–$10,000, with income, family size, liquid assets, tenure of dwelling unit, value of home, city class, and other variables held constant.

[b] Minus figures indicate that the average amounts spent by the 65-and-over group fell short of those spent by the specified younger age groups with the same income and other family characteristics. Plus figures indicate the opposite.

[c] Excludes alcoholic beverages.

[d] Excludes fuel, utilities, and household operation.

[e] Includes gas, oil, and repairs as well as automobile purchases.

Source: Reprinted from Table 2 in Jean A. Crockett, "The Older Person as Consumer," in Aging and the Economy, ed. Harold L. Orbach and Clark Tibbitts (Ann Arbor: University of Michigan Press, 1963: copyright by the University of Michigan), p. 137. Basic data were drawn from the U.S. Department of Labor, Bureau of Labor Statistics, Survey of Consumer Expenditures, 1950.

ployee families in the after-tax income range $1,000–$10,000, with income, family size, liquid assets, tenure of dwelling unit, value of income, city class, and other variables held constant.

In terms of total consumption, the 65-and-over families spent, on the average, $300 to $400 less than the younger families during 1950. For food, they spent less than the 35–49 group but more than the under-35 group; for housing, clothing, housefurnishings and equipment, automobile expense, personal care, and reading, recreation, and education, they spent less than the two younger groups; and, as might be expected, they spent more than the two younger groups for medical expense. It is interesting to note that the largest differences occurred in expenditures for housefurnishings and equipment, and for automobile expense—a difference ranging from $100 to $200. It is also interesting to observe that the 65-and-over families spent, on the average, only up to $50 more than the younger families on medical expense.

While these pieces of evidence are not definitive, on the basis of comparable family size, income level, and the like, inferences still may be made that different consumption patterns exist among the different age-of-head groups and that families headed by a person 65 and over tend to spend less than the younger families.

Homeownership and Mortgage Debt Status of the Aged in Perspective

Since property-tax concessions to the aged are under consideration, it appears necessary to compare the status of the aged and the non-aged with respect to their homeownership and mortgage debt obligations. In 1960, approximately one-half of persons under 65 were heads of owner-occupied dwelling units, but more than two-thirds of persons 65 and over were in this category. While one-third of those under 65 owned their homes free of mortgage debt, the proportion for the aged was over five-sixths. To the extent that homes owned by the aged were mortgaged (one in six), the average outstanding debt (first and junior mortgages) per homeowner property for those 65 and over was in the neighborhood of $4,400 in 1960, whereas the debt for those under 65 amounted to about $7,600. The average outstanding mortgage debt for the three youngest groups (under 25, 25–34, and 35–44) was almost twice that of the aged ($8,100, $8,700, and $8,100 respectively).[6]

Thus, the aged seemed comparatively better off than other age groups from the standpoint of homeownership. First, homeownership was 30 percent higher for the aged than for persons under 65. Second, the aged owned two and one-half times as many non-mortgaged homes as the younger groups. Third, as noted earlier, the average outstanding debt on homes owned by the aged was $4,400, considerably lower than the debt of the younger homeowners, which was $7,600.

Net Worth of the Aged in Perspective

It was indicated earlier that asset or wealth holdings of taxpayers must be one of the indices of their ability to pay. It is, therefore, appropriate to consider the net worth of the aged in relation to that of other age groups.

The Federal Reserve Board of Governors recently published a study of the net worth of consumers by age groups for 1962. According to the study, 25 percent of the families headed by a person 65 and over had a net worth between $10,000 and $24,999; another 25 percent had a net worth of $25,000 and over. The mean for the group was $30,-718 and the median, $10,450. The median net worth of the group 65 and over, $10,450, was surpassed only by that of families with heads 55–64 ($14,950) and 45–54 ($11,950); it was larger than the median net worth of families with heads under 25 ($270), 25–34 ($2,080), and 35–44 ($8,000).[7] It appears, therefore, that, in comparison with other age groups, the aged were, on the whole, in better economic circumstances as measured by net worth.

Tentative Conclusion

In the light of the above comparative study of several aspects of the economic status of the aged, the case for property- (and other) tax concessions to the aged appears tenuous. Taxpaying ability of the aged, especially with respect to their favorable position on the score of net worth, may be exaggerated, however. An important part of their net worth consists of homeownership. If the assets held by the aged (homes, in particular) cannot or will not be converted into currently spendable income, the contribution of these assets to the economic welfare of the aged will consist solely of the imputed income or rent.

The preceding discussion suggests that a dilemma exists with respect to the high incidence of homeownership by the aged. Ownership of homes by the aged enhances their economic position on the one hand but subjects them to property taxes on the other. This is true, of course, for homeowners of any age, and it poses a problem only when there is insufficient income out of which to pay taxes. The problem is more acute, however, for aged homeowners with insufficient incomes, because they have little or no prospect of (high) future incomes.

Home Liquidation Plan: An Unconventional Thought

As pointed out earlier, if the assets are not converted into current income, their contribution to the welfare of the aged is limited to the imputed income. Conversion of a home into spendable money normally requires its sale. Sale of a home would cause difficult adjustment problems, however, when the aged move into a new physical, as well as human, setting. For reasons of sentiment and convenience, the aged may be justified in their apparent resistance to moving. It is on these grounds that some writers have argued that homes should not be included in a measurement of the economic welfare of the aged. Other writers have argued that, if homes are included when measuring economic welfare, only the imputed rent should be taken into account. From an economic point of view, however, it seems illogical to exclude home equities, which account for a significantly larger proportion of the wealth of the aged than of other age groups.

To solve this dilemma, a tentative plan for *voluntary, gradual* home-liquidation is offered for consideration.[8] In essence, this plan would enable aged homeowners to borrow, if they so desire, on the basis of their equities in the home and their life expectancy. The loan would be repaid with interest when the owner dies or when the home is sold. The most important provision in this plan is that, if aged homeowners exhaust their equity-based borrowing capacity, they would be allowed to remain in their homes until death or until they move out voluntarily. This plan would, however, require a fundamental reexamination of the role of a home as an asset which may be liquidated to produce current income for purposes such as taxes, living expenses, medical care, gifts, and travel. The institutions necessary for this type of financial operation—both private and government organizations in the housing market—are already in existence. If private enterprise can and will provide this service, no government participation will be needed. If private enterprise cannot or will not do it alone, the government may offer guaranteeing functions. If private enterprise will not engage in such an operation, however, the role of government may be one of direct lending.

For the sake of brevity, only the philosophy and principle of a possible dissaving plan are pointed out above, and there could be many variant plans. Moreover, the implications and consequences of this plan—including such considerations as the motives for saving and intergenerational transfers—are omitted from the present discussion. It should be emphasized that the suggested dissaving plan is not a panacea for the financial difficulties of all the aged, but it would be very helpful to those who may be called "income-poor but property-rich" if they choose to participate.

Concluding Remarks

In this brief paper, the arguments for property-tax concessions to the aged on grounds of low income and high housing expenditures have been discussed in the light of certain statistical findings. This analysis suggests that the case for tax favors seems tenuous, because the economic circumstances of the aged as a group appear to be better than those of most other age groups. The relatively superior net worth of the aged may not truly represent their taxpaying ability, however, since home equities constitute an important part of their net worth. If these assets cannot or will not be converted into currently spendable incomes, their contribution to the welfare of the aged does not go beyond the imputed income. Conversion of a home into current income normally requires its sale and thus particularly causes many problems for the aged. On the other hand, the assets of the aged, including homes, represent the culmination of a savings process prior to old age, and a gradual dissaving process may be a sensible way of meeting some of the financial problems during old age. Although the institutions capable of financing such an operation—both private and government agencies in the housing market—are in existence, this dissaving plan will require a fundamental rethinking of the role of assets in old age.

Notes

1 This paper summarizes certain findings of the author's research project on the taxation of the aged in 1963–64 with a Brookings Research Professorship, Brookings Institution. Additional support was received from the Bureau of Business and Economic Research and from the Institute of Government and Public Affairs, both at UCLA. The views expressed here are those of the author.

2 For a convenient resumé of income- and property-tax laws favoring the aged, see Yung-Ping Chen, "Preferential Treatment of the Aged in Income and Property Taxation," *American Journal of Economics and Sociology*, 25, No. 1 (January, 1966), 27–38.

3 For discussions of certain difficulties with the present exemption laws, see Yung-Ping Chen, "Present Status and Fiscal Significance of Property Tax Exemptions for the Aged," *National Tax Journal*, 18, No. 2 (June, 1965), 162–74. For discussions of hypothetical exemption schemes, see Chen, "Homestead Tax Exemptions for the Aged with Special Reference to the Revenue Effects of Alternative Exemption Laws in California," in *Taxation of Property in California* (Sacramento: State Office of Printing, 1964), pp. 164–201.

4 U.S. Department of Labor, Bureau of Labor Statistics, *Survey of Consumer Expenditures*, 1960–61 (BLS Report Number 237 Series; Washington, D.C.: U.S. Government Printing Office, 1963).

5 Jean A. Crockett, "Older People as Consumers," in *Aging and the Economy*, ed. Harold L. Orbach and Clark Tibbitts (Ann Arbor: University of Michigan Press, 1963), p. 137.

6 U.S. Bureau of the Census, *Housing of Senior Citizens*, Vol. 7 in *U.S. Census of Housing, 1960* (Washington, D.C.: U.S. Government Printing

Office, 1962) ; and U.S. Bureau of the Census, "Residential Finance," *Homeowner Properties,* Vol. 5, Part 1, in *U.S. Census of Housing, 1960* (Washington, D.C.: U.S. Government Printing Office, 1963), pp. 4, 9, 13.

7 "Survey of Financial Characteristics of Consumers," *Federal Reserve Bulletin,* 50, No. 3 (March, 1964), 291.

8 Argued in more detail in Yung-Ping Chen, "Property Tax Burden of the Aged: An Unorthodox Solution" (mimeo. available on request).

Appendix: Summary of Existing Laws Granting Property-Tax Concessions to the Aged

Indiana grants an exemption of $1,000 of assessed valuation on a homestead assessed at $5,000 or less, owned and occupied by a resident 65 and over (with ownership for at least one year) if his total gross income from every source (including any income of his spouse) does not exceed $2,250.

Maryland law gives its local governments the authority to grant a tax credit based on age or income. This authority is exercised at present in seventeen counties and the City of Baltimore. The eligibility requirements and the forms and amounts of "tax credits" differ among these political subdivisions. (a) The required period of residence is five years in all of them, except in Worcester County which requires ten years. (b) The age requirement is generally 65 years of age, but it is 68 in Carroll County, 70 in Somerset County, and 62 years for females in Cecil County. (c) The income test—which sets the upper limit of annual income a taxpayer may have without losing the tax privilege—ranges from $1,200 to $4,000. (d) Twelve counties and the City of Baltimore allow a credit against the assessed valuation (in effect, an exemption), ranging from $1,500 in Somerset County to $5,000 in Prince Georges County and Montgomery County. (e) Three counties allow a credit against taxes otherwise liable, ranging from $30 in Frederick County to $50 in Wicomico County and $65 in Washington County. (f) A third form of tax credit is offered in two counties: Kent County grants a tax credit of 20 times the tax rate and Baltimore County a credit of 30 times the tax rate.

Massachusetts allows an exemption of $4,000 of assessed valuation on a homestead assessed at $14,000 or less, owned and occupied for at least five years by a person 70 or over who has lived in the state for the preceding ten years if net income from all sources, both taxable and non-taxable, does not exceed $5,000 for a married couple and $4,000 for a single person.

Michigan exempts $2,500 of state equalized valuation on a homestead assessed at no more than $10,000 of state equalized value, owned and occupied by a person 65 and over who was a resident of the state for at least the seven consecutive years immediately preceding the exemption if his gross income—including any income of his spouse and co-occupant and concurrent owner of the homestead—does not exceed $5,000. Gross income means the total income subject to, and all income specifically excluded from, the federal income tax.

New Jersey allows a tax credit of up to $80 against the property tax on the self-owned dwelling of a person 65 or over who has been a citizen and resident for at least three years and whose annual income does not exceed $5,000 (defined to include money from whatever source, covering, but not limited to, realized capital gains and the entire amount of pension, annuity, retirement, and social security benefits).

Oregon exempts the first $10,000 of the true cash value of the principal residence of a person 65 and over if his gross receipts are less than $2,500 (defined to include, but not limited to, pensions, disability compensation, retirement pay, public welfare and social security payments, and receipts from sales or from services rendered). In addition, Oregon allows tax deferment to those who are unable to obtain a complete exemption or to those whose income is over $2,500. To claim tax deferment, the homestead must not be income-producing or have any delinquent property taxes on the property. The deferred taxes become a lien against the property until the death of the owner or the sale of the home or a status change of the property (i.e., when it is no longer a homestead or when it becomes income-producing). The deferred taxes are charged with an interest rate of 6 percent per annum.

Wisconsin grants property-tax relief in the form of income-tax credits and refunds to persons 65 and over, either homeowners or renters. For the homeowner with household income of $1,000 or less, the relief amounts to 75 percent (up to $300) of the property tax in excess of 5 percent of the household income. The relief is 50 percent (up to $300) of the property tax in excess of 5 percent of the first $2,000 of household income and 20 percent of all household income over $2,000 if the household income is over $1,000. Household income is defined as income of all the persons who are related to and live with the aged taxpayer. Income means the sum of adjusted gross income; net income from sources outside the state; alimony; support money; cash public assistance and relief; the gross amount of any pension or annuity (including railroad retirement, social security, and veterans disability payments); non-taxable interest received from the federal government or from any of its instrumentalities; workman's compensation; and the gross amount of "loss of time" insurance. Income does not include gifts, or surplus food or other relief supplied by a government agency, however. An aged renter also benefits from the above provisions, except that his property-tax liability is assumed to be 25 percent of his gross rent (i.e., the payment in cash or in kind solely for the right of occupancy). In cases where the amount of property-tax relief allowed exceeds the income tax otherwise payable, refunds are issued to the aged owner or renter.

14. Clarence W. Nelson

Broader Lessons from the History of Lake Superior Iron-Ore Taxation

Although iron-mineral land is merely one among many types of property in the United States, it has had a history of special attention as an object to be taxed on its value in place. Many types of property are widely distributed: buildings, farm land, forests, and many kinds of mineral deposits. Valuable deposits of iron, in contrast, have been concentrated in a handful of states, and, until the mid-1950's, foreign competition in domestic iron-ore markets was inconsequential. The special property-tax treatment of iron lands, well publicized through prolonged controversy, has sprung from two factors: localization of the bulk of the values under a few sovereign taxing authorities and the enormous value of the deposits. In short, the prize was tempting, and competitive consequences of increased taxation were of relatively small concern to taxing authorities.

The United States portion of the Lake Superior iron-mining district is a fairly compact region, its resources divided highly unequally among Michigan, Wisconsin, and Minnesota. It has been responsible for more than 3,500,000,000 gross tons of iron ore out of a total of 4,250,000,000 gross tons shipped from United States mines in something over a century of record. Before examining and interpreting historical experience with the taxation of iron-ore deposits in these three states, however, we must first define some basic terms to be used.

Value and "Surplus": Some Definitions

I suggested above that special tax handling of iron-ore properties developed in part because of the enormous values creditable to iron lands. In general, "value" of a resource is a value as found, in place and without any conversion process involving labor or capital applied to it. One computes this value, where required, as a residual, or a kind of "surplus," after all of the costs and claims required to convert the resource have been deducted.

I shall refer to an uncreated or unproduced value in place as "technical surplus." To define this term within an *ex ante* framework of investment decision-making, a projection will be made of the future annual flows of monetary funds that would result from a potential iron-mining operation. The projected annual amounts with which we deal must be "real" cash transactions—i.e., excluding such accounting artifices as depreciation, depletion, and other capital-consumption allowances—recorded to the year in which money actually changes hands. These transactions may be grouped conceptually into a half dozen or so major classes pertinent to investment analysis (see Figure 14.1). Each year, t, in the project will, in general, have a different value for each of the financial flow classes. Plant and equipment investment, K_t, will be high in the early years, low or zero in later years; revenue from sale of product, P_t, will be low or zero until the plant construction period is over and operations are built up to capacity. The flow of equity capital (F_t where $t = 1, 2, \ldots, n$; n being the number of years the project is expected to run) is derived as a residual and can either be positive (net funds flowing into the project) or negative (net funds flowing out of the project). Because the classifications of transactions on both sides of the diagram are fully exhaustive, the total dollar flows from the various "sources" of funds must be equal to the total dollars flow into the various "uses" of funds, hence,

$$F_t = - P_t - B_t - E_t + K_t + T_t + C_t + R_t. \tag{1}$$

The series

$$F_1, F_2, F_3, \ldots, F_n$$

will, in general, show large positive values in the first few years (indicating net owner investment) and moderate negative values over the remainder of the project (net owner recovery—"owner" refers to the possessor of equity interest, who often is lessee rather than owner of the mineral property). A series of this general sort has an associated profitability criterion, the expected rate of return, which is defined as that value, r, for which

$$F_1(1 + r)^{n-1} + F_2(1 + r)^{n-2} + \ldots + F_{n-1}(1 + r) + F_n = 0. \tag{2}$$

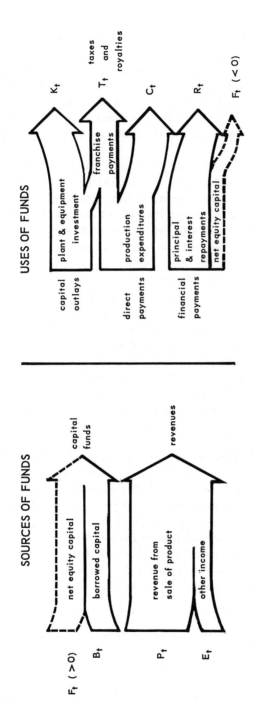

Fig. 14.1—Grouping of funds flows for *ex ante* investment analysis.

The logic of this definition might be seen in an analogy in which the positive F_t amounts are payments into a savings account that pays interest compounded annually at the rate, r, and where negative F_t amounts represent withdrawals. The rate r, which enables us to reduce to zero in the final year the balance of all the entries and withdrawals dictated by our flow series (taking account of any interest earnings that may have accrued), is the internal rate of return for that particular series.

We postulate a hypothetical "prudent investor" who determines some minimum rate of return that would make the project as appraised an attractive investment to him—considering the risks he judges to attend this particular investment and the investment alternatives open to him. Call this rate r^*. If exploitation of the ore deposit promises a rate of return at least as high as r^* when all known factors are considered, the investor would undertake, or would be willing to undertake, the mining and marketing of the ore.

We might note that, for any proposed project, the outlays for plant and equipment, K_t, as well as payments for direct production factors, C_t, are more or less *technical* results of the ore deposit considered, kept to a minimum by appropriate engineering practice. In the absence of taxes and royalties (and assuming no borrowed capital is involved), the expected stream of owner funds is largely determined by technical cost factors in combination with the market price that can be obtained, f.o.b. mine, for the ore produced:

$$F_t = -P_t + K_t + C_t \tag{3}$$

Once this projection of the flow of equity capital, F_t, has been made, equation (3) can be used in essentially all practical cases to compute a unique rate of return, r. If r exceeds r^*, then a "technical surplus" is defined to exist for the property in question. Technical surplus is measurable as any stream of payments, S_t, which, if required of the investor in addition to his technical outlays, K_t plus C_t, would reduce the computed rate of return from the project to the minimum acceptable rate, r^*. Any series, S_t, which changes the flow of equity capital in equation (3) as follow:

$$F_t^* = -P_t + K_t + C_t + S_t \tag{4}$$

is technical surplus if the following conditions then hold:

$$f(F_t, r) = 0,$$
$$f(F_t^*, r^*) = 0,$$

and $r > r^*$, with the function, f, being that defined by equation (2) and F_t being defined by equation (3). Note that "surplus" is defined in general as a stream of future annual amounts, and only as a special case would it be a single, present amount.

Usually the investor planning a mine project faces the payment of certain known taxes and has agreed to pay royalty at some rate fixed by long-term contract. He, therefore, incorporates information on these payments, and on payments based on technical requirements, into his calculation of the funds stream:

$$F_t = -P_t + K_t + C_t + T_t, \tag{5}$$

which has an associated rate of return, r'. As long as the *ex ante* franchise-payments stream, T_t, does not exceed the technical-surplus stream, S_t (that is, $r' \geq r^*$), the project is still attractive to the investor.

Technical surplus is thus open to advance capture up to its full equivalent by any agency with the power to say: "Pay me if you want to operate this mine." Since such agencies, the taxing authority and the holder of mineral rights, generally possess an enforceable legal right to "enfranchise" the project investor, the term "franchise payments" is used in Figure 14.1 to cover taxes and royalties.

The decision-making process within this framework is a continuing thing, performed initially, as we have illustrated, in order to determine whether a mining project is to be undertaken, but also performed anew with each change in conditions or expectations in order to determine whether a project is to be continued. One very important result of the decision-making framework employed here is that the technical surplus stream, S_t, takes an appreciable positive jump after the initial outlays of the investor have been made. This means that, once the opening expenditures for plant and equipment are completed, additional surplus becomes eligible for capture as franchise payments. The investor seeks to safeguard himself, of course, by fixing the royalty payment in advance through long-term contract, though no such arrangements can be consummated with the taxing authorities. When a midstream boost in taxes is made, the investor may continue to operate the property on the basis of his continuing *ex ante* appraisal in spite of the fact that his overall historical experience with the project indicates a historically realized rate of return that is much below his *ex ante* minimum requirement (or is even a negative rate).

In summary, we have defined technical surplus as a measure of value of an iron-ore deposit in place. Value, in general, is a stream of future amounts which is determined by a production plan; by a rate of return required by a hypothetical investor; by prices an ore will command when brought to the surface; by the technical costs and outlays required to bring ore to the surface; and by the foreseeable franchise payments that will be required for the privilege of bringing ore to the surface and selling it. According to our definition, the stream is not unique; there may be any number of equivalent streams.

Value and Wealth: Historical Development

The iron wealth of the Lake Superior district is found in its several recognized iron formations, which are bedded sedimentary rock formations varying in thickness from a few tens of feet up to one thousand or more feet. The iron formations comprise a variety of rock types but share the basic trait that they contain unusual concentrations of iron minerals, iron constituting 20 percent to 35 percent by weight of the formations. Localized within the iron formations are scattered secondary concentrations of iron, either at the surface or at depth, that constitute ore bodies assaying 40 percent to 65 percent iron by weight. Throughout the region, bedrock-iron formations in most locations were concealed from the eyes of early explorers by a variable cover of glacial drift, pervasive forest, bogs, and brush. In many locations, however, these distinctive iron formations were exposed to view as bare rock, and, at a few locations, secondary ore concentrations were in view.

Copper was already being mined in Upper Michigan by the early 1840's, and its potential wealth stimulated exploration and land acquisition. Within a decade, government surveyors running section lines into the Lake Superior wilderness had discovered half of the district's major iron ranges by locating and identifying iron formation. Within a few years of the end of the Civil War, both publicly and privately financed explorers, timber cruisers, geologists, and surveyors had sufficiently well delineated the areal distribution of iron-rich rock that the broad patterns of location of the district's iron formation were known. Legal title to most of these mineral lands passed from public domain into private hands long before there was substantial direct exploitation of the deposits. Much of the mineral land was originally obtained for its timber, but its mineral rights were severed and retained for subsequent disposal by early timber interests. Substantial acreages were obtained early, purely in anticipation of future realization of mineral value.

In spite of the fact that, at mid-nineteenth century, the district lay mostly in virgin wilderness, its iron lands known only in the most casual way and with neither developed markets nor transportation systems, attempts to exploit it came quickly and costs rapidly improved. As a consequence, immense technical surpluses were associated with iron-mineral lands in the Lake Superior district from the earliest years of their development.

The first iron deposits were discovered in 1844 by government surveyors on the present Marquette iron range in Michigan. Attempts to mine and locally smelt the ores found at that time were made in 1847–48, and test shipments were made to Pennsylvania in 1852. In March, 1853, this *ex ante* preview was given in a prospectus entitled "Exhibit of the Condition and Prospects of the Lake Superior Iron Company": "The ore lies mostly above the surface; and for excellence is generally of a uniform character and is blasted out like rock in vast masses. The cost of mining it for years to come will not exceed 10 cents per ton. At present prices, the ore is worth at Cleveland and Erie $10 per ton. Should its value at these places ever be reduced to $5 per ton, which is not at all probable, the business of the company even then would be highly profitable." [1] In 1855 (the year that the shipping canal around the rapids at Sault Ste. Marie was completed), quoted rates to haul ore from the mines to the lake shipping port of Marquette were $3.00 per ton, while lake shipping rates to Cleveland and Erie (where ore sold at $10.00) were quoted at $3.00 per ton, leaving a mine price of roughly $4.00 per ton. Within five years, the Cleveland ore price had been cut to $6.00 per ton. This reduction, together with a cut in rail rates to $.87 per ton and in lake freight to $2.00 per ton, placed the average mine price at $3.13 per ton with a greatly expanded volume of shipments. Thus, by the early 1850's, the *potential* to exploit the district's iron lands had been proved, and that potential gave immediate value to mineral lands wherever delineated.

The ore mined at this early stage was that geographically and geologically most accessible—at the surface, close to the lake, and from the easternmost iron range of the district. An immense acreage of mineral tracts was still untouched, containing ore deposits increasingly remote from lower lake markets—increasingly remote in the sense of geographic distance, of depth from which the ore would have to be mined, and, finally, of the amount of processing that would have to be done on the crude ore before it could become a marketable product. In anticipation of the latter possibility, considerable expanse of iron formation itself became attractive property to secure in spite of its relatively lean 20 percent to 35 percent iron content—especially if mineral title could be divorced from surface ownership and the inevitable surface property tax avoided—not only as a potential site of a yet-to-be-discovered high-grade ore body, but also as a potential commercial lean-ore operation. By the early 1870's, magnetic taconite, a part of the basic iron formations of the eastern Mesabi, was already being investigated as a possible ore source. In the late 1880's Thomas Edison had constructed an experimental mill on the Marquette range for concentrating magnetic-iron formation.

Mineral lands occupied only a small fraction of total land area in the district's wilderness, and the potential mineral wealth they contained was very unevenly distributed within them. At least 170,000 acres of bedrock-iron formation awaited mapping. A minimum of 5,780 government "forties" included some iron formation either at the surface or at moderate depths in bedrock (see Table 14.1). This figure represented something under 1 percent of the total number of forty-acre tracts eventually defined by government survey in the larger region encompassing all of the principal ranges.

Table 14.1—Estimated Surface Acreage of Iron Formation
in Major Lake Superior Iron Ranges [a]

Range	Approximate iron-formation acreage	No. of government 40's with surface iron formation
Marquette	21,600	770
Menominee	26,400	870
Gogebic	8,300	330
Vermilion	6,700	390
Mesabi	96,600 [b]	2,980
Cuyuna	12,300	440
Total	*171,900*	*5,780*

[a] Estimates made by author based on various published geological maps.
[b] Pre-1950 open-pit acreage about 12 percent of surface area.

Such forties often passed from public domain into private hands for prices of $50 to $60 through homesteading and pre-emption laws. After the Civil War, land companies or timber companies often hired "professional homesteaders" to secure forties in aggregates up to thousands of acres at costs of $160 to $200 per forty. If a forty had a fine stand of timber on it—as many of them did—stumpage alone, for resale or for harvest, could have a value of several hundred dollars. But the real harvest lay beneath the tree roots, for the values of some of the mineral forties reached as high as $8,000,000 at one point or another in the first century of their development.

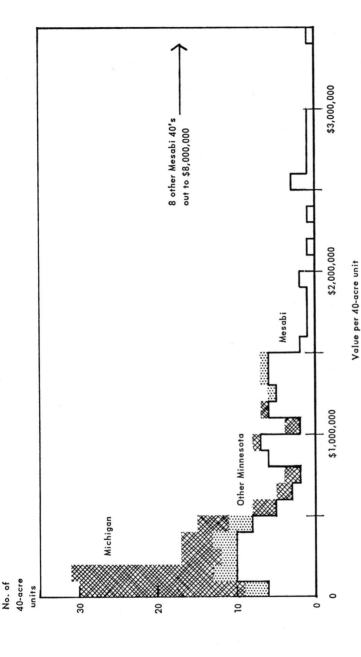

Fig. 14.2.—Frequency distribution of principal 40-acre iron-ore properties according to state-appraised full and true values, 1920 (interval—$100,000).

From valuation figures prepared by the states of Michigan and Minnesota, we can get a rough notion of the distribution of values at an intermediate historical point, 1920. Figure 14.2 portrays the spread of value per forty-acre unit for the principal mining properties on the tax rolls of the two states. The values shown are roughly equivalent to our technical-surplus stream, S_t, discounted to a present worth. The distribution of value is highly skewed, yet the values of all of the nearly 200 forties included in this tally were vastly greater than the values of well-stocked timber lands.

Quite obviously, mineral values in 1920 were largely concentrated in the Mesabi range. Since these values played such a dominant role in our mineral-tax history, I want to take just a moment to examine the historical period when the enormous magnitude of Mesabi's surplus began first to be recognized—that is, the decade following 1890.

At this point in the history of the Lake Superior district, taxes were of little moment in producers' calculations and there were still plenty of bargains to be picked up in the form of leases or mineral fee; yet the great wealth in iron-mineral lands was beginning to be recognized. Minnesota state geologist N. H. Winchell reported in 1891—one year prior to the first shipments from the Mesabi range—that: "The net profit of a successful iron mine is often very great, in proportion to the money invested. There is a large amount of money lost, it is true, in fruitless investigation, but it is small compared to the income from successful mines." [2] In his 1892 report, after estimating net profit for the Chandler underground mine on the Vermilion range to be $1.00 per ton, Winchell goes on to comment: "These figures are approximate and are given merely for the sake of indicating the entire feasibility of mining at a profit on the Mesabi where the cost of mining will be considerably less than at the Chandler, but the royalties higher." [3]

Winchell's comment about Mesabi royalties is especially interesting because it reflects the rapidity of Mesabi discovery and development, as well as the speed with which royalty claimants sensed and cashed in on the large technical surpluses. The State of Minnesota had title to several thousands of acres of iron-formation lands, which became subject to lease at a royalty rate of $.25 per ton of ore produced under a law lobbied through the legislature in 1889 by Alfred Merritt. The Mesabi's first ore discovery, the Mountain Iron mine, was revealed the following year, and, by 1892, more than a dozen properties (mostly forties) had already been subleased, subject to production royalties ranging, for the most part, from $.50 to $.65 per ton. (Royalty on the Chandler underground mine, by comparison, was $.35 per ton.) One of the most favorable of the subleases in the list of 1892 was that of the Missabe Mountain property (4 forties) with an advance royalty of $75,000 and a minimum specified output of 450,000 tons which, if met, would yield over $292,000 annually. Other, privately held Mesabi lands soon commanded royalties from $.75 to $1.00 and more per ton.

One way in which the "enfranchisers" captured part of the huge surplus, therefore, was through royalty contracts which conveyed an operating franchise in return for the promise of a stream of annual payments. In addition to designating the royalty rate and an advance cash payment, most contracts specified a minimum annual production designed to guarantee a substantial annual income to the royalty recipient. Aside from the state, most holders of mineral fee were the early timber operators or their families. Some chose to sell their mineral interest for cash rather than to lease. The Wright & Davis interests, for example, which held more than 25,000 acres along the Mesabi (including some of the range's richest mineral lands), sold the mineral fee to James J. Hill in 1899 for $4,117,000. Needless to say, that payment of nearly $6,900 per forty yielded a rather tidy return on lands which had originally been secured for less than $400 per forty and had already returned more than the purchase price in value of timber removed. As tidy as that transaction may have been, it was but a fraction of the surplus subsequently conveyed by royalty contracts to the Hill trust.

To the extent that surplus is not captured in franchise payments under a royalty contract or by cash sale of the mineral fee, the rate-of-return expectations would appear to the producer-investor to be enhanced beyond his minimum requirements. Some producing companies acquired title to substantial property holdings prior to 1900 or 1910 under very favorable conditions.[4]

Iron-Ore-Property Taxation: Pattern of Evolution

Property taxation of iron lands in the Lake Superior district evolved through three or four broad phases that were fairly parallel in each of the three states. The first special tax measures for iron ore, logically, were adopted in Michigan where both statehood and mining development came earliest. But leadership in iron-ore-taxation activity was soon assumed by Minnesota—also quite logically—after the true facts of geographic maldistribution of mineral wealth became apparent. Wisconsin, which had the least to gain from special tax measures relating to iron-mining properties, also did the least in that regard.

The evolutionary path of iron-ore taxation seems to have described roughly a broad and incomplete circle in which tax environment went from encouragement of industry to tax exploitation and then back toward encouragement of industry. These shifts in emphasis, and the factors underlying them, are our principal concerns in the remainder of this paper.

The Period of Light or Nominal Taxation (pre-1907)

During the early developmental years in Lake Superior iron mining, the states adopted very lenient tax postures with respect to iron mining, and, to the extent that mineral lands were given special mention in tax codes, the mention was usually favorable and was designed to encourage infant industry. The mining or fee interest often wrote and lobbied through the early laws affecting them. For a time, both Michigan and Minnesota exempted the iron lands from property taxation and provided for a specific tax, or severance tax, on ore as mined.

In Michigan that form of taxation was adopted on copper production as early as 1846. Some Civil War era attempts to induce in-state smelting of iron ores by providing a fairly steep tonnage tax on any raw ores shipped from Michigan were soon determined to be unconstitutional, and the state established in 1871 a nominal $.01 per ton tax on iron ore produced, which prevailed until 1891. A similar $.01 per ton in-lieu tax prevailed in Minnesota from 1881 to 1897. At these nominal rates, the tax was obviously not regarded as an important source of revenue, and there was certainly no public awareness of the immense surpluses which might be captured as a prize through taxation. At that time, the endeavor to cash in on the great wealth to be found in mineral lands was still a game for private hands to play. We have noted previously that private royalty contracts during the 1890's were consummated at rates of $.65 per ton and upwards for Mesabi range properties. During the Gogebic range boom in the mid-1880's, royalty rates had already reached $.75 per ton.

As part of a tax reform compromise effected after a change in political control in the state government, Michigan dropped its specific tax in 1891, thus placing iron mines under a general property tax for both state and local purposes. Minnesota dropped its specific tax in 1897; its law of 1881 had been determined to be unconstitutional because it conflicted with the state's uniformity-of-taxation clause. From then on, all three states taxed iron-mineral properties under their general property-tax laws. But the era of light-to-nominal taxation continued yet for a season—until roughly 1907, though increasing sentiment against it had begun to build through the 1890's. At this stage, local communities on the iron ranges were generally company towns administered by company representatives who also performed the valuation of mine properties. Valuations were low, *ad valorem* rates were low, and the resulting tax take can be fairly described as light.

Tightening the Tax Screws (1907–25)

Within the first decade of the twentieth century, a whole new public posture displayed itself, and a new phase in the district's mineral-tax history was ushered in. The historical factors that gave rise to the new attitude were many. A decade of corporate consolidation, culminating in 1901 in the formation of United States Steel Corporation, had concentrated mining operations, mining capital, leasehold rights, and a substantial portion of mineral rights in a handful of major corporations. Other large blocks of mineral fee had been assembled into other fee-holding trusts or corporate interests. As the public became increasingly aware during this period of the corporate acquisitions of mineral wealth, the revelations adversely affected public opinion. For one thing, the public image of the beneficiary of windfall mineral wealth had now changed from that of "Mr. Everyman, Prospector-Next-Door," to that of "Mr. Giant, Wall-Street-Trust Absentee Owner." For another, publicity arising from court suits and Congressional hearings left many people with the impression that some of the major transactions had a few ethical deficiencies. There developed a feeling that someone deserving, if not the public, had been bilked. Furthermore, mineral values revealed in testimony by United States Steel in chancery suit in 1902 as well as in later Congressional hearings underscored the fact that only a small part of the Corporation's mineral wealth in the Lake Superior district appeared on public tax rolls.

Tax commissions were formed in each of the states around or shortly after 1900. The commissions made thorough studies of tax systems within their respective states and, in particular, sponsored studies of iron-mining-property valuation. Already aware of substantial undervaluation of mineral properties, the commissions called in professional mining engineers and geologists to help set up scientific procedures for evaluation of mineral lands. It seemed to be recognized that proper valuation of mineral lands was a technical problem that could be accomplished only by expert technical personnel. For this reason, the commissions usually provided for periodic appraisal or reappraisal of the properties by professional personnel from the state universities, geological surveys, or state tax departments. Although local assessors have not always been required by law to accept the state's valuations, they have generally accepted them without question.

In 1906, iron mines in Minnesota were appraised at $64,486,400. Minnesota's tax commission was the first to institute engineering valuations in 1907, and, in that year, iron mines were assessed at $189,459,700.

In 1911, Michigan's Board of State Tax Commissioners heard consultant J. R. Finlay's recommended valuations for iron mines and partially adopted the recommendations. Using the old method of valuation, local assessors had valued iron mines at $19,623,500. This figure was revised to $85,642,500 by the Board of State Tax Commissioners. About 1911, the Wisconsin Tax Commission employed the state geological survey to determine iron-ore values for state-income-tax verification. Later the survey was employed to prepare valuations for iron mines for property-tax purposes, which were then certified to local assessors by the state.

The result of all these expert appraisals of iron-ore properties was to multiply several-fold the value of iron-ore properties on the public tax rolls. The goal was to place mine valuations on a theoretical parity with other property within each state, at a "cash" or "market" value. The undervaluation of most locally owned property— for which local tax assessors were notorious—was generally more than equalization methods could cope with, however, and, as a result, iron-mineral lands were immediately providing a higher fraction of local tax bases than the laws theoretically required them to. To this extra-legal tax discrimination against iron-mining properties, Minnesota added a legal discrimination in 1914. This required a change in the uniformity clause in the state's constitution (the clause, you will recall, that had earlier forced abandonment of the specific tax as unconstitutional).

In 1906 such an amendment to the Minnesota state constitution was passed—the so-called "wide open tax amendment" [5]—which replaced the older wording: "all taxes . . . shall be as nearly uniform as they may be," with the wording: "Taxes shall be uniform upon the same class of subjects . . ." [6] The result of this change, as intended, was to make it possible for the legislature to define iron ore as a special class of property and to treat it differently from other property for purposes of taxation, with administration of the tax laws subject only to the very general constraints of the "due process" and "equal protection" clauses of the federal Constitution. After Minnesota's Classified Assessment Law [7] went into effect in 1914, parity meant, in the eyes of the law, that iron-ore property should appear on public tax rolls at a higher fraction of its market value than was required for any other class of property. The factors for iron-ore-property valuation relative to three other major classes of property were established as follows:

2.0 × household goods and personal property;

1.5 × farm property, industrial materials, and unplatted real estate;

1.25 × urban and other property.

Discrimination was thus legally built into Minnesota's property-tax system. Needless to say, the characteristic outcome of local assessors looking at the property of their friends and neighbors, coupled with the essential ineffectiveness of equalization procedures, was that iron-mining properties assumed several times the weight on public tax rolls that would have resulted if true dollar-for-dollar equality had been sought and attained. A combination of the enormous value of ore in place in many mine towns and other local taxing districts—especially on the Mesabi range—and of the valuation bias, both legal and extra-legal, described above quickly created a condition in which mineral values comprised up to 95 percent or more of many local tax rolls.

The stage was thus set, and the next step is probably as predictable as the next move in a typical Hollywood script. (The action that occurred, let me suggest, was a good deal more fascinating than many a Hollywood script.) In brief, a sort of populist revolt occurred in the iron-range communities. Early in the 1900's most range towns were company towns, called "locations." Most of these locations were populated by European immigrants brought in by the mining companies specifically to work the mines, but local government was run, for the most part, by mine-company management. Around 1912, in a kind of political rebellion against the old order, the voters in some range communities gained political control of the town for an anti-company leadership and, by their own determination, set local-government expenditure patterns. Mill rates were easy to adjust to match almost any expenditure level and still remain virtually painless to non-mining property. A strange mixture of inter-town rivalry, range solidarity, and an ethic unique in America caused the political rebellion in the range towns to develop into something of a movement. Extravagance in spending, duplication of services, and expenditure of public funds for unnecessary purposes had already become an advanced art by 1920, when Minnesota's total *ad valorem* tax on iron ore reached $20,800,000—over three times the amount of this tax in 1910.[8]

There were, of course, protests. One of the more common defenses used when rationales were offered for the sudden and heavy dip of the public hand into the mineral coffer, was the "natural heritage theory." Essentially, this theory espoused the point of view that the values in mineral lands were windfall, unearned and uncreated by any specific endeavor, and, as such, were a natural heritage that should inure to the benefit of the general public rather than to the few who were legally empowered to claim them through historical happenstance.

The proponents of the natural heritage theory were faced with one slight difficulty, however. They could not agree upon who the beneficiaries of the tax-captured mineral surplus should be. Minnesota iron-range delegations descended on the legislature biennially (a practice that had occurred even earlier in Michigan) to stave off downstate attempts to cut in on the wealth by passing a state tonnage tax. Such pilgrimages paid off for nearly a half-dozen bienniums, but downstate proponents of a special state tax on iron ore gathered sufficient strength in 1921 to write such a tax, called an occupation tax, into state law, independent of the property tax. That same year the legislature passed per-capita limits to city, village, and school-district levies which were directly aimed at curbing iron-range spending. The limits, however, tended to serve as targets to those range communities whose spending had been relatively low.

Although the battle between the iron-range and downstate areas of Minnesota was prolonged and bitter, both sides seemed to have come out winners in terms of burgeoning revenues. Range communities depended on and got most of the proceeds of the iron-ore property tax, while the state government received the bulk of its revenue through two principal media: the Occupation Tax, passed in 1921, and the Royalty Tax, passed in 1923.[9] While these might technically be classed as excise taxes rather than as property taxes, their effect, as well as their primary goal, was indistinguishable from that of the *ad valorem* levy.

Minnesota's annual Occupation Tax initially applied a 6 percent tax rate to a semi-net income base—that is, it allowed some deductions permissible under an ordinary corporate-income tax, but disallowed others. One of the items deductible as an expense was royalty paid.

Two years later, the annual Royalty Tax was passed as a companion measure to the Occupation Tax. Its rate was set at 6 percent on royalty paid during the year. The net effect of this tax in combination with the Occupation Tax—in general, though not in detail—was simply to eliminate royalty as an allowable deduction on the Occupation Tax. With the establishment of Minnesota's Royalty Tax, the second major period in the Lake Superior district's iron-ore-tax history ended.

Neither Michigan nor Wisconsin enacted special taxes aimed only at iron mining, though bills to that effect were introduced from time to time, and Wisconsin's constitution was amended in 1927 in such a way as to permit the legislature to establish minerals under a separate classification for tax purposes.

The Philosophy of Discriminatory Tax Treatment

Before moving on to the more current history of iron-ore taxation, we ought to briefly examine what it was that was being taxed by the successive tax incursions of the 1907–25 period—and perhaps to offer a few interpretations of the philosophy of the special taxation of minerals on which the measures then undertaken seemed to be based.

Since outright sales of mine properties were infrequently made, the problem of determining full and true market value for assessment purposes was resolved in the three states by estimating the maximum amount a "prudent investor" should pay for a particular property at hypothetical sale. According to our earlier argument, in a state where neither taxes nor royalties were required, a proper amount would be the technical surplus stream, S_t, because that stream (or its equivalent) could be imposed as an additional expense while leaving the investor the minimum required return for his funds. When royalty and taxes are a required adjunct of the operation, however, the expected stream of such franchise payments must enter the investor's calculations exactly as if they were technical costs, so that the value of the property under more general conditions is equal to technical surplus, S_t, diminished by the stream of expected franchise payments, T_t.

The practice of the states is interesting, for it attributed by implication a sort of illegitimacy to the occupation of royalty collecting. The states drew upon established engineering methods of valuing mineral properties for purchase. The details of the approach differ from state to state, although they all belonged to the same family of estimates, involving the dual-interest-rate Hoskold formula.[10] Both Michigan and Minnesota started with an estimate of future revenues, deducted an estimate of future capital outlay and deducted an estimate of future operating expenses. (The details of the Wisconsin format are considered confidential, so they were not available for this paper.) The total value derived at this point, if discounted over the expected life of the project, is roughly the equivalent of technical surplus. From this point on in their computations, however, the treatment of expected future franchise payments shows some interesting departures from the method we have suggested above.

Both states made a deduction for all estimated state and local taxes. Minnesota deducted estimated federal income tax, but Michigan did not. Both states agreed in rejecting future royalty payments as a legitimate deduction in spite of the fact that royalties may be just as much of a cost to the mine operator as wages or payments for supplies are. Finally, the net value of the property after allowable costs were deducted (usually reduced to a net income per ton) was discounted over an estimated future production period to give the desired hypothetical cash value for assessment purposes.

There are a number of technical differences between the Minnesota and Michigan methods, and there are differences between the "class rate" method used by Minnesota during the first three to four decades after 1907 and the "court's method," which Minnesota later adopted after tax suits were brought by various mining companies in the 1930's. In each state, the methods contain devices which introduce a relative conservatism into the estimates.[11]

By its Royalty Tax of 1923, Minnesota sought to tax the royalty recipient directly. This measure clearly demonstrated the general public feeling that the private fee owner was somehow collecting an unearned surplus value from mineral lands and that a tax upon the royalty would divert a part of this back to public uses. Those who might have espoused this construction of the law were soon to be disappointed, however, for the United States Supreme Court, in affirming constitutionality of the Royalty Tax law in *Lake Superior Consolidated Iron Mines* v. *Lord* [271 U.S. 577 (1925)], interpreted the tax as being, not on royalty, but *on land* measured by the royalty. Most mineral leases in effect in the state were worded in such a way that, as a result of this ruling, the producer-lessee, and not the fee owner-lessor, was obligated to pay the tax. Later court tests affirmed this result.

We might mention one other rationale for discriminatory tax treatment of iron-mineral properties, the "diminishing value" theory, which received a certain amount of public recognition during the period 1907–25. While it perhaps never had the popular appeal of the natural-heritage theory, the diminishing value idea may have had some intellectual appeal to those who might have been troubled by the fact that the natural-heritage argument provided no basis for distinguishing between surpluses attributable to mineral lands and those attributable to, say, downtown real estate. If we go after one, why not go after the other? The diminishing value theory gave an answer. Unlike the value of urban land, which, presumably, would not—or, at least, need not—decline, the value of mineral land would be constantly diminishing—and, once the mining was done, the state would have nothing to show for it but a hole in the ground. It therefore seemed only fitting to tax mineral land more heavily than other land, and to put the surplus so collected into some permanent embodiment that would profit future generations when a hole in the ground would not. Consistent with this theory, a substantial portion of Occupation Tax revenues in Minnesota was designated by law to go into permanent state trust funds.

Regardless of how one explains the transition to heavy taxation, however, once the district's tax systems were implemented by the addition of the royalty tax there began a long period of slow, irregular adjustment among the taxers and the taxed, including even a new concept—tax relief. One modest example was the Minnesota law of 1937 that altered the 1914 classified assessment law to the extent of reducing the assessment ratio (ratio of taxable value to full and true value) for certain lower-grade ores to the same ratio prevailing for some non-mineral classes of property. But another one of the measures that grew out of this gradual change in temper proved to be of such far-reaching significance that it essentially defines the final historical period we shall consider.

The Rise of In-Lieu Taxation (1941——)

The act that began a distinctive new era for both industrial history and iron-ore-tax history was the Minnesota Taconite Tax Law of 1941.[12] We do not have time to describe in detail the setting for the passage of this act, but, briefly: around the mid-1930's, some of the extensive acreages of low-grade mineral land on the eastern Mesabi range had begun to recapture the interest of several major steel companies as a possible commercial source of ore. Fresh memories of the tax exploits of both state and local governments made Minnesota appear an unhappy place in which to make major fixed investments on projects that were not "sure things." It is safe to say that the *ad valorem* tax was by far the biggest deterrent—particularly in the immediate context of the depression years of the 30's, when the dollar demands of this tax rolled merrily on, almost unabated, while the production-tied occupation and royalty taxes plummeted with the spirit of the times. Since the taconite lands in question had essentially no special mineral value for *ad valorem* tax purposes, a law was passed providing for a nominal production tax in lieu of property taxes on the lands and any production facilities that might be constructed thereon.[13]

The objective of the law was clearly to induce industry to locate where none had existed before, and the law did two things. (*a*) In place of property taxation, it applied a production tax of roughly 5 cents to 6 cents per ton of product, depending on its grade. (In years in which production did not exceed 1,000 tons for any one property, the law specified that it pay an *ad valorem* tax but that valuation of the property be so assessed that, in conjunction with the prevailing mill rate, it pay no more than $1 per surface acre of mineral land in the property; this provision was ostensibly included to meet constitutional requirements.) (*b*) It removed control over tax rates from local hands to the state legislature. Because the tonnage tax was to replace the property tax as a public revenue source, proceeds were to be divided (equally at first) between four participants: the state, the county, the school district, and the local governmental unit. The law did not alter the applicability of occupation and royalty taxes to taconite production.

The effect of the enactment was to give Minnesota two separate systems for the taxation of mineral land: one applied to conventional ores and facilities and a second (containing the in-lieu provisions) applied to a special class of ultra-lean ores. Not for several years was commercial plant construction undertaken, and, in the meantime, the 1941 law had little practical impact by way of property-tax exemption. Though in-lieu tax treatment entered unpretentiously, it now seems destined to become the principal method of iron-ore taxation used in the Lake Superior district. Such a transition is indeed well on its way, and some of the more interesting problems inherent in the change have yet to be squarely faced.

One reason that in-lieu taxation has grown in importance is that legislatures have extended it to additional classes and localities of ores. The Minnesota legislature granted the first extension (of no particular practical effect to date) of in-lieu treatment to deposits of iron sulfides in 1947.

By about 1950, it was becoming clear that huge commercial taconite installations were about to be constructed in Minnesota. Michigan and Wisconsin, in 1951 and 1953 respectively, then passed laws providing special in-lieu tax treatment of low-grade iron ores which were rough equivalents of Minnesota's 1941 law.[14] (This law, incidentally, required several revisions during the 50's in order to clarify its intent, to allow for conditions unforeseen in earlier years, and to allow for distribution of a greater proportion of the proceeds of the taconite tax to local taxing units.) Technically, the 1951 Michigan enactment only set a maximum *ad valorem* tax for a property, but the maximum was computed as a nominal production tax, and the language was changed in later revisions (e.g., the 1959 law which adopted much of the construction of Wisconsin's 1953 law) to call it a "specific tax, in lieu." [15]

The most interesting in-lieu legislation in Minnesota during this period was that which enriched the in-lieu family by creating a class of *special* in-lieu assessments on taconite operations. Several such acts, assessing a total of $20,000,000 against two taconite companies for school district and municipal facilities near their plants, were passed by the Minnesota legislature.[16] As a result, the combined in-lieu payments to date have worked out to be something other than nominal.

By 1958, Wisconsin had greatly enlarged the class of ores eligible for in-lieu treatment, and, in 1961, it extended in-lieu tax benefits to electric utilities serving low-grade ore operations, prorated on their power sales.[17]

In 1959, Minnesota extended in-lieu tax treatment to a broad class of intermediate grade materials called "semitaconite," [18] and, in subsequent legislatures, it included certain limited additional classes of ore in the in-lieu classification, usually to aid small operations or special conditions. In 1963, Michigan extended in-lieu specific tax measures to underground ores beneficiated or treated even by simple means.[19]

The foregoing recitation, then, documents the successful growth of this second system of property taxation which began in 1941 with the taconite in-lieu tax in Minnesota. The extension of this system by legislative edict has now gone proportionately much further in Wisconsin and Michigan than in Minnesota, though all three states still maintain dual systems of iron-mineral taxation: some properties taxed on traditional *ad valorem* concepts and others taxed through a specific tax, in lieu.

The constitutionality of Minnesota's 1941 in-lieu law has never been tested. Mining companies who might feel unequally taxed within their class as *ad valorem* taxpayers are unlikely to test it because it might result in a loss of the important gains in property-tax exemption. Yet the question of whether the existence of dual systems means inequality under the state constitution may soon be of only academic interest. For one thing, legislatures have been disposed to continue in-lieu extensions. Economic factors may play an even more important part in resolving this question, however. A technologically induced attrition of the *ad valorem* base, represented by conventional iron ore, has been occurring. The earlier in-lieu laws were themselves responsible, indirectly though significantly, for these results. The high-quality pellet into which crude taconites were ultimately converted proved to be so outstanding in the blast furnace that ordinary ores which had been acceptable in the past were progressively driven off the market as pellet facilities were completed.

In fact, a group of major steel companies who were developing new mines for conventional ores in Quebec-Labrador actually dropped their previously announced plans to expand output of natural ores of 55 percent iron in order to process and produce pellets from taconite-like deposits averaging 35 percent iron. To the layman this may indeed seem like a peculiar reversal—what had been high grade was now low grade, and what had been low grade was now high grade. Yet it happened because it made technological and economic sense, and the resulting shift has had inevitable implications for mineral-land values, rents, or surpluses. Effects have shown up in dramatic ways since 1957. The expected future values to be derived from many ore properties so deteriorated that scores of mines on all of the district's ranges were closed and leases dropped. To further shrink the mineral-tax base, declining expectations of return forced substantial reductions in per-ton valuations on most of the mines that remained active. Tonnage depletion has, of course, taken its toll also.

Taconite lands, on the other hand, accrued significant values—technical surplus if you will—as these developments occurred. For example, the State of Minnesota owned considerable taconite lands and leased them, under a law passed in 1941,[20] at a royalty rate of about $.15 per ton. Royalties on private taconite lands appear to have averaged about $.30 per ton in 1940–41. One large block of 9,000 acres of privately owned taconite lands was subleased to Reserve Mining Company in 1939 for a one-third share of whatever net profits might arise, in lieu of any per-ton royalty figure. In recent years, taconite royalties have ranged from $.65 to $.85 per ton on most private properties, and a dispute over the profit-sharing arrangement for the 9,000-acre Reserve Mining Company block—punctuated by arbitration and court cases—was finally resolved in 1961 to the effect that per-ton royalties were to be paid. The amount of the royalty worked out to about $1.00 per ton, plus $.25 per ton paid to a prior mineral fee interest. In recent years, state and local tax payments, including the special in-lieu assessments, have ranged in the neighborhood of $.35 per ton of pellets produced.

Thus, judging by the willingness of investors to undertake commercial projects when faced with known franchise payments of $.75 per ton of product—or even of twice that amount—there are today many 40-acre tracts of the better taconites that have attributable surpluses on the order of $1,000,000 to $4,000,000. Such surpluses rank these tracts in dollar magnitudes with some of the very best natural-ore tracts listed in our 1920 tabulation earlier (ignoring adjustments that may be appropriate because of differences in price levels).

To summarize the interpretations of this paper in broad historical perspective, we seem once again to be in a sort of pioneering stage with respect to a new era of mineral industry in the Lake Superior district. Historically rapid improvements in cost-price relationships have opened up new classes of ores and bestowed on them large mineral values where little value existed earlier. It seems as though the district now, as a century ago, has immense tonnages of ores yet to be mined on its iron-mineral lands. It also appears that the values are as maldistributed as ever—the Mesabi range apparently is destined to remain "queen bee" in the new era of development, as she was in the old. Finally, the new era—like the first one—was inaugurated in an environment favorable to the expansion of industry. In lieu of property taxes, nominal specific taxes were enacted for the purpose of inducing a new generation of industry to enter and to grow. Interpreted in this fashion, the district's iron-mining tax picture appears to have swung back to an old starting point. Now, where do we go from here?

I do not think the answer to this question has yet been written. Some new dimensions have been added to the current situation, however, which suggest that the case for tax restraint is much stronger this time. For one thing, there has been something of a public commitment to tax restraint by the district's leading tax collectors—the State of Minnesota and the iron-range communities. For another, the former monopoly of the Lake Superior district as an iron-ore source has been broken; there are now several other sources capable of supplying much of this country's needs with ores which are, in quantity and quality, at least the equal of those in the Lake Superior district. Finally, the recent severe retrenchments in employment in the region's mining districts have created considerable support for the idea that it may be locally profitable to trade some "tax dollars" for "wage dollars." While times may indeed have changed, however, human nature probably has not—which suggests that some of the most interesting problems in the history of Lake Superior iron-mining taxation are perhaps yet to be faced.

Notes

1 Quoted in Crowell and Murray, *Iron Ores of Lake Superior* (4th ed.; Cleveland: Penton Press, 1920), p. 71.

2 N. H. Winchell and H. V. Winchell, *The Iron Ores of Minnesota* (Minnesota Geological and Natural History Survey, Bulletin No. 6; Minneapolis: Harrison & Smith, state printers, 1891), p. 212.

3 H. V. Winchell, *The Mesabi Iron Range* (20th Annual Report, Minnesota Geological Survey; Minneapolis, 1892), p. 44.

4 For an interesting account of early land and mineral dealings see Fremont P. Wirth, *Discovery and Exploitation of the Minnesota Iron Lands* (Cedar Rapids: Torch Press, 1937).

5 "Brief History of Iron Ore Taxation," *Report of Legislative Commission on Taxation of Iron Ore Submitted to the Minnesota Legislature of 1955* (December 20, 1954), pp. 18–19.

6 Minn. Const., art. IX, § 1 (pre-1906), and Minn. Const., art. IX, § 1 (post-1906), quoted in David R. Roberts, "Tax Valuation of Minnesota Iron Ore," *Minnesota Law Review*, 34, No. 5 (April, 1950), 389.

7 Minnesota Laws (1913), c. 483.

8 See Warren Aldrich Roberts, *State Taxation of Metallic Deposits* (Cambridge, Mass.: Harvard University Press, 1944). Additional historical material on the Minnesota tax arrangements may be found in *Report of the Minnesota Interim Commission on Iron Ore Taxation Submitted to the Minnesota Legislature of 1941;* and Deane A. Millman, *A Brief History of Iron Ore Mining and Taxation in Minnesota* (St. Paul: Minnesota Department of Taxation, 1964).

9 Minnesota Laws (1921), c. 223, and Minnesota Laws (1923), c. 226.

10 For good explanations of the Hoskold formula see *Report of the Interim Commission on Iron Ore Taxation Submitted to the Minnesota Legislature of 1941,* pp. 58 ff.; Roland D. Parks, *Examination and Valuation of Mineral Property* (4th ed.; Reading, Mass.: Addison-Wesley, 1957), pp. 190–213; and Roy G. Blakey, *et al., Taxation in Minnesota* (Minneapolis: University of Minnesota Press, 1932), pp. 244–47.

11 For discussion of methods of computation of iron-mining taxes by the two states, see *Report of Legislative Commission on Taxation of Iron Ore* to Minnesota state legislature (February 15, 1961); and Parks, *Examination and Valuation of Mineral Property,* Appendix A (on Michigan system).

12 Minnesota Laws (1941), c. 375.

13 See E. W. Davis, *Pioneering with Taconite* (St. Paul: Minnesota Historical Society, 1964). The idea of exempting taconite lands and production facilities from the general property tax and placing instead a nominal production tax on them was pushed most energetically by Dr. Davis of the University of Minnesota Mines Experiment Station, who was also instrumental in developing part of the technology that eventually bestowed great mineral value upon these same lands. Largely as a result of his efforts, the in-lieu tax bill—written by a mining-industry attorney and with some modification by University faculty members—was sponsored by legislators from the iron range and passed.

14 Michigan Public Acts (1951), Act 77; and Wisconsin Laws (1953), c. 110.

15 Michigan Public Acts (1959), Act 147.

16 See, for example, Minnesota Laws (1955), cc. 391, 423, 429, 514, 540, 576.

17 See Wisconsin Laws (1957), cc. 485, 595; Wisconsin Laws (1959), c. 231; and Wisconsin Laws (1961), c. 553.

18 Minnesota Laws (1959), Ex. Sess., c. 81.

19 Michigan Public Acts (1963), Act 68.

20 Minnesota Laws (1941), c. 546.

Part IV Conference Hour Discussions

Introduction

The fourteen papers in this volume were read and an
informal discussion followed each of these presenta-
tions. General conference hours were also held each
afternoon, at which time conference participants
further explored and clarified aspects of property taxation. The following section is a summary of these
discussions. The discussions follow the general order
in which the topics are discussed in the preceding
chapters. These discussions explore particular new
and troublesome points in considerable depth. They
also synthesize portions of individual papers. The
reader will benefit greatly from the wide range of experience in property taxation possessed by the participants.

Eli Schwartz

Conference Hour Discussions

Israel Labovitz: In our morning discussions I noted a few topics that appear to be worth further exploration.

For example, I noticed that in the discussion John Shannon did not go so far as to advocate complete state assessment of all taxable property. Although this, in one sense, would be a return to earlier methods, it might well be considered in this day of automatic data processing and other techniques for handling large volumes of clerical work.

Jewell Rasmussen: I'd like to have us take up first the question of the role of the property tax given the trend of income taxes and sales taxes.

Labovitz: Are there any other topics that anyone would want to call attention to?

Economic Neutrality of Property Taxation

Morris Beck: I would like to expand a bit on the theme of the conversion of the property tax from a capital-based tax to an income-based tax. The sort of thing that has been tried for a few years in New Jersey in connection with commercial rental property.

I think very few people in this field realize that this is an opportunity, if not to reform, certainly to revise drastically the taxation of commercial property, i.e., everything but the single-family homes. It would substitute a gross-receipts formula for at least a portion of the capital-based property tax.

The particular method used in New Jersey is not important. We will tax the land-value component at its temporal value; but, instead of taxing the building—the improvement—under the conventional procedure, we substitute a gross-rent tax. The city fathers in Newark are quite convinced that this reform is absolutely necessary to attract investment to the city. Without this tax incentive, investors will shy away from the city and will instead build their office buildings and apartments outside the city where the tax rates are lower.

The effective tax rate in the City of Newark, by the way, is 6 percent, and I don't think there's another city in the country—not even Milwaukee—which comes close to this.

John Denton: Doesn't this type of tax discriminate against the individual with a speculative type of business?

Beck: It definitely favors the new builder, or rather it favors the investor who is able to acquire urban renewal land and also to obtain the advantages of this new provision. It does discriminate against the owners of existing property, the competitors who, incidentally, have objected quite strenuously to the provision.

Denton: It also discriminates in favor of, let us say, a downtown department store where an appraiser would normally take a lower capitalization rate on earnings as against an outlying venture where you have a higher capitalization rate but lower earnings and a lower capital value.

Beck: It discriminates against the downtown department store which does not come under this provision but not against a firm that wishes to build a new store downtown.

Denton: This tax method applies only to new construction?

Beck: Only for new firms operating under the urban renewal.

William Vickrey: Thus for new firms, in lieu of the tax on the improvements, you have a tax on gross receipts of some sort?

Beck: Right. A 15 percent tax on the gross receipts for a limited period; say, fifteen years.

Vickrey: How gross are the gross receipts or gross rents?

Beck: Well, these are realized receipts. In other words, if receipts are very low in the initial years, if the apartment house has a high vacancy rate, the owner still pays only 15 percent of the gross rent or receipts.

Vickrey: Does this include the outlay for maintenance or other expenses?

Beck: No deductions. Fifteen percent of gross income, which is really gross rent. No allowances for expenses.

Vickrey: In the case of a grocery store, is that 15 percent of gross sales?

Eli Schwartz: It is 15 percent of his gross rents.

Beck: Without this device he might be paying as much as 25 or 30 percent in the form of the conventional property tax so this is a tax saving.

Vickrey: This provision is optional or—?

Beck: Yes, it is optional, and it's a matter of contract between the municipality and the investor.

Vickrey: The point is that it's an optional affair. You don't have to use it unless it's to your advantage as contrasted with assessment at the usual rate on all of your property value.

Yung-Ping Chen: The argument for this arrangement is much like that for infant industries, isn't it?

Beck: Right.

Chen: I wonder what happens when you get close to the end of the fifteen years, the end of the period? Is that infant still or—?

Beck: I'll let you know in 1975.

Vickrey: The other point I would like to bring out is this seems to imply a duplicate assessment of the land value, since—as I understand you—this exemption applies only to the property tax on the improvement and not to the tax on the land.

Beck: Yes.

Vickrey: But yet this tax which is in lieu of the property tax on improvements is on the gross rent which presumably includes a return on the land value.

Beck: I think there is an element of duplication here. However, the land value will be assessed at a very low figure since it has to be urban-renewal land.

Schwartz: To respond to that a bit, I would point out that if this were not done, if there were not a separate tax on the capital value of land, but merely a pure gross-rent tax, it would be possible to put in a very cheap improvement on land of considerable value and simply make a return on this investment. This would be a waste of resources. You have to have some tax on the land in order to get use corresponding to the value of the land.

Vickrey: I have no objection to this. I'm just pointing out there's a Henry George element in this scheme.

Labovitz: Before we discuss the idea of using gross rents further, could we let Mr. Stiles get in?

Lynn Stiles: It seems to me the point relating to Newark brings us to a very important question.

I gather that the purpose of the Newark plan is to encourage building and development within the City of Newark which will, in time, boost tax revenues within the city. It seems to me this casts the municipality in a rather odd role. Shouldn't we be disturbed about the allocative implications of a scheme of this kind?

It seems to me that the nub of the thing is that, as far as the City of Newark is concerned—or any other municipality for that matter—new investment and commercial or industrial facilities presumably confer a long-run windfall gain on the city's fisc. The city apparently decided that the ultimate income to be derived from new building and development would be greater than the immediate income from the property tax.

Now what are we doing with the fiscal system or institution that works in this fashion? Oughtn't we to be disturbed that the property tax *in its ordinary working* gives rise to a situation where these choices must be made? Oughtn't we to be striving toward neutrality of the revenue system at the local level in terms of its impact on investment decisions and investment location decisions?

Mason Gaffney: Are you referring to the fact that a new building yields a fiscal surplus?

Stiles: Apparently. Otherwise why does the City of Newark seek to stimulate development?

Gaffney: Or any city? What alternative system do you have in mind?

Denton: He's suggesting a kind of neutrality.

Stiles: Well, I don't know. It just seems to me to be somewhat disturbing that we use a means of supporting local government that entails these intrusions upon decision-making with respect to the location and form of commercial and industrial investment.

Harold Groves: The thought occurs to me that we have talked for a long time about the top limit on the property tax. Maybe Boston and Newark have reached it. What we may be running into, especially if the life blood of central cities is further drained away by suburban development, is general property tax by contract rather than by law.

We originally confronted this in the case of some railroads, especially those in Canada and the Illinois Central, among others, in this country. Also, the tax on the new development in Boston, the Prudential Building, is based upon a long-range contract with the city. I don't know how the courts square this with old constitutional traditions of uniformity. Maybe neutrality, Mr. Stiles, is a luxury you must forego if you are desperate enough to get something new in a town. At any rate, maybe this is the new era, and maybe we are approaching the long-awaited ceiling on the property tax which so many people have talked about. Previously it always seemed to fade away into the distant horizon. I don't suppose this is imminent but it might be a subject for a conference a few years from now if trends continue.

Beck: Actually the definition of neutrality is very important in the

Newark situation. Prior to the enactment of this incentive, which seems to be designed mainly for central cities, the investment went to the surrounding communities. The central cities simply could not compete. Newark's 6-percent tax rate could not compete with a 3-percent tax rate in neighboring East Orange. Where was the economic neutrality prior to this? There simply wasn't any because of the underlying economic forces which direct investment away from the city core.

This legislation may introduce new inequities, but it, at least, attempts to correct an existing distortion in the pattern of the allocation of investment.

Stiles: Doesn't this reflect back on the target of uniformity itself?

It had occurred to me earlier to sound a discordant note on this. It seems to me that uniformity is a good word. It's like motherhood and Albert Schweitzer and so on. You can't be opposed to uniformity, but it seems to me that the assessment-ratio technique of measuring uniformity can be misleading. Certainly, through the studies of ratios of dispersions and ratio distributions, we can satisfy ourselves on the degree to which the statutory or constitutional standard is observed in practice. The ratio technique does not discriminate between dispersion ascribable to sheer inefficiency and incompetence in the assessment process and dispersion of a systematic character attributable to a deviation from the strict standard spelled out by law. It should be remembered, however, that the legal standard is 100 years old, and, given today's conditions, a deviation from this standard may be necessary. Conditions today may be such that the across-the-board uniformity spelled out in century-old constitutions is just absurd, and, left to their own devices, the assessment authorities are going to have to make concessions and work toward systematic extra-legal departures from uniformity. This deviation will show up in the dispersion coefficient in the same manner as the non-uniformity ascribable to incompetence.

However, these are two different things. It seems to me it's very important for us to get the role of the uniformity requirement in proper perspective. I submit that it's high time we questioned it rather than regarding it as something that's just axiomatically desirable.

Groves: When we get to general property tax by bargain, then I think I'll be in favor of taking everything to Washington.

Benjamin Bridges: I've thought about neutrality and what it means in terms of industry location. I think the general opinion is that business tends to pay more in taxes than it gets in services, and that individuals tend to pay less in taxes than they get in government service. The locality likes to obtain industry to get this fiscal bonus.

In terms of neutrality one might argue that we ought to move toward a crude approach to benefit taxation. There is a case for classifying the property tax with one kind of rate for residential property, another kind of rate for commercial property, and maybe another kind of rate for industrial property.

By attracting industry, individual localities may be able to obtain advantages in addition to the fiscal bonus [the taxes]; for example, if they have any kind of unemployment, they gain more employment and more income. I don't know that we can really say what effect—for better or for worse—one locality's moving its taxes in one way or another is going to have on resource allocation.

Maybe areas will start competing for industry and the competition will drive localities into tax systems that are really more neutral in terms of resource allocation. It seems to me you can make some kind of case for classifying the property tax in terms of a benefit approach.

John Shannon: As Mr. Beck pointed out, New Jersey is attempting to take some of the rough edges off its property-tax load by trying to relate productivity of commercial property to tax load.

Wisconsin, in a different field, is attempting to do the same thing with respect to the residential property-tax load as far as the elderly are concerned. For all practical purposes (Wisconsin people can check me), the legislature last year indicated that, if an elderly person carries a residential property-tax load that exceeds 5 percent of the total family income, it would consider this an extraordinary contribution to make to the common welfare, i.e., to the state or local government. In such a case, the state will reimburse the elderly person the amount that it considers excessive. This adjustment was geared into the income tax. I think this represents another example of ingenuity at the state and local level—an attempt to try to convert this *ad valorem* beast [the property tax] so that it does not do too much violence to a consensus as to what is a reasonable tax load. I believe that we'll see more of this approach.

Labovitz: Are there other comments?

Bernard Sliger: Is this [the gross-rent tax base in New Jersey] sort of a takeoff on the timber-yield tax? It sounds a little bit like it.

Beck: It is, yes.

Vickrey: In Caracas, a few years ago, I found a situation where the property tax was limited to the areas that were benefited by certain essential services. If you did not have street cleaning services, garbage collection, and street lighting, you paid no property tax in Caracas.

Perhaps we might think more in terms of benefit taxation; that is, only those properties that have available the benefit of certain public services would be subject to tax.

To return to the Newark situation, it seems to me that a city such as Newark, which has a very high proportion of commercial and industrial property, ought not to be in financial difficulty unless there is a tremendous amount of service to a poor segment of the population that can't pay its own way. Ordinarily, industrial enclaves, such as Teeterboro, have very low tax rates. I'm a little at a loss to see how the situation in Newark developed unless that community has a very poor population which cannot pay its own way, and, as a result, taxes were imposed on industry which were far beyond what it could afford to pay—and beyond the value of any form of government services it receives. This appears to me to be a problem not really of the property tax but a problem of the divisions of functions and finance between the local government and the state.

Denton: As I recall, Newark has a number of vacancies. I wonder whether it is a good place to test Professor Beck's theory that the property owners with existing improvements are not likely to gain from stimulating new construction. It just increases the excess competition. Isn't it true that in Newark the vacancies were extensive and are extensive? Has this stimulus to new construction created more vacancies?

Beck: No. As a matter of fact, the law has not yet, in the four years it's been in operation, stimulated very much in the way of new construction. Professor Vickrey, without knowing the town, guessed correctly on two points, however.

Number one, Newark happens to be the collection point or the port of entry for low-income migrants from the South and from Puerto Rico. Therefore, health and welfare costs are extremely high. The city has to bear these costs, not the state.

Secondly, the basic problem in the State of New Jersey is the extremely unfair and intolerable division of fiscal responsibility between state and local government. The State of New Jersey finances only one-third of the total costs or total expenditures of state and local government. There is no broad tax base. There is very little money provided by the state for public services. The problem would be solved or certainly alleviated if the state government assumed its proper share of responsibility—properly measured in terms approximating national or nation-wide averages.

Stiles: I was just going to ask whether we couldn't agree among ourselves that the extent of the problem of a city like Newark is complicated by its having to bear health and welfare costs with respect to a segment of its population over which it really has not had, at any time, any direct control. Here is the strong case for assumption of responsibility by some unit other than the city—if not the state, perhaps the federal government. After all, the phenomena that have given rise to the migration of poorer southerners to the northern industrial cities is certainly something over which the city of Newark could have exercised no control, and even the State of New Jersey could have done nothing to stem this.

Truly, isn't it the case that, when we saddle the City of Newark with fiscal responsibility for this migration, we aggravate the very problem? To the extent Newark's tax rate rises to reflect these welfare costs, there will be a discouragement to further development of the city.

Assessment Ratios

Denton: Could we hear from Mr. Doering a little bit about these 94 multipliers to which he referred earlier?

Werner Doering: Well, almost every time the Wisconsin legislature must make a decision on rate limits or debt limits or whether a fourth-class city qualifies for aid, one of these multipliers must be calculated. These involve apportionments and determination factors on the full value of the assessed property in various kinds of districts; moreover, there are many other overlapping districts. The multipliers are basically debt limits, rate limits, and other determinations that are decided on other bases than taxes. For instance, a qualification for fourth-class city depends on the population as well as a certain amount of full value of property.

Labovitz: In some states they run into the several hundreds where you have individual statutory rates under different provisions.

Doering: They are rate limits, debt limits, apportionments, and these things called determinations.

Shannon: But the key thing here is, in order to secure uniform application throughout the State of Wisconsin, they rely on the findings of the state tax department. That's the crux of the issue. At the same time, local assessors, for tax purposes, can use any percentage of current market value they want. This is an attempt to get the best of both possible worlds.

Labovitz: If any assessment the local assessor chooses is allowed, is there any limitation on dispersion of assessments or on the average?

Doering: There's no statutory limit to dispersion. All the legislature says is that the taxation shall be uniform and taxpayers may petition the tax commissioner for reassessment if they feel that the assessments are not uniform. It's up to the tax commissioner then to investigate and decide whether the assessments there are uniform or beyond: "not in substantial compliance with the law."

Labovitz: I understood that in Minnesota there was a rule that would prevent a taxpayer from using the state-determined assessment ratios as proof of his contention that he was unfairly assessed. Is that kind of prohibition in existence in Wisconsin?

Doering: Well, there's no statutory reference saying that the taxpayer may enter the state ratio in evidence. However, in cases that have come to the Supreme Court, they have taken testimony as to what the average level might be in this particular community. Then they looked at the assessment ratio of the appellant's property; in other words, they have taken judicial notice of the ratio.

Vickrey: This provides a remedy in case one particular property is assessed relatively high; but it provides, in most cases, no remedy that a taxpayer can take if he feels somebody else has been the beneficiary of an unduly low assessment, does it?

Doering: Well, there is a statutory provision whereby three people may petition the tax commissioner to have another property raised. In other words, the tax department may intervene into a local assessment if three signers petition and say John Jones is assessed too low. This doesn't happen frequently.

Irving Howards: This sounds very similar to a situation which we have presently in the State of Illinois. Many people who are from this state know it better than I. Here also we have a report from the local and county assessors and normally the application of so-called multipliers by the department of revenue.

Sadly, however, the state's activities in this area have not been as cleancut as has been implied. There's been no particular virtue, I'm afraid, in Illinois at least, in having a state enter into this. Indeed, if one tries to analyze the equalization factors in Illinois, one discovers that they can bear economic analysis only up to a point. Then the political facts of life inevitably step in. The state and local governments take account of these particular facts of life and uniformity varies with the needs of the state at that particular time.

For example, if additional monies are needed by the school districts, it's interesting to see how quickly the uniformity factors go up—i.e., the multiplication factors. The general observation is that I see no particular virtue or no unusual efficiency in having the state step into these, because the state is, after all, a governmental entity. It's subjected to the same kinds of political pressure as the local governments.

Intensity of Use of the Property Tax

Paul Alyea: I wonder if we might get back to this question of the role of the property tax generally.

I have spent the last thirty-one years in states that do not practice property taxation. The effective rates in Alabama and in South Carolina range on the average between .5 percent and, perhaps, .7 percent. The problem there, most everybody would agree, is that the property tax is not playing a proper role. But what should it be? I can tell you some of my tentative conclusions, and I'd like to have some reactions.

Thinking in terms of pushing the rate up to the point where it would not discourage investment or cause any disinvestment, and keeping in mind that a committee of the National Tax Association some years ago suggested a 1-percent effective rate for personal property, I believe that in these states they could raise the revenue of property taxes by 50 percent, perhaps by 100 percent, without getting the effective rate on improvements and personal property beyond the point where it would discourage investment. After that, I think they should look to land values.

Sliger: Just to bring out something on the role of the property tax. If the recent Heller and Pechman proposal* has any validity, the federal government is going to have more money than it can spend in the next ten years.† The state and local governments will have the need and not the money. We will have a channeling of funds from the federal government to the state and local governments. Is this not going to cause a diminution in the role of the property tax? We won't need the property tax at the state level to the extent we need it even now.

Of course, on the other hand, Selma Mushkin has thrown some cold water on the Heller and Pechman proposal.‡

---

* Walter Heller, *New Dimensions of Political Economy* (Cambridge, Mass.: Harvard University Press, 1966), Chap. 3.

† This situation has changed recently (1966) as a result of the expansion of federal expenditures by over $20,000,000,000 to meet the costs of the fighting in Vietnam.

‡ Selma J. Mushkin and Eugene P. McLoone, *Local School Expenditures: 1970 Projections* (Chicago: Council of State Governments, 1965).

Shannon: One of the objections to the Heller proposal is that it would postpone the day of reckoning for many state governments as far as putting their own fiscal houses in order. Some people are concerned that New Jersey might not have to face up to the fact that it needs a broad-based sales or income tax if they were bailed out conveniently by a federal windfall. I believe, politically, there will be some kind of tax-effort strings attached to any kind of general-purpose grant that flows from the federal government. From here on out you will see quite a bit of interest in attempts to define what is a reasonable state and local tax effort as a condition for any type of "no strings attached" federal sharing.

Sliger: Of course, it's possible that New Jersey should not have to face up to the problem, along the same line of argument that Newark should not have to face up to it. But, it seems to me, it's always difficult to arrive at what is the proper state share of fiscal responsibility. In Louisiana you have exactly the opposite situation to that in New Jersey. Some parishes—counties—put up as little as 4 percent of the money for their primary and secondary education, and so there the argument is that the local governments are not putting up a proper share. Just to use a consensus as a proper share doesn't seem to me to be very satisfactory, either.

Schwartz: There are many anti-property-tax views. I'd like to put in a few words in its defense. Of all the taxes it is most predictable. It does give local communities a solid base for planning. There is something to be said for a certain amount of local independence and fiscal responsibility, and the best tax for that purpose is the property tax.

Secondly, since property-tax revenues are mostly spent on local improvements, education, and services, the effect is very much to enhance the value of property in those areas that have an adequate property-tax base and use the revenues properly for social expenditures. If the property tax were such an absolute deterrent, we would find those areas with the high property taxes considered the least desirable areas to locate and live in. However, I think that there is no correlation of this sort at all. On the contrary, we find that in many communities and areas with a fairly high property tax, where there is good recreation, good education, good local services, the value of property does not go down, but rises. If, in a given area, the demand for local government services is being at the moment short-changed, if the area is inadequately served, the effect of a rise in taxes directed to proper government effort might be to raise the value of property.

Groves: I have always thought that the limit to the general property tax in terms of an impractically high rate must be relative rather than absolute. For example, I presume that, if everybody paid a 6-percent property tax, or if all business paid the 6-percent property-tax rate, business would adjust to that quite easily.

But the problem is the differential rates, and there are two areas in which they occur. One is between different parts of the country, and the other is between the central city and the suburbs. I expect the latter is the more critical of the two, because location with regard to broad regions is more or less conditioned by non-tax factors. The question is, who can tackle the metropolitan problem? Will it be the municipalities themselves, facing up to very powerful vested interests? I guess the answer is no. Will it be the state legislatures after reapportionment? Possibly.

But I expect what it's going to come down to is that the federal government will raise its income taxes in the suburbs and use the funds to help solve some of the problems in central cities. In this respect, if federal government goes to the heart of the metropolitan problem, I think the Heller plan probably will serve a very useful purpose.

Rasmussen: I hear a great deal of discussion about downgrading the property tax. To me, it doesn't make any sense to replace a property tax with another consumption tax. I am like Mr. Schwartz. I think there is a solid role for the property tax in our tax structure. I do think we should gradually reduce the amount of tax on improvements and put more of the tax onto land value. I think we can move in that direction very definitely. However, I think we need a philosophy about the property tax. I don't think we have a real philosophy about the property tax. I'd like to see a developed philosophy of the property tax relating it to the present structure of our urban problems and our growth problems.

Future Role of the Property Tax

Labovitz: I hope that we can return to the question that Jewell Rasmussen raised—the question of the broad role of the property tax in our general fiscal structure. Jewell, would you want to start?

Rasmussen: In view of the fact that in the next couple of decades we are going to be faced with terrific pressure for revenues at the state and local level, I see no advantage, considering the fairly high levels now of sales taxes, in extending this type of tax. What then should be the role of the property tax in financing state and local government, particularly local government? What do we do with such problems as urban renewal, and the problem that Barlowe mentioned of the metropolitan-fringe, suburban-area situation?

Labovitz: I take it you don't agree with Lynn Stiles that the property tax ought to be abolished.

Rasmussen: Not at all. I do have some sympathy, as a matter of fact, with removing the tax on personal property and with reducing taxes on improvements. How we do it, I don't know. I think it would be a mistake to get away from a tax on the land value.

There's a general feeling that the tax on property can't go any higher. I find no basis, however, for the idea that there's a ceiling on the property tax. The ceiling does not exist, I am sure, when we move to a land-value base.

Labovitz: You see a continuing role for the tax at the local level.

Rasmussen: I certainly do.

Labovitz: Lynn, would you like to expand on your arguments?

Stiles: I certainly am not prepared to predict that the property tax is due to disappear, much as I would like to see it at least transmuted into a different form than the present one. I suspect that we are stuck with it as far ahead as we can look, but I think that some of the unfortunate effects of the property tax are associated with the use made of it in the support of a multitude of small governmental bodies. It seems to me that all of us must be concerned with the effect that the property tax has on the pattern of land use in many areas. Chicago is a prime example because of the multiplicity of governmental units in the area.

Labovitz: Is it the existence of the property tax or the way it is administered that is the problem?

Stiles: I think it's more a matter of its administration. I hold no brief for the way the property tax is administered in the Chicago area. To the extent that we have concentrations of industrial and commercial investment locked up within the borders of small school districts and other special-purpose units, the properties, for all practical purposes, have dropped out of the tax base of the metropolitan area. These properties are sealed off in tax colonies.

These tax colonies provide a form of *de facto* tax exemption in many little pockets within the metropolitan area. This problem has a way of feeding on itself because these concentrations of investment and the low tax rates that they produce create a lure to additional investment. One solution might be massive consolidation of governments so that we could spread the industrial-commercial assessments into the tax base of a much broader area. Nevertheless, there are distinct advantages to small-area, small-population units. If people want small local-government units, I'd hate to see the structure of local government drastically altered just to offset the tendency the property tax has to distort land use.

Labovitz: If I can interrupt you, on the particular abuse that you are referring to, wouldn't it be a less extreme ameliorative measure if you reimposed a state levy and distributed the proceeds?

Stiles: Of course, the schools are the major culprits. They account for about 80 percent of the property tax in the Chicago metropolitan area. If we had a uniform state rate or a uniform county-wide rate for school purposes, we could iron out most of the differentials that seem to affect land use. This is one possible solution: something resembling fiscal federation.

Labovitz: Or just wider rate areas.

Denton: If the fiscal problem of the schools is answered, most of the other problems are relatively minor. So, if you had county school rates, the other municipalities would be adequately financed out of their own tax base.

Labovitz: That's why I wonder, Lynn, if you do not have other reasons besides the tax-colony problem for wanting to get rid of the property tax. There are less drastic solutions to this tax-colony problem.

Stiles: Well, I am impressed too, by George Mitchell's contention that the valuation of property for tax purposes is inherently impossible.* This is, perhaps, the reason that exceedingly serious administrative difficulties seem to be present wherever the property tax exists.

It isn't just a matter of singling out Illinois for bad administrative practices, tempting as it may be to do so. I think that it's at least to be said in favor of Illinois that its dirty linen is evident for all to see. Other jurisdictions are in just as bad shape as Illinois, you may be sure, but they are keeping quiet about it.

Labovitz: Does anyone else want to pursue this?

Raleigh Barlowe: My comment is related to the general problem. I think there may be a need for some sort of overall limitation on the property-tax rate. I don't expect to see the tax abolished. However, I

---

* "While I feel now, as I look around the scene of today, that this is where I came in twenty-odd years ago, I strongly doubt that either I, or any other observer, twenty-odd years hence [i.e., 1976] will gain the same impression. The property tax will by then have become an all-but-forgotten relic of an earlier fiscal age." George Mitchell, "Is This Where We Came In?" in National Tax Association, *1956 Proceedings of the Forty-Ninth Annual Conference on Taxation,* ed. Ronald B. Welch (Sacramento, 1957), p. 494. See also pp. 487–93, esp. pp. 490–91.

think there are some definite problems. Property taxes have been going up for some time, and there is danger in this if we think in terms of a possible serious recession. A situation could be developing just as serious as the experience of the 20's and 30's when one-fourth of all the land in some of the lake states actually did tax revert. More than half the land was tax delinquent for a good many years.

Tax Shifting and Burden

Gaffney: In what sense do you believe that the property tax on farm land is regressive?

Barlowe: I have only seen one study on this matter. I'd be happy if we had a study which related the census classifications by economic class of farms to amount of taxes paid; then we could develop some relationships on this problem. I have not seen a study carried out thoroughly in this manner.

We did conduct a small study in Michigan based on our farm-account records of 1957 involving about 940 to 950 farms. In this particular study, we broke the farms down into income classes at $1,000 or $2,000 intervals, ranging from under $2,000 to $10,000 or more. After we placed property taxes on this base, we had an indication of regressivity at least for that one year's records. Unfortunately, we didn't carry the study on to 1958 and 1959 and 1960. In 1957 we had 33 out of about 940 farmers with negative incomes. I assume, if you carried the study to 1958 or 1959, you would find that these people would be back in the positive-income class, or, presumably, they wouldn't stay in farming. At any rate, the lower-income farms for that one year, 1957, seemed to be paying about 34 percent of their income as property taxes, excluding those with negative incomes. Taxes were 90 percent of income if you average in the negative-income classes. The tax burden for the $2,000 to $3,000 net-income class was around 14 percent. It dropped off to about 5.5 percent at the $10,000-or-more income class. The general average was about 8 percent for the entire sample.

Labovitz: Just to avoid any confusion: your measure of regressivity is regressivity with respect to the income of the owner of the property rather than, let's say, the value of the farm or some other measure.

Barlowe: That's right. There was a parallel study, which we used, developed with local consumer data from the City of Lansing. We were able to relate property taxes paid by residential owners within the city to family incomes. We had rather good income data, and we found the same regressivity in residential-property ownership taxes as in farm-property taxes.

Vickrey: Measures of regressivity calculated on these bases are subject to the regression fallacy. In addition, in this particular case, one would also have to consider where the burden of the tax ultimately rests. In a case of the property tax on farms, a good case could be made for the assertion that a fair share of the property tax on land value is capitalized, whereas the tax on improvements may be passed on to consumers.

The latter part of the analysis [the passing on of the property tax on improvements to consumers] would be a bit more tenuous. However, I think we should be hesitant about accepting a conclusion of regressivity on the basis of the kind of data you describe.

Barlowe: I'm not sure we even used the term "regressive." I think we were just indicating a relation: the proportion of net income, before payment of taxes, which was taken by property taxes.

Labovitz: Bill Vickrey has referred to the regression fallacy. I'm not sure what he's referring to is really clear to all of us. Perhaps he ought to expand on this a little.

Vickrey: I think—particularly in the case of farming, which is notoriously subject to variations in annual income from crop prices, weather, etc.—the fact that you find farms that have, in any particular year, little or no income but nevertheless pay taxes may merely mean that you have selected out those farms that happened to have had a particularly poor year. This would not in itself indicate that over a series of years the tax was, in fact, regressive, either—as I would prefer to define the term—in the sense of measuring effective rates against property value or in the sense of the ratio of the tax to net farm income over a period of years.

Stiles: It might be preferable then to calculate regressivity by using a total wealth measure—which would be less likely to display fluctuation from year to year.

Labovitz: The issue is whether, when you measure regressivity, you should use as your base a wealth concept, an income concept, or an expenditure concept.

Rasmussen: The concept of the regressivity of the property tax has traditionally been related to wealth. The percentage of assessment on the larger-value properties has been smaller than the percentage assessed on lower-value property. I think the income base is a bit misleading in this context.

Gaffney: When we take income as the base, we are implicitly assuming that income is the proper tax base. In the case of the property tax, however, we have another assumption.

Rasmussen: A farmer that has a poor year is going to have a high ratio of property tax to income, certainly. This is not necessarily what we mean by regressivity in regard to the property tax.

Barlowe: Shouldn't we remember, though, that all taxes are paid out of income?

Vickrey: It is true that all taxes are paid by giving up some form of outlay or expenditure, but should expenditures be the base?

Barlowe: Let me turn your question around. Is that any reason to disregard income when we talk about regressivity?

Gaffney: Well, there is an interesting fact. If you order people on the basis of their income, in your highest group you have people whose property holdings are relatively high. A number of studies indicate that, when economic units—families or individuals—are ordered by income, the holdings of property rise with income faster than income. This would seem to indicate that the property tax would not be regressive. Your result surprises me, although I've seen other studies that had results of the same kind in respect to income but not in respect to holdings of assets. It may be that many of the assets escape the property tax.

Labovitz: Mr. Chen.

Chen: I hate to belabor the point; however, the conventional or popular notion of the comparison of the regressiveness of property tax and the regressiveness of sales tax has been related to income.

Rasmussen: No, not on the property tax. That's not right for the general property tax. Sales tax, yes; but not property. I challenge you on that.

Chen: How could the property tax be regressive on the basis of relative over-valuation of simple low-value properties if we avoid or eliminate assessment problems? Properties are assessed equally or uniformly and taxed at one rate, and it's proportional. The rate would result in revenue from properties which would be proportional exactly in the same sense as sales tax when we use the purchase prices as the base, 4 percent on the dollar. On $10, it's $.40. It would be proportional, wouldn't it?

Labovitz: This is correct about the concept. However, I think Rasmussen is referring to Seligman's old indictment of the tax,* and

---

* In his *Essays in Taxation* (10th ed.; New York: Macmillan, 1925), Edwin R. A. Seligman was more emphatic about regressivity in the burdens of the property tax relative to incomes or wealth than about regressivity in terms of the value of individual parcels of property. He quoted the Kentucky state auditor's report of 1887 in support of this observation: "And in general it may be said, with our state auditors, that 'the property of the small owner, as a rule, is valued by a far higher standard than that of his wealthy neighbor' " (p. 28).

also to other people's observations, that the tendency of assessors is to assess large properties at a smaller percentage of their market value than small properties. Therefore the tax, in practice, becomes regressive in relation to the size of the property.

Chen: Let me give you an example, and see whether I'm missing something. There is a great deal of agitation for property-tax concessions to the aged, 60 and over. There are states now which give preferential treatment to the aged. The argument in favor of this concession is that the aged, being retired, have very low income but that their property taxes are high because, as a group, they have larger holdings of homes. Therefore, the tax is a regressive burden on the aged, and we have had to help them out by exemption or other methods. Now isn't this argument based on an income measure?

Gaffney: I think when you make a statement like that you are really saying the property tax is not the income tax.

Chen: What about the sales tax being regressive?

Gaffney: The sales tax isn't the income tax either. However, I think something left out of these studies, such as the one that you cited, Barlowe, is that 50 percent of the population doesn't own any property. Therefore they are not included in the data.

Labovitz: On the other hand, we leave out the taxation of business property when we make these comparisons, because we make no specific assumption about the shifting and incidence of property taxes.

Gaffney: Nevertheless, if you look at a Lorenz curve * showing the concentration of income in the United States and compare it with a Lorenz curve showing the distribution of property, almost any kind of property, you obtain a higher concentration of property than of income. This holds true even if you eliminate the people who don't own any property. If you included them, you'd get something even more extreme. From this evidence I find it very hard to believe that the property tax could be regressive when compared to the income tax.

Schwartz: I do not think the property tax will ever be justified as a progressive tax relative to income. I do think that, relative to income, it does show up as regressive. The reason for this is that, although your heavy wealth owners hold income-producing property, the tax burden on these holdings is largely shifted forward to the renters. People who own no property and rent housing are still paying a large portion of the property tax in their rent.

---

* The Lorenz curve is used to illustrate equality of distribution. If property holdings were equally distributed, the curve would be a straight line rising at a forty-five degree angle from the point of origin. A Lorenz curve showing property holdings would be flat near point of origin and rise sharply near terminus. A property Lorenz curve would be more concave than an income Lorenz curve.

I would justify the use of the property tax on other bases. One, for example, is that a large part of the value of property is socially induced because of local government expenditures, i.e., social capital that goes into the area. I think that we are justified in recapturing some of the increment in property value for the general fisc. I would not, however, try to justify the property tax as a progressive tax.

Gaffney: You are really shifting grounds, though, because these gentlemen are concerned about progressivity.

Schwartz: I think you'd have to concede that, in general, the property tax is probably regressive. All studies of the expenditure for shelter in family budgets indicate that it's a higher percentage of lower budgets, a lower percentage of the higher-income groups, and therefore I can't help but believe——

Gaffney: As a matter of fact, Margaret Reid's book * comes to a different conclusion, but I don't think it's the main point. As you move from the slums out to Fox Point, which is our [the Milwaukee] gold coast, you find that the houses become bigger but, as you suggest, not in proportion to income. However, the people out there in Fox Point own the property downtown in many of the slums. If you include that, the situation changes. The budget studies do not include ownership of other property.

Schwartz: I don't believe the owners of rental properties pay the tax burden on it. They may write out the checks to the tax collector, but they are not really paying the tax.

Vickrey: Again you have to distinguish sharply between the property tax on improvements and the property tax on land values. Although you may make a fairly good case for the proposition that the tax on improvements is shifted to the tenant, it's very difficult to make much of a case for a proposition that a land tax is shifted to tenants.

Schwartz: The land tax is probably absorbed by the owner although it may not be absorbed by the present holder. It may have been capitalized as the tax went up historically; whoever was holding the property at the time absorbed the rise. I would say a good part of the tax was shifted back a long time ago in lower capitalizations.

Vickrey: Then you have the question: are land speculators as a group part of the wealthier section of the population or are land speculators drawn primarily from the poorer section of the population? I favor the first hypothesis.

Barlowe: The evidence isn't complete on that.

Alyea: I wonder if I might make two observations here. One is that

* Margaret Reid, *Housing and Income* (Chicago: University of Chicago Press, 1962).

we are forgetting that, when examining the problem of equity, even an elementary public-finance textbook would consider the entire tax system and not separate taxes.

The second point is that the question of equity is probably not too important today. Currently we are more interested in the effect on taxable capacity, on income generated, and on income received. When we approach the question of the role of the property tax in this manner, our problem is to compare the effect of the property tax, as it is practiced, on income generated, on investment, on payroll, etc., with the effect alternative forms of taxes have on them. As a result of this approach, a major problem is the one brought out previously. What is the economic limit of property-tax rates? At just what point will investment be discouraged and taxable capacity be reduced if we increase the property tax?

Labovitz: Of course, this presumably involves a comparison with other, alternative taxes.

Rasmussen: That's exactly the point.

Alyea: Let me say one thing more. Forgive me, Professor Vickrey, if I'm wrong, but did you not say several years ago that, for a capitalistic society, we were acting in a very peculiar manner, with an anticapitalistic property tax and corporate and business taxes? Am I correct on that?

Vickrey: Yes. I would maintain that, so far as some of these taxes are concerned, the burden is not on anybody here present. The burden may be on the future wage earner.

Labovitz: By some of these taxes, do you mean the property taxes or taxes generally?

Vickrey: Well, suppose we assume that property taxes have the effect, not of changing the net rate of return, but of requiring economic reactions that leave a net rate of return to the owners more or less unchanged. There will be a shift in the composition of the national income in the direction of more consumption and less capital investment. In the long run, this leads to a reduction in the marginal productivity of labor because of the relative shortage of capital. The long-run result is lower wages.

Stiles: And this is something we need to worry about now?

Vickrey: Well, if one is going to refuse to worry about the future, any tax system that promotes current consumption at the expense of investment should be favored. In effect, such a system removes all the burden from the present and places it on the future.

Stiles: Yes, still our span of concern is pretty much confined to our own lives and, say, the lives of our children, isn't it? Are we capable of responding to developments that will only affect generations beyond those we know?

Vickrey: Well, if we are not capable of responding, then we had better consume our substance in riotous living.

Labovitz: What should be the application of the property tax to business property, and what differentiations would be desirable between this and other types of property? Also there is the kind of situation that Mr. Stiles described in the case of railroad property, where there are incentives to hold on to property upon which you have very little or no taxes. This arises because of the method of valuation used for utility properties which sets the tax base of the utility at the capitalized value of its earnings.

Barlowe: Can we seriously consider abolishing the property tax on business? This is the very heart of the property tax in a good many taxing areas. We already accuse the property tax of being purely a tax on shelter.

Labovitz: If you do not consider abandonment of the tax on business property, then what can be done to rectify or to improve it?

Support of Education

Barlowe: Well, the property tax was once used to take care of practically all state-government functions as well as local; the states have pretty much abandoned it, however. I think the next logical step would be to shift the cost of schools away from the property tax.

Karl Falk: This brings up the whole question of grants and aids from the federal and state governments as sources of revenues. This ties in again with the comments that the tax system has to be considered as a whole.

Labovitz: Are you making a plea for more grants?

Falk: In California, the legislature is presently discussing tax reform and, among other things, has sidetracked the discussion of shifting taxes from improvements on the land. They are saying something like: "Well now, wait a second. First, we have to settle on alternative sources of revenue: e.g., an additional cigarette tax. Perhaps we will take care of the school problem at a state level or we may send it back to communities." In each case the property tax's role would change.

Labovitz: Doesn't the suggestion that the school-finance burden be taken off the property tax substantially mean that, on the average, over the country about half the property tax would be eliminated?

Barlowe: I think it does.

Rasmussen: More than half.

Sliger: Let me point out a danger. I come from a state, Louisiana, that supports about 75 percent of primary and secondary education at the state level. I mentioned one parish in the county, where only 4 percent of school support comes from the local unit. You have some real problems when you have this situation. Those of us who are in public higher education should be concerned about this. In this situation, there isn't much money left over for higher education, which traditionally has been supported by the state. When you are paying so much at the state level for primary and secondary education, higher education may get left behind. So just from a vested interest, I think we should—

Alyea: Just a footnote to that. I think he's talking about a single earmarked fund which supplies all the financing for all education. This is our problem.

Labovitz: Of course, over the last several decades, there has been a considerable shift to state and federal financing of public education and, for that matter, some private education, and so—

Sliger: Of course, in Louisiana they think they are right, and the others are just moving toward them.

Labovitz: The property tax is still a very mighty fiscal engine for the support of local education in most areas.

Denton: It would be interesting to estimate whether the grants that we envision coming from the federal government are going to be of a magnitude to make a significant difference to local areas. For example, the present War on Poverty, figured as a percentage of present welfare costs, I think, is only about .5 percent. Relatively insignificant.

Labovitz: .5 percent of what?

Denton: Of the total amount spent in the United States for welfare.

Now is there any likelihood that the funds that will be available for schools from the federal government will really be a significant factor in holding down local rates?

Falk: In the California case, I had in mind more state aid rather than federal.

Denton: But the states are already, at least our state is already, in a bind for revenue [for lower education and junior colleges].

Falk: Yes, but the needs are growing. The property tax is simply unable to raise sufficient revenue for local education. We have had to go to more and more state aid as well as federal.

Labovitz: Why is your state, California, unable to provide the revenue? What are the constraints?

Falk: The property tax could if you are not going to limit yourself to a ceiling. Much depends upon what you do elsewhere. In Los Angeles, they talked about taxpayer strike. They hit a ceiling down there a few months ago.

Labovitz: A tax ceiling or a figurative ceiling?

Falk: Both.

Denton: At least part of the pressure in our area comes from tax-sheltered communities. In the San Francisco Bay area there are some communities which have assessed values of $18,000 per capita, although the average runs about $1,200 per capita.

Gaffney: Emeryville is one of the high-per-capita-assessment areas.

Denton: Emeryville, exactly, and they have worse situations in Los Angeles.

If we could set county-wide school taxation, a great deal of the pressure would be removed. Whether we can get it or not, I don't know.

Schwartz: Is it in the Los Angeles area that they have a township boundary drawn to contain just a factory? The whole township, for example, is a strip two blocks wide and a mile long—just factories in it.

Denton: They have one dairy city and one industry city.

Rasmussen: These are not inherently economic units. They are simply administrative things; they are not really cities.

Denton: Once they are incorporated, they have a life that is difficult to extinguish.

Labovitz: Mr. Stiles' suggestion was to wipe out the property tax altogether. However, for dealing with this particular kind of situation, there are at least the alternatives you mentioned, the county-wide or state-wide rate.

State-Wide Property-Tax Rate

Gaffney: I'd like to put up a very timid trial balloon—to suggest tentatively, and for purposes of discussion, that the property tax be returned to the state level.

Labovitz: Do you mean the levying of the tax or simply state-wide assessment?

Alyea: The levying.

Gaffney: And the funds used to support state government.

Labovitz: In addition to local-government effort?

Gaffney: In addition to local government.

Rasmussen: Or in lieu of it?

Gaffney: There are various possibilities. You might collect centrally and distribute the funds as we do for the income and sales taxes. Initially, when the property tax was in flower in the nineteenth century, it was a state tax and a means of asserting the sovereign's interest in the real estate within its borders. It had a definite redistributive function. The thought was that real estate was a kind of public trust.

Schwartz: A major source of wealth.

Gaffney: And that the sovereign had an equity in it which was asserted through taxation. Then the taxing power was split up into localities. Soon we discovered that some localities had more per-capita assessments than others, and then we felt we should find some other means of redistributing wealth. We turned to other taxes at the state level which were justified because the property tax was confined to the localities, some of which were rich and some of which were poor.

Now I have often wondered why the property tax cannot be returned to the state level and used as it was in the nineteenth century.

Labovitz: In Illinois in the 1850's, when the state adopted a fairly heavy property tax to provide a state-distributed fund for schools, I'm convinced the intent was not solely the support of schools. The school people supported it, but the intent was to spread taxable valuations over the state so that there wouldn't be some school districts without resources and others with more than ample resources. What you are suggesting is that there might well be a recurrence of this kind of policy.

Gaffney: One of the major criticisms regularly levied against the property tax has been that some districts were richer than others. This is really a criticism of a locally levied tax.

Rasmussen: My state, Utah, has virtually done this now. The gap is very narrow now between the highest and lowest rate in the state.

Gaffney: How was this done? By gerrymandering?

Rasmussen: No, by state levies.

Denton: Your state levy is more significant than the local levy?

Rasmussen: In many cases, yes.

Arthur Becker: As I see it, the answer to Doctor Gaffney's question is that, if we were to centralize the property tax at the state level, there would be very little room for providing government services at the local level. The local governments really have no other source of revenue but the property tax. The local units could render their services exclusively on the basis of state aids and grants. This is a possibility. However, I don't know that the localities could have quite the same flexibility in providing the quality and quantity of services that they do at present.

Reed Hansen: You find that true here in Wisconsin under your equalization formula?

Becker: The advantages to certain high-tax communities of this recent device of property-tax equalization have just about been absorbed. I understand that, this year, the communities are back to the level that they were before.

Hansen: Is there an infringement on home-rule concepts?

Becker: No, not particularly. Of course, they haven't carried equalization very far. However, this is not quite the same thing as turning the property tax over to the state. The local governments would have nothing left if that were done.

Vickrey: Well, if the income tax is made available to local governments, as it has been in a number of areas both in this country and abroad, you could get away from reliance on the property tax and still maintain local autonomy and local responsibility.

Becker: Perhaps our basic problem is the level of government that provides the school service, rather than the level of government that exercises the tax. Perhaps the difficulty occurs when the local government provides school services which should be provided by county units, or maybe even by larger state units. Then, if the state reenacted the property tax, it could finance education on a more equal basis.

I don't think it would be desirable to take the property tax entirely away from local communities if, by various reforms, at least part of the discrepancies could be eliminated.

Labovitz: My understanding is that Doctor Gaffney was not necessarily recommending complete, sole use of the property tax at the state level; that would be an extreme version of his proposal. Is that correct?

Gaffney: That's very correct.

Household Tax Exemption

Chen: I believe I may have given the wrong impression to some participants that I am advocating exemptions similar to veteran's exemptions for older homeowners. I wish to clarify this.

As do most economists, I feel that exemption or preferential treatment of certain classes of taxpayers is not the most effective way of dealing with certain problems. Therefore, I am not necessarily advocating property-tax exemptions for elderly people.

More specifically, I think Sliger's paper, in agreement with the report of the Advisory Commission on Intergovernmental Relations, suggests that direct payments would be a better approach than exemptions. I believe that this ideally is the best approach. However, bearing the political processes in mind, this may be very difficult to achieve. If we assume that it is very difficult to get rid of all preferential treatment of certain classes of people, then I believe there may be ways and means to modify our exemption techniques so as to more closely achieve the original purpose.

Just one illustration. In regard to possible exemptions for the aged, typically, as in veterans exemptions, the law specifies three requirements. One is the requirement of residence. The second is a limitation on the amount of exempt valuation—$2,000, $3,000, or $4,000. Lastly, there is usually a requirement of a low income.

Typically, an exemption law for the aged allows a homeowner of 65 or older who has an annual income of less than $2,000 or $3,000 an exemption up to the amount of assessed valuation of perhaps $5,000. This type of technique may not be the best one. There are other techniques that might be used.

There are six states that have exemptions for the aged. Michigan is the latest state that has passed a law. However, I do not advocate the kind of legislation they passed.

By the way, in reply to Dr. Rasmussen's objection that property-tax exemptions do not help the renters, perhaps we should be aware of the fact that Wisconsin passed a law last June to give tax relief to renters as well as to homeowners.

Rasmussen: To the renter also?

Chen: Yes, 25 percent of the rent paid for occupancy of their residence can be deducted.

Labovitz: From taxable income?

Chen: Yes. It's a deduction from the state income tax for people over 65.

Labovitz: Is it all people 65 or over or those with small incomes or—?

Becker: There's a needs test here. You can have no more than a specified annual income in order to be eligible.

Labovitz: Is it analogous to the exemption given homeowners?

Becker: Except that this is actually a cash refund, which is available from income tax. Even if an income tax is not paid, there is still a cash grant. Let's say a needy person doesn't pay any income tax. He still gets a "refund" in order to help him cover his rent or property-tax payments. This is the way it operates.

Rasmussen: I just want to clarify one point. Under our present federal-income-tax law, the homeowner is allowed to deduct taxes; however, he doesn't have to pay income taxes on the imputed income from his home. If he were a renter, he would not obtain these advantages. Locally, we now give the homeowner a tax exemption on his home also. I think we allow too much for the homeowner as opposed to the renter. This is my concern.

Chen: I share your concern.

Becker: I think that, given the political popularity of all these exemptions—whether homestead exemptions or exemptions for veterans or for the aged—perhaps the most practical approach to the problem is to advocate that the eligibility requirements be eased so that everybody gets an exemption. This would indicate how ridiculous the whole thing is.

Investment and Land-Value Taxation

Gaffney: I think that the impression may have been left that Professor Alyea's argument was primarily a microeconomic one—i.e., that exemption from taxes on buildings would accelerate investment in the jurisdiction that provided such exemptions at the expense of other jurisdictions that did not. If all jurisdictions exempted buildings, there would be no net increase in investment.

Labovitz: This morning I said, in effect, that Professor Alyea was talking of attracting industry to locate in a given place, and, therefore, the advantage was transitional. While there might be some residual advantage to those who first made the shift to straight land taxation and away from taxation of improvements, once you have universalized the system there was no possibility of using the tax system to attract net new investment.

The other comment I made concerned the earlier portion of his paper which dealt with the existing *ad valorem* tax system on both land and improvements. I thought he had rather dismissed the marginal effects of the higher tax burdens on establishments already in existence, i.e., on their decisions whether to disinvest or whether to increase investment, or to continue to operate at a given level.

Gaffney: The opinion you stated, then, was not that a general reduction of taxes on buildings would not have macroeconomic impact.

Labovitz: No, it was not. I just would not feel competent on that point.

Gaffney: Well, I would like to introduce a very small dose of Keynesian economics at this point. It would seem that one of the concepts of Keynesian thought is the prescription that the maximization of investment opportunities or the marginal efficiency of capital was a highly desirable thing—perhaps the key to the solution of many of our macroeconomic problems. The exemption of buildings from taxation, I should think, would do a great deal to make real goods a more attractive way to hold assets than money, which is already exempt from property taxes in most jurisdictions. Therefore, the exemption of buildings from taxation, if it were universalized, would have strong positive effects of a macroeconomic sort.

Labovitz: I am undoubtedly on thin ice when discussing Keynesian analysis; however, I will come back to Mr. Burkhard's comments. There are many areas in which one can invest under the present tax system which are not subject to *ad valorem* taxation. It seems to me there's an underlying assumption that investment in improvements on land is somehow necessarily a way of maximizing efficiency. It may be that investment in Research and Development (R. and D.), for example, contributes equally as much to economic progress as investment in improvements on land does.

Gaffney: There you get into the microeconomic question. If buildings are taxed and R. and D. is not taxed, investors are biased toward R. and D. and away from buildings. Maybe we need fewer slums instead of R. and D.

Schwartz: Instead of someone developing self-motorized toothbrushes and investing in new gadgets, more investment in slum clearance might be a more socially desirable investment, and our present tax laws discriminate against that. Is that right, Dr. Gaffney?

Gaffney: Yes.

Taxation of Extractive Industries

Barlowe: I would like to move to an aspect of mineral taxation. It was alluded to in Clarence Nelson's paper, and I think it warrants further discussion. The problem is the relationship between our tax policies on depletable resources such as mines and the use of the funds from such sources.

As I look around the country at the present time, with the exception of pockets of poverty in some of our cities, the major areas of rural poverty are found in regions where we have had exploitive forest or mineral industries—for example, the coal industry of the Appalachians and the minerals and timber of the northern lake states. I wonder whether we could construct special tax systems on mining which would put money aside to be used later to help redevelop the economy and create jobs.

As I remember, Minnesota had an iron-range-development commission. They were supported partially out of the taxes of the iron mines. I would like Dr. Nelson to comment on whether they have been able to provide new jobs in the iron-mining parts of the state.

Clarence Nelson: Yes, I can comment on that. There was an organization, called the Iron Range Resources and Rehabilitation Commission, established in about 1939. I think 5 percent of the occupation tax was earmarked for this unit. The objective of the commission was to encourage the development of other resources and industries in depressed or problem areas, i.e., the northern part of the state. They defined nineteen counties, most of which did not have iron-mineral resources in them, as the iron-range area and then proceeded to encourage research and development in the use of the existing resources. There were several plants to which they loaned money. They had the power to make interest-free loans. There are some empty plants (some of them sold for scrap later on) that testify to some of these early efforts. The Commission was a principal aid in inducing certain small industries to come into the area. However, in terms of the total, it's safe to say they made a very small dent in the underemployment and unemployment problems that developed in the area. The Commission came to a standstill, and the fund ended. The record of accomplishment on the whole was not particularly good. I'm not sure that it is necessarily the wisest public policy to build up a rehabilitation fund. It might be better to use the funds for current consumption and then, at a later date, borrow funds, if necessary, to relocate people or industry.

Just one final comment. The depletion of the mineral resource is inescapable in the long run, but as I indicated, the end, which once appeared imminent in Minnesota, is not yet at hand. Now we are beginning to mine and process a crude rock, and the reserves that were originally used up are but a small fraction of the new reserves remaining.

We are now working on reserves of billions and billions of tons, and this is only what is available under our current technology (from about 1950). With the new taconite process we have unlocked more tonnage of reserves in the Lake Superior district than we ever had previously on the books or that could have been shipped under the old technologies. What lies beyond, who can say? Iron mining has been extended into the indefinite future with respect to commercially extractable minerals in the Lake Superior district.

Rasmussen: No doubt. However, there were many millions of dollars spent over 40 to 50 years to develop taconite. This is a reinvestment of sorts.

Nelson: In the study that I'm working on, I will attempt to deal with this in considerable detail, and I hope to shed some light on it. An important role was played by the funds spent by the University of Minnesota in developing some of the new technology.

The private companies have also spent considerable sums, but I think, if we work out the return on this investment, the sums are not very large relative to the return. The investment would prove to have been highly profitable to the original investors if there were some way the parties who invested in the original development of the technology could recover some of the surplus created. One private mineral contract with a taconite company, for example, calls for a royalty of around $1.25 per ton of product. This is an enormous surplus which accrues to a party who had the foresight to hang on to his mineral title. However, presumably he did nothing in the way of investment toward creating the new technology that opened up the economic value of the taconite. The rent collector is always there, able to capitalize on the natural resource.

Barlowe: You have mentioned the great potential of taconite. Under the present Minnesota laws, does it represent the same taxpaying potential as the old iron deposits did?

Nelson: This is a moot point. Generally, no, because the in-lieu provisions which apply appear to be considerably more lenient than the *ad valorem* taxes. They are less capable of taking any of the surpluses that I indicate now exist.

Secondly, the state occupation and royalty taxes that apply to the taconite operations also are more lenient than those that apply to the standard ore operations because of provisions that have been worked into the law over a long period of time.

Labovitz: However, you imply that, if these industries had continued to be taxed under the straight *ad valorem* system, there might not have been this kind of development.

Nelson: This might have been a possible outcome. Or the development wouldn't have happened now. It is possible that the encouragement that the in-lieu system offered made the decision to invest immediately in the development of taconite mining possible.

Barlowe: Dr. Nelson, I think you should brief us a little more on this Minnesota taconite amendment. I believe, as soon as the vote was announced, four or five big iron companies announced they were going to start operations or were going to expand.

Nelson: We can't be sure. However, the state had made a commitment to tax restraint. This was one of the elements that encouraged production.

Supposedly, the earlier 1941 law itself was a kind of a commitment to treat this whole class of properties under the special provision. The implied promise was that the state would not reverse itself and burden the operators with other types of taxation. The so-called taconite amendment, which was approved by the voters of the state overwhelmingly in our last election, has been incorrectly reported or described in the press as a tax guarantee. It has been mislabeled by proponents as a tax guarantee and by the opposition as a handcuffing or straitjacketing of the state's power to tax.

The amendment grew out of several years' effort on the part of companies to obtain concessions and guarantees with regard to taxation for the taconite plants that they were considering building. The earlier hopes of the companies, as expressed in their testimony to legislative committees at each of the sessions, was for constitutional guarantees that they would not be taxed excessively. The actual measure passed was a compromise.

The new amendment controls the second system of taxation on the taconite companies, the occupation tax and the royalty tax. However, we also have the in-lieu taconite tax itself, $.05 to $.06 cents a ton.

Gaffney: Can you describe that one? Is that also a severance tax?

Nelson: That would be the severance tax in lieu of the property tax.

Gaffney: It is a specific tax?

Nelson: Yes.

Labovitz: Is it in lieu of a property tax on the plant?

Nelson: It is quite broad. It covers the plant, a port they might build, a power plant, quite a bit of works.

Gaffney: In other words, the taconite plant itself is exempt from property tax.

Nelson: As well as the deposit, the lands.

Rasmussen: These are true severance taxes.

Nelson: Now along came the proposed amendment. There was an existing law. The amendment itself simply says we will not change this law for 25 years.

The law itself prohibits an increase in the excise-type taxes, the royalty and occupation taxes, at more than a given rate. Moreover, the given rate is spelled out by a peculiar formula over any future period.

However, the law and the amendment specifically exclude any limitation on the specific tax, the in-lieu tax. Thus, the existing legislation does not represent a guarantee. The state is at full liberty, in the spirit and letter of the law, to change the in-lieu tax. In fact, they could repeal it and put the whole taconite system under the old *ad valorem* tax system. Also, they could move the present rate of $.05 to $.06 a ton up to $.20 or $.30 a ton. In this sense, there is a certain amount of misinformation about the nature of the amendment. It only covers the excise-type tax.

I want to make one final observation. After the favorable vote on this so-called guarantee, four or five companies announced plans for plant expansion. However, there were two companies who made decisions to build early in the year, without waiting to find out the outcome of the vote. One was the Ford Motor Company associated with the Grub Evolith Taconite Company. They went ahead and constructed their plant on the Mesabi Range. There was another company, McCloud Steel, which decided to invest money in an operation in Upper Michigan before waiting for the vote. There is evidence, therefore, that some major investors were willing to make decisions before finding the outcome of the vote on the "tax guarantee."

Falk: I want to ask a specific question and then lead into a more general one.

The question that intrigues me is to what extent increased economic activity is induced by tax policy and to what extent tax policy follows structural changes—i.e., improved technology or an increase in foreign supplies?

My own particular interest happens to be in cities and slum clearance. The question arises whether property taxation could be used as a tool to aid slum clearance instead of employing an overt subsidy. My first question relates to this one, because I generally find it difficult to measure a causal relationship between a tax and changes in the economic environment. Does the tax cause the economic change, does it follow it, or is it completely incidental to it? Are other, extraneous forces more important? Can we use property-tax reform as an incentive to eliminate slums?

But to come back to your own situation, would you care to comment on the evidence? You have given some illustrations that there is a causal relationship.

Nelson: I will make a rough generalization. I would say there was a definite and relatively strong relationship in the taconite case. In the early stages of the industry, the tax environment was an important and real factor in the decisions to go ahead, and, presumably, it is also a factor at this time.

I would also say that industrial motivation created the tax environment. By the mid-30's a couple of major corporations had begun to be interested in the taconite properties. In 1939, Reserve Mining Company, for example, signed a lease with the owners of a 9,000 to 12,000 acre tract of taconite. There was a relationship between the principals in the commercial development, the legislature, and the people on the Mesabi Range, that carried the taconite-tax reform through in 1941.

Labovitz: So you feel there was a definite causal relationship?

Nelson: Yes, and the direction it took was from industry interest in tax reform to changes in the tax law.

Rasmussen: Wasn't there a past history of increases in state taxes that the industry was afraid of?

Nelson: Oh, very definitely. That is the background.

Tax-Exempt Government and Non-Profit Institutional Property

Richard Lindholm: Apropos of Dr. O'Bannon's paper and the comment Rasmussen made relative to the complicated formulas that the federal government has developed for paying taxes on its property holdings, it occurs to me that this is a possible area where the federal government can assist state and local governments. Many economists have recommended that the federal government do so by some method—given the productivity of its tax system and the rapid growth of the national economy. Given this premise, a relatively simple procedure might be for the federal government to pay the going rate of property tax on the land it holds in various states and localities around the country. The federal government would do this only if the state were to tax all other land, including the land which the states themselves are utilizing. This would assist the state and local governments in obtaining more funds and, at the same time, would provide perhaps a more efficient allocation of a rather important economic resource. It would encourage the proper use of land by any holder, whether private institution, state government, county government, or federal government. These groups of landholders, as Dr. O'Bannon's paper indicated, are expanding in our society.

Labovitz: You will find, I am afraid, very little enthusiasm in Congress for the payment of a federal property tax as an alternative to grants and other aids.

One of the reasons that the National Association of County Officials was slow to go on record in favor of a comprehensive proposal to reduce intergovernment tax exemptions was that, in transmitting the proposal to the Congress, the Director of the Bureau of the Budget had mentioned that this touched only one aspect of the whole, broad, complicated problem of intergovernmental tax immunities. He mentioned three or four other areas, such as the tax treatment of federal, state, and local personnel and the exemption of the interest on municipal bonds from the federal income tax.

Lindholm: However, suppose we begin to obtain people educated in our schools and colleges who look at the whole economy and can critically examine all these various special privileges and nonsensical things that have developed, such as the exemption of interest on municipal bonds, but not of interest on other types of securities? Suppose they begin to look at these special privileges from a broad, general point of view? We may develop in the United States an environment that will make possible general tax reforms.

Gaffney: Lindholm, is it your proposal that the states tax federal property, land?

Lindholm: Yes. This development would place all land on the tax roll.

Labovitz: Well, one problem is that this would be very haphazard. There are many states where it would be an important source of revenue and many states where it would be unimportant.

Lindholm: It would vary from state to state, that's certain. All things vary from state to state.

Schwartz: The State of Connecticut would not benefit at all, and Arizona would get a tax on the national park at the Grand Canyon.

Howards: There is a search for some method of bringing federal money back to the states. It is sometimes suggested that it come back on a per-capita basis. Lindholm is suggesting it come back through more adequate, fair, and equitable property taxation.

This has some interesting ramifications. Suppose the federal government paid this money on the basis of assessed value of property, not in an absolute amount. Then Connecticut has a problem. But, if you used either the comparative ratio of assessed value to true value or the assessment ratio as a base for paying the federal tax, you would encourage competitive overvaluation.

Barlowe: In some of the states there would be a drive to create many new, unnecessary units of government because the federal land is often blocked together. These local government units would provide very little in actual local services.

Labovitz: These are just some of the complications. The amount of money that the federal government might distribute because it owns real property might not be sufficient to provide the incentive you are envisaging here. Even in some of the eleven western states [which contain about 90 percent of federal land holdings—excluding Alaskan holdings] the implicit free market value of the federal real estate may not be very large.

Barlowe: One could look at it another way; Dr. O'Bannon pointed this out. A number of grants in aid, federal-government subsidies, are geared to make some adjustment for states that contain large concentrations of federal land. For example, we contribute 95 percent of the cost, under the Federal Highway Act, in the public-land states as against 90 percent in other states. I suspect there are other subsidies of this nature that, in the long run, equal—or more than equal—what the federal government might pay in property tax.

Labovitz: One of my colleagues made an estimate for one of the states to determine the difference between subsidies received and possible tax collections by including federal property in the state and local government property-tax base. It indicated that the state would actually lose money in the form of special provisions in federal grants if all the federally owned public domain were turned over to the state.

Rasmussen: In the western states, I found that two of them would receive more in property taxes, taking into account just the payments that related to land.

Labovitz: It's quite evident from these discussions that there's ample material here for many doctoral dissertations. Dr. Barlowe implied earlier in the discussion that it might be worthwhile if some graduate student would make a study of the saving of a portion of the mining tax proceeds to finance redevelopment. One might compare the effects of this kind of policy with the welfare fund policy of the United Mineworkers in West Virginia and Kentucky.

Are there any other last words, the time for adjournment having come?

Gaffney: I would like to sum up by returning to Professor Rasmussen's suggestion about developing a property-tax philosophy. There are probably two aspects that should be considered in this philosophy —distributive equity and allocative efficiency. The property tax actually comes out fairly well on these grounds when compared with some alternate taxes, particularly if it is applied at a fairly high level of government.

The grasshoppers who landed on the fertile field can be taxed to help the ones who landed on the sandpile. The land tax especially is a method of taxing the fertile field without adding to marginal costs of the grasshoppers there. It can thereby redistribute surpluses without artificially directing the allocation of resources away from the rich field which, of course, is where all of us grasshoppers would like to be.

Index

Index